STUDY AND LISTENING GUIDE

FOR

CONCISE HISTORY OF WESTERN MUSIC

AND

NORTON ANTHOLOGY OF WESTERN MUSIC
THIRD EDITION

STUDY AND LISTENING GUIDE

FOR

CONCISE HISTORY OF WESTERN MUSIC
BY BARBARA RUSSANO HANNING

AND

NORTON ANTHOLOGY OF WESTERN MUSIC
THIRD EDITION
BY CLAUDE V. PALISCA

J. PETER BURKHOLDER

W. W. NORTON & COMPANY
NEW YORK   LONDON

ISBN 0-393-97171-6 (pbk)

W. W. Norton & Company, Inc.
500 Fifth Avenue, New York, N.Y. 10110
http://www.wwnorton.com

W. W. Norton & Company, Ltd.
10 Coptic Street, London WC1A 1PU

1 2 3 4 5 6 7 8 9 0

CONTENTS

READ THIS SECTION FIRST

The purpose of this *Study and Listening Guide* is to help you learn the material in *Concise History of Western Music* (CHWM) by Barbara Russano Hanning and acquaint yourself with the music in the *Norton Anthology of Western Music*, 3rd edition (NAWM), by Claude V. Palisca. Each chapter of this *Study and Listening Guide* is coordinated with a chapter of CHWM and several pieces in NAWM.

There is much to know about the history of Western music and much to discover in the music itself. The best way to learn it is to follow some simple rules of successful learning.

1. Know your goals. It is easier to learn and to chart your progress if you know what you are trying to accomplish.
2. Proceed from the general to the specific, from the main points to the details. We learn best when what we are learning relates to what we already know. That is easiest when we start with the big picture.
3. Do not try to do everything at once. Trying to do too much, too fast makes learning difficult and frustrating. Divide the task into units small enough to grasp at one sitting. Do not cram for tests; study every day.
4. Write down what you learn. You will retain information and concepts much more readily if you write them down for yourself rather than merely read them or hear them or highlight them in a book. The mental act of putting ideas into your own words and the physical act of writing out names, terms, dates, and other information create multiple pathways in your brain for recalling what you have learned.
5. Apply what you know. You learn and retain the skills and knowledge that you use.
6. Review what you know. We learn through repetition.
7. Have fun. You learn better and remember more when you are having fun. This does not mean goofing off, but rather means allowing yourself to enjoy the process of learning, mastering, and applying concepts and skills, whether riding a bike or discovering music history.

This study and listening guide is designed to help you do all of these, through the following features.

Chapter Objectives

Each chapter begins with an outline of what you should learn from reading the texts and studying the music. These are the central issues confronted in the chapter. When you read the objectives before studying the material, they will pinpoint what you are trying to achieve. When you reread them after you have read the chapter, studied the music, and worked through the study questions, they can help you to evaluate your achievement. They direct you to the big picture, so you do not miss the forest for the trees.

Chapter Outline

The chapter outline shows how the corresponding chapter in CHWM is divided into sections, summarizes the main points in each section, introduces important terms and names (highlighted in *italics*), and indicates which selections in NAWM relate to each topic. By reading the outline *first*, you begin with an overview of the subject. Then, as you read the chapter, the details presented there will flesh out the general concepts presented in the outline. Since you have already read the main ideas in the outline, as you read the text you are beginning to review and reinforce what you have learned, while increasing the depth of your knowledge. When you have finished a section or chapter, reread the outline to make sure you grasp the main points. The outline will also be useful as you review.

Study Questions

The readings are full of information, and it may sometimes be difficult to figure out what is more and less significant. The study questions are designed to help you focus on the most important issues and concepts addressed in each section of each chapter and to apply those concepts to the music in NAWM. Material related to any of the questions may be found in a single place in CHWM or scattered throughout the section. Relevant material may also be found in the analytical discussions of individual pieces in NAWM.

Questions are grouped by topic, and each question focuses on a single issue. This divides each chapter into units of manageable size and allows you to proceed step by step. Questions vary in kind, from fill-in-the-blank questions to short essays that ask you to synthesize material and apply it to the music, or exercises that ask you to sing or play through the music. Tackling the material in small units and doing a variety of things in each section can help to make your work more fun.

Write down your answers. Space is provided to answer the study questions in this book. Writing down what you learn, rather than merely reading or highlighting the text, will help you retain it better. This is particularly helpful for recalling terms, names, and titles in foreign languages, since spelling them out for yourself will make them more familiar.

The study questions are not review questions, to be filled in after you are done reading and have closed the book. They are guides to the reading and to the music. After you have read a section of the text, or while you are reading it, work through the relevant study questions, rereading the text for answers as needed. Always respond to the questions in your own words, rather than copying from the text; this will help you to master each concept, making it your own by phrasing it in your own way. If there is something you do not understand, return to the reading to find the missing information, or ask for help from your instructor.

Some study questions ask you to define or to use terms that are introduced in the text. There is rote learning in every subject, and in music much of it is of terminology. Each musical repertory has its own specialized vocabulary, often borrowed from Italian, Latin, French, or German. You cannot communicate with others about this music without mastering these terms.

Many questions ask you to apply to the pieces in NAWM concepts and terms that are presented in the text. In this way you will to get to know the music better and will reinforce your grasp of the concepts and terms by applying what you know to the music itself. These study questions on the music are set off in boxes headlined *Music to Study*. Each of these subsections begins with a list of the pieces in NAWM under consideration, indicating the location of each piece on the recordings that accompany NAWM (by number and track on the compact disks and by number and side on the cassette tapes).

You should listen to each piece in NAWM several times, including at least once before reading about it and at least once afterwards. The heart of music history is the music itself, and a major part of your study should be listening to and becoming familiar with the music.

Terms and Names to Know

Near the end of each chapter is a list of important terms and names that appear in the texts and are highlighted in italics in the chapter outline. Most of these are covered in the study questions. They are listed separately here to help you review and to test your retention of what you have learned. In addition to these names, you should know the composers and titles of the pieces you studied. Use the lists in reviewing at the end of each chapter and in reviewing for examinations.

Review Questions

Each chapter ends with review questions that ask you to reflect more generally on the material you have learned. Most of them are like essay questions that you might encounter on a test. These may be used as springboards for discussion in class or with your study group, or as essay questions to use for practice as you study for examinations. Others are exercises that ask you to pull together information from several places in the chapter.

How to Proceed

The following procedure is recommended, but any procedure that helps you learn the most effectively and efficiently is the right one for you.

1. As you start each chapter, read the **chapter objectives** first to see what is expected of you.
2. Read through the **chapter outline**. Notice the topics that are covered, the main points that are made, and the terms that are introduced. Important new terms and names are given in italics.
3. Read the "Prelude" at the beginning of the chapter in CHWM and the "Postlude" at the end. These summarize the chapter and sometimes provide historical background. (Since the "Postlude" repeats material already given, it is usually not included in the chapter outline.)
4. Now work through the chapter section by section, as marked by roman numerals in the chapter outline and centered headings in CHWM.

5. Start each section by listening to the pieces in NAWM that are listed in this section of the outline. Read through the text and translation before listening to vocal pieces, and listen to every piece with the score. (If you have time, you might first listen to each piece without the score, and you might also sing or play through the piece yourself.) This lets you encounter the music first, just as music. Later, you will come back to it and apply the principles you learn in reading the text.

6. Next, read the section in CHWM, using the chapter outline as a guide. As the text refers you to pieces in NAWM, look again at the music and read the analytical discussion of each piece.

7. Work through the **study questions** for this section. Refer again to the music when the questions direct you to do so, and study the music or review CHWM and the analytical discussions in NAWM to find the information you need to answer the questions. (Instead of reading first and then working through the study questions, you may find it more convenient to answer the study questions as you read through the text.)

8. When you have answered the study questions, review the chapter outline for this section and look over your answers. If there is anything you do not understand, refer back to the text, or make a note of it in the margin and ask your instructor for help.

9. Listen to the music again, and check your answers to the relevant study questions. Then congratulate yourself for finishing this section. You may move on to the next section, or save it for another day.

10. At the end of the chapter, reread the "Postlude" in CHWM for a summary. Then review by checking your knowledge of the **terms and names to know,** rereading the chapter outline, and reviewing your answers to the study questions. Read the objectives again to make sure you have accomplished them. Read the **review questions** and write brief answers in outline form, or use them as practice essay questions before examinations.

Note to the Instructor

This *Study and Listening Guide* is designed to walk the student through the material in CHWM and NAWM step by step. Not every teacher will want to include all the content covered in the texts, and each teacher is likely to emphasize different aspects of the music and its history. Each instructor is encouraged to tailor this study guide to the needs of the individual course.

The study questions are designed to be used as guides for the student, as the basis for work in drill sessions, or as problem sets to be handed in. There are many questions, so that each significant topic can be covered. The instructor is encouraged to select which of the questions students should do on their own, which they may omit, and which should be handed in, if any. The review questions can also be used in several ways: as guides for individual review, as model test questions, or as short writing assignments in or out of class. For courses in which this *Study and Listening Guide* is a required text, permission is granted to use any of the questions on examinations.

ACKNOWLEDGMENTS

Any book is a collaborative effort, and teaching materials are especially so. This *Study and Listening Guide* is adapted from a similar guide, published in 1996, for *A History of Western Music,* 5th edition, by Donald Jay Grout and Claude V. Palisca, and the *Norton Anthology of Western Music,* 3rd edition, edited by Claude V. Palisca. That guide originated in a group of study questions for the first twelve chapters of the previous edition of *A History of Western Music,* which I developed in collaboration with my teaching assistants for Music History and Literature I at Indiana University School of Music in fall 1993, Brian Bourkland, Nicholas Butler, Kirk Ditzler, Gesa Kordes, and Mario Ortiz-Acuña. I am grateful for their cooperation, their suggestions, and the questions of theirs that remain here in some form.

I am grateful also to my teaching assistants in fall 1995, John Anderies, Nicholas Butler, Pablo Corá, David Lieberman, Felicia Miyakawa, and Patrick Warfield, who used the first draft of the study guide for *A History of Western Music* and offered very helpful feedback. My students and my colleagues Austin B. Caswell and Thomas Noblitt provided encouragement and useful comments.

Thanks also to Claude V. Palisca for helpful advice and for permitting me to consult materials he had developed, Michael Ochs for guidance on format and content, Gabrielle Karp for providing up-to-date drafts, galleys, and proofs of the new editions of *A History of Western Music* and the *Norton Anthology of Western Music* as they became available, and Kristine Forney for her suggestions. In preparing this adaptation for Barbara Russano Hanning's *Concise History of Western Music,* I am grateful to Martha Graedel and Kathy Talalay for providing materials to work with prior to publication. Thanks finally and as always to Doug McKinney for his unlimited patience and support.

MUSIC IN ANCIENT GREECE AND EARLY CHRISTIAN ROME

1

CHAPTER OBJECTIVES

After you complete the reading, study of the music, and study questions for this chapter, you should be able to:

1. identify several elements of Western music and theory that derive from the music of ancient Greece or Israel;
2. describe in general terms ancient Greek music and ideas about music;
3. explain why the Greeks linked music to numbers, astronomy, and poetry, and how they thought it affected a person's character and behavior; and
4. summarize early Christian attitudes toward music, including the role of music in the church, the place of music among the liberal arts, and the relation of audible music to the mathematical proportions that govern nature and humans, and explain how these views relate to ancient Greek views of music.

CHAPTER OUTLINE

Prelude (CHWM 1–3)

Knowing the history of music can help us understand it. Western culture has roots in ancient Greece and Rome. Although little ancient music survived, ancient writings about music, particularly music theory, had a strong influence on later centuries. This ancient heritage was passed on in part through the early Christian Church. The continual influence of ancient ideas and practices on music of all later periods makes it appropriate to begin our study with music in the ancient world.

I. Music in Ancient Greek Life and Thought (CHWM 4–8, NAWM 1–2)

In ancient Greece, music was linked to the gods and divine powers.

Etude: Ancient Greek Instruments: Kithara and Aulos
There were three main instruments, played alone or to accompany singing or recitation:

1. The *lyre*, a plucked string instrument associated with Apollo;
2. The *aulos*, a reed instrument associated with Dionysus and Greek drama (as in NAWM 2);
3. The *kithara*, a larger relative of the lyre.

Music was used in religious ceremonies, and festivals and contests were also important parts of Greek musical life. *Aristotle* and others opposed the rise of professional musicians and the increasing virtuosity and complexity of music, and later Greek music became simplified. **Music: NAWM 2**

1. Extant Greek music

About forty pieces or fragments of music survive, most from relatively late periods. Greek music was *monophonic*, but was often performed in *heterophony*. It was usually improvised, not read from notation.

2. Greek theory

Greek music theory had a profound effect on music of the Middle Ages. *Plato* and Aristotle wrote on the nature and uses of music, and music theorists described musical materials and ways of composing.

3. Music and number

Pythagoras (ca. 500 B.C.E.) is credited with having discovered that the basic consonant intervals were produced by simple number ratios of 2:1 for the octave, 3:2 for the fifth, and 4:3 for the fourth.

4. Music and poetry

Music was closely tied to poetry, which was usually sung. The rhythms of a melody follow the rhythms of its text, and the pitch contour follows the inflections of a speaking voice. **Music: NAWM 1**

5. The doctrine of *ethos*

The Greeks held that music could directly affect character (*ethos*, related to the English word "ethics") and behavior.

6. Theory of imitation

Aristotle wrote that music represents the *passions* or states of the soul and arouses passions in the listener. He felt that music that stimulates undesirable attitudes should be avoided.

7. Music in education

Plato gave music an important role in education, arguing that the right kind of music disciplined the mind and aroused virtue. Aristotle also endorsed music for entertainment and for its role in dramatic catharsis.

8. Music and politics

Like Plato and Aristotle, the church fathers and modern politicians have opposed certain kinds of music because of the effects attributed to them.

9. The harmonic system and tetrachords

The Greek musical system laid the foundation for later Western systems with such concepts as notes, intervals (including tones, semitones, and thirds), scales, and modes. Greek scales were constructed from *tetrachords*, groups of four notes spanning a perfect fourth. There were three *genera* (plural of *genus*, meaning type) of tetrachords: *diatonic*, *chromatic*, and *enharmonic*.

II. The Early Christian Church: Musical Thought (CHWM 8–12)

1. Rome's decline
As the Roman empire declined and collapsed, the Christian Church became the main cultural force in Europe.

2. Church fathers and the dangers of music
Christian writers and scholars known as the church fathers saw in music the power to inspire piety and to influence the character of listeners. Many early church leaders opposed listening to music for pleasure.

3. Transmission of Greek music theory
Greek theory and philosophy were summarized and passed on by early Christian writers, notably Martianus Capella and Boethius.

4. Martianus Capella
Martianus helped to codify the *seven liberal arts*: the three verbal arts called the *trivium* (grammar, dialectic or logic, and rhetoric) and the four mathematical disciplines called the *quadrivium* (geometry, arithmetic, astronomy, and harmonics, or music).

5. Boethius
The heritage of Greek music theory was transmitted to the Middle Ages primarily through *De institutione musica* (The Fundamentals of Music) by *Boethius* (ca. 480-524).

Etude: Boethius's Fundamentals
Boethius listed three kinds of music: *musica mundana* (cosmic music), the orderly numerical relations that control the natural world; *musica humana* (human music), which controls the human body and soul; and *musica instrumentalis,* audible music produced by voices or instruments.

III. The Early Christian Church: Musical Practice (CHWM 12–16)

The early Christian Church absorbed musical practices from Greece and other cultures, but its leaders rejected pagan uses of music and excluded instrumental music from church services.

1. The Judaic heritage
Although Christian worship was not based directly on Jewish ceremonies, there are parallels, including a symbolic sacrifice, a ceremonial meal, the reading of Scripture, the singing of *psalms,* and the practice of assigning certain readings and psalms to specific days of the calendar.

2. Christian sacrifice
In the Christian Mass, worshipers shared wine and bread, representing the blood and body of Christ, as his disciples did at the Last Supper.

3. Psalms and hymns
As Christianity spread, the Church absorbed influences from many areas. Among the most important were psalm singing and *hymns* as used in Syria and later cultivated in Byzantium and Milan.

4. Eastern churches
Each region of the church in the East developed its own *liturgy* (set of texts and rites). *Byzantium,* later called Constantinople, was the capital of the Eastern Roman Empire from 395 to 1453, and its musical practices influenced the West.

5. Western churches and chant dialects
Between the fifth and eighth centuries, each region of the Western church also developed its own liturgy in Latin. Along with a separate liturgy, each region had its own repertory of liturgical melodies, called *chants*. From the ninth century on, most of these regional dialects were replaced with a common liturgy and set of melodies authorized by *Rome,* home to the pope (the bishop of Rome).

6. Ambrosian chant and responsorial psalmody
One chant dialect that survived was the Ambrosian, centered in Milan. It is named after St. Ambrose, who introduced *responsorial psalmody* to the West, in which a soloist sings the first half of a psalm verse and the congregation responds by singing the rest.

7. Rome's musical dominance
Chant melodies were passed down orally at first, then began to be written down, starting in the ninth century. Rome was the dominant influence because several popes worked to standardize and preserve the melodies through a papal choir and the Schola cantorum, a group of teachers who trained church singers.

8. Gregorian chant
Gregorian chant is the standard repertory of liturgical chants from the ninth to the sixteenth centuries. It was named for Pope Gregory I or II.

Etude: The Restoration of Gregorian Chant
Modern editions of Gregorian chant were prepared in the late nineteenth and early twentieth centuries by monks at the Benedictine *Abbey of Solesmes* in France. Today, Latin is seldom used in Catholic services, and the chants are seldom heard.

Window: Sounding and Silent Harmony (CHWM 14–15)

The ancient Greeks linked music and astronomy, since both depended on numerical proportions. This is embodied in Plato's notion of "the music of the spheres." These ideas persisted through the Middle Ages and Renaissance.

STUDY QUESTIONS

Music in Ancient Greek Life and Thought (CHWM 4–8, NAWM 1-2)

1. What were the three main instruments used by the ancient Greeks? How was each played, and on what occasions was it used? Which instrument was associated with Apollo, and which with Dionysus?

     a. _____

     b. _____

     c. _____

2. When did Pythagoras live? According to legend, what did he discover?

3. In Greek musical life, how was music related to or dependent upon poetry?

4. According to Plato and Aristotle, how could music affect a person's character and behavior? Why was it important that certain kinds of music be promoted and other kinds suppressed? What is the relevance of this debate for our own time?

5. What are some of the concepts in the Greek harmonic system that are part of later Western systems of music?

6. What is a *tetrachord*? What are the three *genera* of tetrachord?

Music to Study
> **NAWM 1:** *Epitaph of Seikilos*, skolion/drinking song (ca. 1st century C.E.)
> > CD 1.1 (Concise 1.1)   Cassette 1.A (Concise 1.A)
> **NAWM 2:** Euripides, from *Orestes*, fragment of *stasimon* chorus (408
> > B.C.E., the date of the play, or 3rd to 2nd century B.C.E., the date of
> > the papyrus on which the music is preserved)
> > CD 1.2   Cassette 1.A

7. How do the *Epitaph of Seikilos* (NAWM 1) and the *stasimon* chorus from Euripides' *Orestes* (NAWM 2) exemplify the characteristics typical of Greek music as described in CHWM, pp. 4–8 and the summary on p. 16? (Note: One way they are not typical is in being notated, rather than improvised or transmitted orally.)

The Early Christian Church: Musical Thought (CHWM 8–12)

8. What attitudes toward music were held by the leaders of the early Christian Church? How do these views compare to the views of Plato and Aristotle?

9. How does music fit into the seven liberal arts? Why is music (or harmonics) grouped with the mathematical arts, rather than with the verbal arts?

10. Why was Boethius important for music in the Middle Ages?

11. In Boethius's view, what was *musica instrumentalis,* and how did it relate to *musica mundana* and *musica humana*? How does this view compare to ancient Greek ideas about music?

12. What parallels do you notice between Jewish religious practices and the liturgy and music of early Christian worship?

13. How far back does hymn singing go in Christian worship?

14. When did chant melodies begin to be written down? _____

    How were they transmitted before notation was developed?

15. What is *Gregorian chant,* and what did it replace? Why is it seldom heard in Catholic churches today?

16. What is the significance of the Abbey of Solesmes for Gregorian chant?

Window: Sounding and Silent Harmony (CHWM 14–15)

17. In the Greek conception, what were the links between music, numbers, and astronomy? How did these concepts influence European thinkers in the Middle Ages and Renaissance?

TERMS TO KNOW

Terms Related to Ancient Greek Music

lyre
aulos
kithara
monophony, heterophony

doctrine of ethos
tetrachord
genus (pl. genera): diatonic,
   chromatic, enharmonic

Terms Related to Music in the Early Christian Church

liberal arts, trivium, quadrivium
musica mundana, musica humana,
   musica instrumentalis
psalms
hymns

liturgy
chant
responsorial psalmody
Gregorian chant

NAMES TO KNOW

Pythagoras
Plato
Aristotle
Boethius

De institutione musica
Byzantium
Rome
Abbey of Solesmes

REVIEW QUESTIONS

1. According to the summary in the "Postlude" (CHWM, pp. 16-17) and other parts of the chapter, what are some basic characteristics of ancient Greek music? Which of these are shared with other ancient musical traditions?

2. What does ancient Greek music have in common with our music? What are some similarities between Greek music and ours? What are some similarities between Greek music theory and common-practice music theory?

3. What are some Greek ideas about the power of music and its role in society that are still relevant today?

4. How did early Christian writers, including St. Augustine and Boethius, view music? How do their attitudes compare to those of the ancient Greeks, including Plato and Aristotle?

5. What are some of the sources of Gregorian chant, the repertory of melodies used in the Western church? What were the contributions of the Judaic tradition, Syria, Byzantium, and Europe? How did Gregorian chant come to be standardized?

CHANT AND SECULAR SONG IN THE MIDDLE AGES, 400–1450

2

CHAPTER OBJECTIVES

After you complete the reading, study of the music, and study questions for this chapter, you should be able to:

1. describe in general terms the liturgical context for plainchant in the Roman Church, including the main outlines of the Office and the Mass;
2. read a melody in plainchant notation;
3. describe several varieties of Gregorian chant and explain how the shape and manner of performance of some chants relate to their liturgical function;
4. characterize the eight church modes by their final, tenor, and range and identify the mode of a given chant or song;
5. name some of the kinds of secular musicians active during the Middle Ages and the regions and social classes from which they came;
6. describe some examples of medieval secular song by troubadours, trouvères, *Minnesinger,* and *Meistersinger*; and
7. name and briefly identify a few of the people who contributed to the repertory of medieval monophonic music.

CHAPTER OUTLINE

Prelude (CHWM 18–19)

Two large repertories of song survive from the Middle Ages: the chant of the church, or *plainchant,* and secular songs, including those of the twelfth- and thirteenth-century *troubadours, trobairitz,* and *trouvères.*

I. Roman Chant and Liturgy (CHWM 19–23, NAWM 3–4)

Chant was created for religious services in the Roman Church, and the shape of each chant is determined by its role in the service. There are two main types of service in the Roman liturgy, the Office and the Mass.

1. The Office

The *Office* or *Canonical Hours* evolved from group prayer and psalm-singing. Eight Offices are celebrated at specified times each day, of which Matins, Lauds, and especially *Vespers* are musically the most important. Offices feature the singing of psalms and *canticles* (songs of praise from the Bible, such as the *Magnificat* at Vespers), each with an associated chant called an *antiphon*. They also include the singing of hymns and the chanting of lessons (passages from Scripture) with musical responses called *responsories*. **Music: NAWM 4**

2. The Mass

The *Mass* is the most important service. It opens with introductory prayers and chants, continues with Bible readings, responses, and the creed, and culminates in a symbolic reenactment of the Last Supper of Jesus and his disciples. The texts for certain parts of the Mass, called the *Proper,* change from day to day. The texts of other portions, called the *Ordinary,* are the same each time, although the melodies may vary. (For this reason, the Proper chants are called by their function, such as Introit or Communion, while the Ordinary chants are named by their first words, such as Kyrie or Credo.) **Music: NAWM 3**

3. The notation of chant

Notation helped to standardize chant melodies and promote uniformity. (It also reduced the need for memorization and made chant easier to learn than it had been when it was passed down orally.)

Etude: Modern Chant Books and Notation

Music for the Office is in a book called the *Antiphonale,* music for the Mass in the *Graduale.* The *Liber usualis* contains music for both. Plainchant notation uses a four-line staff, two movable clefs, and various noteshapes called *neumes,* which may indicate one or more notes.

II. Classes, Forms, and Types of Chant (CHWM 24–32, NAWM 3–7)

Chants can be classified in several ways:

1. by the type of text (biblical or nonbiblical, prose or poetical);
2. by the manner of performance (*antiphonal, responsorial,* or *direct*);
3. by the number of notes per syllable (*syllabic,* mainly one note per syllable; *neumatic,* 1–5 notes; or *melismatic,* with many syllables having many notes); or
4. by the form (balanced phrases, strophic form, or free form).

Chant melodies often reflect the inflection and rhythm of the words. Each melody divides into phrases and periods, following divisions in the text. Phrases tend to be archlike, rising, sustaining, then falling.

A. *Chants of the Office*

1. Psalm tones and Doxology

Psalm tones are formulas for singing the psalms in the Office. There is one psalm tone for each church mode (plus one "wandering tone"). Most of the formula consists of recitation on the *tenor* or *reciting tone* of the mode, with an initial figure at the beginning of the first verse and cadential figures to mark the middle and end of each psalm verse. The *Lesser Doxology,* praising the Trinity, is sung at the end of each psalm, using the same psalm tone.   **Music: NAWM 4c, 4e, 4g, and 4i**

2. Antiphonal psalmody and antiphons
In performing psalms in the Office, the half-verses alternate between different halves of the choir, a practice called *antiphonal psalmody.* Each psalm is paired with an *antiphon* (a term derived from antiphonal singing), sung before and after the psalm. There are also independent antiphons used on other occasions.   **Music: NAWM 4b, 4d, 4f, and 4h**

B. *Chants of the Mass*

1. Introit
In the Mass, the *Introit* and *Communion* were once full psalms with antiphons (more elaborate than Office antiphons). The Introit now has only one verse (plus the Doxology), and the Communion has none.   **Music: NAWM 3a and 3i**

2. Gradual and Alleluia: Responsorial performance
The *Gradual* and *Alleluia* are responsorial, alternating between soloist (or solo group) and choir. Both are highly melismatic (note the link between solo performance and melismatic style), with a single verse framed by a *respond.* The respond for the Alleluia is always the word "alleluia," ending with a long melisma called a *jubilus.* The *Tract* (a series of psalm verses in melismatic style), originally a solo, substitutes for the Alleluia in periods of penitence. The *Offertory* was originally an antiphon with psalm, but lost its verses and is performed responsorially. (Those chants that originated as antiphonal psalms originally accompanied actions; those performed by soloists were associated with the reading of lessons from the Bible.)   **Music: NAWM 3d, 3e, and 3f**

3. Chants of the Ordinary
The chants of the Ordinary began as syllabic melodies sung by the congregation. Now they are sung by the choir. The *Gloria* and *Credo,* with their long texts, remain mostly syllabic, while the others are more elaborate. Because of their texts, the *Kyrie, Sanctus,* and *Agnus Dei* have three-part sectional arrangements.   **Music: NAWM 3b, 3g, and 3h**

C. *Later Developments of the Chant*

Because of the rise of new cultural centers in western and central Europe and the decline of Christian influence in the south, almost all important developments in music from the ninth century to near the end of the Middle Ages took place north of the Alps.

1. Tropes
Tropes are newly composed additions to existing chants. There are three types: adding text to existing melismas; adding music only; or adding both text and music. Tropes flourished in the tenth and eleventh centuries, then gradually disappeared.   **Music: NAWM 7**

2 CHANT AND SECULAR SONG IN THE MIDDLE AGES, 400–1450 13

2. Sequences

Sequences were newly composed chants, usually sung after the Alleluia in the Mass. Like tropes, all but a few sequences were eliminated from the liturgy by the Council of Trent (1545–63).   **Music: NAWM 5**

Etude: Structure of the Sequence
The form of the sequence usually consists of a series of musical phrases, of which all but the first and last are repeated to new phrases of text.

3. Liturgical drama

Liturgical dramas were short dialogues set to chant and performed just prior to the Mass.   **Music: NAWM 7**

4. Hildegard of Bingen

Hildegard of Bingen (1098–1179), a famous abbess and mystic, wrote both words and music for several sequences and for the sacred music drama *Ordo virtutum* (The Virtues, ca. 1151).   **Music: NAWM 6**

III. Medieval Music Theory and Practice (CHWM 32–35)

Treatises from the eighth century through the late Middle Ages tend to focus on practical issues such as performance, notation, and the modes.

1. The church modes

Medieval theorists recognized *eight church modes*, defined by their *finalis*, or *final*, and their *range*. *Authentic modes* have a range that runs up an octave from the final; *plagal modes* run from a fourth below to a fifth above the final. There is one plagal and one authentic mode on each of four finals: D, E, F, and G.

Etude: More about the Medieval Church Modes
Each mode also has a *tenor* or *reciting tone*. The note B was sometimes flatted, making the modes on D and F resemble modern minor and major. Medieval theorists applied Greek names to the church modes, which were more commonly identified by number.

2. Solmization and the Guidonian hand

Guido of Arezzo (ca. 991–after 1033) devised *solmization* syllables to help singers recall where whole tones and semitones occur. With some alterations, these syllables are still used. The *Guidonian hand* assigned a pitch to each joint of the left hand as a tool to teach notes and intervals.

3. The staff

The musical staff (which evolved from earlier systems of using lines to indicate relative pitch) allowed precise notation of relative pitch. This made it possible to learn a melody directly from the written page.

IV. Nonliturgical and Secular Monody (CHWM 35–42, NAWM 8–12)

1. Goliard songs

Early forms of secular music (from the eleventh and twelfth centuries) include *Goliard songs,* songs with Latin texts celebrating the vagabond life of students and wandering clerics called Goliards.

2. Conductus

Conductus is a term used for any serious, nonliturgical Latin song, sacred or secular, with a metrical text and a newly composed melody.

3. Chanson de geste

The *chanson de geste* was an epic narrative poem sung to melodic formulas. An example is the *Song of Roland,* the French national epic.

4. Jongleurs

Jongleurs or *ménestrals* (minstrels) made a living as traveling musicians and performers, on the margins of society.

5. Troubadours and trouvères

Troubadours (feminine: *trobairitz*) were poet-composers active in southern France in the eleventh and twelfth centuries. They wrote in the language of the region, called *Provençal* (or *langue d'oc* or *Occitan*), and were from or associated with the aristocracy. Their counterparts in northern France, called *trouvères,* wrote in the *langue d'oïl,* the ancestor of modern French, and remained active through the thirteenth century. The songs of both groups are varied in structure and topic. Many trouvère songs include a *refrain,* a segment of text that returns in each stanza with the same melody.

6. Pastourelle

One genre was the *pastourelle,* which told of a shepherdess pursued by a knight. This evolved from narration to dialogue, leading to musical plays such as *Jeu de Robin et de Marion* (ca. 1284) by Adam de la Halle (ca. 1237–ca. 1287.)   **Music: NAWM 8**

7. Provençal lyrics

Many of the troubadour and trouvère songs were about love. They often depicted a kind of love—called *courtly love*—in which a discreet, unattainable woman was adored from a distance.

8. Bernart de Ventadorn

Bernart de Ventadorn (ca. 1150–ca. 1180), one of the most popular poets of his day, rose from low status to consort with aristocrats. His *canso* (song) *Can vei la lauzeta mover* is well known.   **Music: NAWM 9**

9. Melodic structure

Troubadour and trouvère poems are strophic. The melodies are mostly syllabic with a range of an octave or less. The rhythm of troubadour melodies is uncertain in the notation, but later trouvère melodies have clear rhythms. Various patterns of repetition are used, along with free composition.

10. Beatriz de Dia

Beatriz de Dia (d. ca. 1212) was a countess and trobairitz. Her canso *A chantar* shows the woman's perspective on courtly love. Each stanza has a musical form of a b a b c d b.   **Music: NAWM 10**

11. Minnesinger

The *Minnesinger* were knightly poet-composers active in German lands from the twelfth through the fourteenth centuries. They sang of an idealized love (*Minne*), and their melodies are formed of phrases that repeat in orderly patterns. A common form is *Bar form*: a a b, with the b section often repeating the end of the a section (thus resembling Beatriz's canso). **Music: NAWM 11**

12. Meistersinger

The *Meistersinger* were German poet-composers of the fourteenth through sixteenth centuries, drawn from the urban middle class of tradesmen and artisans rather than from the aristocracy. Their songs were governed by rigid rules.   **Music: NAWM 12**

Window: Eleanor of Aquitaine and Her Courts of Love (CHWM 40–41)

Eleanor of Aquitaine (1122?–1204) was a member of an aristocratic family, granddaughter of a troubadour, wife and mother of kings, and a patron of troubadours and trouvères.

STUDY QUESTIONS

Roman Chant and Liturgy (CHWM 19–23)

1. What are the *Offices* or *Canonical Hours*? From what earlier practice do they derive?

2. What does the *Mass* commemorate?

3. What are the three sections of the Mass liturgy? What is the main focus of each one?

   a.

   b.

   c.

4. What is the *Ordinary* of the Mass, and what is the *Proper*?

5. Example 2.1 in CHWM (p. 25) is a transcription in modern notation of the chant on the facing page. The plainchant notation uses a four-line staff. As in the modern five-line staff, each line stands for a pitch a third lower than the line above it, and the spaces stand for the pitches in between. The first symbol in each line is a clef; here it is a C clef on the top line, indicating that the top line stands for middle C. What pitch does each of the following lines and spaces stand for?

the second line from the top   ____   the bottom line   ____

the space below it   ____   the space below it ____

In plainchant notation, what does a dot after a note signify? (Note: This is a sign added by modern editors and does not appear in medieval manuscripts.)

Musical exercise in reading chant notation (CHWM 24–25)

You do not have to know the names of the different note-shapes. But with a little practice you should be able to read the chant notation. Practice in the following way:

Reading the modern notation in Example 2.1, sing or play on an instrument the first phrase of the chant (the top line of the example). You may omit the words if it is easier for you to do so.

Then sing (or play) the same phrase, using the plainchant notation. Go back and forth between the two ways to notate the phrase until you understand how the plainchant notation indicates the same pitches and rhythms as the modern notation. If you have trouble with any of the note-shapes, check the explanation in the text on p. 23 of CHWM or p. 7 of NAWM.

Go through the same process for each phrase in turn: sing (or play) it first from the modern notation, then from the plainchant notation.

When you are finished, sing (or play) through the whole chant from the plainchant notation. If you get stuck, refer to the modern transcription.

Classes, Forms, and Types of Chant (CHWM 24–32, NAWM 3–4)

6. What manner of performance does each of the following terms describe?

   antiphonal

   responsorial

   direct

   Which type is most often associated with melismatic chants? _____

7. Which of the following chants are from the Mass Ordinary, and which are from the Proper?

Introit _____   Credo _____

Kyrie _____   Offertory _____

Gloria _____   Sanctus _____

Gradual _____   Agnus Dei _____

Alleluia _____   Communion _____

Music to Study
NAWM 3: Mass for Christmas Day, in Gregorian chant
   3a: Introit: *Puer natus est nobis*   CD 1.3   Cassette 1.A
   3b: Kyrie   CD 1.4   Cassette 1.A
                            (Concise 1.2)   (Concise 1.A)
   3c: Gloria   CD 1.5   Cassette 1.A
   3d: Gradual: *Viderunt omnes*   CD 1.6–7   Cassette 1.A
   3e: Alleluia Dies sanctificatus   CD 1.8   Cassette 1.A
                            (Concise 1.3)   (Concise 1.A)
   3f: Offertory: *Tui sunt caeli*   CD 1.9   Cassette 1.A
   3g: Sanctus   CD 1.10   Cassette 1.A
   3h: Agnus Dei   CD 1.11   Cassette 1.A
   3i: Communion: *Viderunt omnes*   CD 1.12   Cassette 1.A
NAWM 4: Office of Second Vespers, Nativity of Our Lord (evening service on Christmas Day), in Gregorian chant
   4b: Antiphon for first psalm   CD 1.13   Cassette 1.A
                            (Concise 1.4)   (Concise 1.A)
   4c: First psalm   CD 1.14   Cassette 1.A
                            (Concise 1.5)   (Concise 1.A)
   4j: Short Reponsory   CD 1.15   Cassette 1.A
   (other sections not on recording)

8. Look at the chants of the Mass and Office in NAWM 3 and 4. Find two examples of primarily *syllabic* chants, two *melismatic* chants, and two that are *neumatic*, frequently using more than two notes per syllable but rarely using long melismas.

syllabic   neumatic   melismatic

_____   _____   _____

_____   _____   _____

9. What are some ways that the music of chant reflects the accentuation and phrasing of the text? For each way you mention, find an example among the chants of the Mass and Office in NAWM 3 and 4.

10. What are *psalm tones*? Where are they used?

11. How are psalm tones shaped, and how do they adjust to suit the many different texts they are used with? Give an example from NAWM 4.

12. What is an *antiphon*? Diagram the way an antiphon and psalm would be performed in the Vespers in NAWM 4, using A for Antiphon, V for each psalm verse, and D for the Lesser Doxology.

13. The Introit, Offertory, and Communion were all once antiphons with psalms. What is the structure of each now? (Use the same symbols as in #12 above.)

    Introit   _____   Communion   _____

    Offertory _____

14. How is the Alleluia in NAWM 3e shaped by musical repetition?

    Which parts are sung by the soloist(s)? _____

    Which parts are sung by the choir? _____

    What is the *jubilus*? _____

15. What is the pattern of musical repetition in the Kyrie in NAWM 3b (as it is performed)? How does this relate to the pattern of repetition in the text?

16. What is a *trope*? What are the three types of trope?

17. Why are there no tropes and so few sequences in the modern liturgy?

Music to Study
 NAWM 5: Wipo, *Victimae paschali laudes,* sequence for Mass on Easter Day
  (first half of the eleventh century)
   CD 1.16 (Concise 1.6)   Cassette 1.A (Concise 1.A)
 NAWM 6: Hildegard of Bingen, *Ordo virtutum* (The Virtues), sacred music
  drama, excerpt: closing chorus, *In principio omnes* (ca. 1151)
   CD 1.17–18 (Concise 1.7–8) Cassette 1.A (Concise 1.A)
 NAWM 7: *Quem quaeritis in praesepe,* trope (liturgical drama) at Mass on
  Christmas Day (tenth century)
   CD 1.19   Cassette 1.A

18. Diagram the form of the sequence *Victimae paschali laudes* by Wipo (NAWM 5).

 In addition to the repetition of complete phrases for successive verses, where else does melodic repetition appear in this sequence?

19. How is melodic repetition used in Hildegard of Bingen's *In principio omnes* (NAWM 6)? How does this song differ from liturgical chant in function and in style?

20. In what sense is *Quem quaeritis in praesepe* (NAWM 7) a trope? Where does it fit in the Mass to which it is attached?

21. What makes *Quem quaeritis in praesepe* a *liturgical drama*? (In what sense is it liturgical? In what sense is it a drama?)

Medieval Music Theory and Practice (CHWM 32–35)

22. The eight church modes are labeled by number and name. Each is defined by (1) its *finalis* or *final*, (2) its *tenor* or *reciting tone*, and (3) its *range*. Give the name, final, tenor, and range for each of the church modes.

Number	Name	Final	Tenor	Range
1	_____	____	____	_____
2	_____	____	____	_____
3	_____	____	____	_____
4	_____	____	____	_____
5	_____	____	____	_____
6	_____	____	____	_____
7	_____	____	____	_____
8	_____	____	____	_____

23. Which modes are *authentic* (indicate by number)? _____

Which are *plagal*? _____

What is the relationship of a plagal mode to its corresponding authentic mode?

24. Using the criteria of final and range, identify (by number) the mode of each of the following chants:

    Quem quaeritis in praesepe (NAWM 7)   _____

    Alleluia Pascha nostrum (NAWM 16a)   _____

    Conditor alme siderum (NAWM 29, verse 1)   _____

25. What is *solmization*? Why was it useful? When was it invented, and by whom? How is modern solmization similar to medieval practice, and how does it differ?

Nonliturgical and Secular Monody (CHWM 35–42, NAWM 8–12)

26. Who were the *Goliards*? Who were the *jongleurs* or *minstrels*? What kinds of music did each perform, and when and where did they perform it?

27. What is a *conductus*? How does it differ from a liturgical chant?

28. What is a *troubadour*? a *trobairitz*? a *trouvère*? When were they active, and what languages did they use? From what social classes did they come?

29. What is *courtly love*?

30. Who were the *Minnesinger*? When and where were they active? How are their songs like troubadour and trouvère songs, and how do they differ?

31. Who were the *Meistersinger*? When and where were they active?

Music to Study
  NAWM 8: Adam de la Halle, *Robins m'aime*, rondeau or trouvère song (ca. 1284)
  CD 1.20   Cassette 1.A
  NAWM 9: Bernart de Ventadorn, *Can vei*, troubadour song (ca. 1170–80)
  CD 1.21 (Concise 1.9)   Cassette 1.A (Concise 1.A)
  NAWM 10: Beatriz de Dia, *A chantar*, canso or troubadour song (second half of 12th century)
  CD 1.22   Cassette 1.A
  NAWM 11: Wizlau von Rügen, *We ich han gedacht*, Minnelied (ca. 1290–1325)
  CD 1.23   Cassette 1.B
  NAWM 12: Hans Sachs, *Nachdem David war redlich*, Meisterlied (ca. 1520–76)
  CD 1.24   Cassette 1.B

32. Describe the melodic characteristics of troubadour songs, using Bernart de Ventadorn's *Can vei* (NAWM 9) and Comtessa Beatritz de Dia's *A chantar* (NAWM 10) as examples.

    How many notes are set to each syllable? _____

    How large a range does the melody typically cover? _____

    Does the notation indicate the rhythm? _____

    How else would you characterize the melodic style?

33. How is the trouvère song *Robins m'aime* (NAWM 8) by Adam de la Halle different in style from the troubadour songs (NAWM 9–10)?

34. How do *Can vei, A chantar,* and *Robins m'aime* use melodic repetition? Chart the form of each (for the first two, chart the form of a single strophe; for the third, use capital letters for repetitions of music *and* text, and lower-case letters for repetitions of music with new words).

    Can vei

    A chantar

    Robins m'aime

35. What is the mode of each of these songs? (Use the mode number.)

    Can vei   _____

    A chantar   _____

    Robins m'aime   _____

36. What is *Bar form*? How is it used in Wizlau von Rügen's Minnelied *We ich han gedacht* (NAWM 11) and in Hans Sachs's *Nachdem David war redlich* (NAWM 12)?

TERMS TO KNOW

In part because the Middle Ages are so long ago and the culture so distant from our own, there are many unfamiliar terms that relate to the music of this period. They are listed below in three groups. The terms related to liturgy will be useful for church music of later periods as well, since the liturgy has shaped church music of every period down to our own time.

Terms Related to Liturgy

Office or Canonical Hours
Vespers
canticle
Magnificat
Mass

Ordinary: Kyrie, Gloria, Credo, Sanctus, Agnus Dei
Proper: Introit, Gradual, Alleluia, Tract, Offertory, Communion
Lesser Doxology (Gloria Patri)

Terms Related to Chant

antiphon
responsory
neume
antiphonal, responsorial, or direct performance
syllabic, neumatic, melismatic
psalm tone
antiphonal psalmody
respond
jubilus

trope
sequence
liturgical drama
mode: the eight church modes
final (finalis)
authentic mode, plagal mode
tenor or reciting tone
solmization
Guidonian hand

Terms Related to Other Monophonic Music

Goliard song
conductus
chanson de geste
jongleur or ménestral or minstrel
troubadour, trobairitz
Provençal or langue d'oc
trouvère

langue d'oïl
refrain
pastourelle
courtly love
Minnesinger
bar form: Stollen, Abgesang
Meistersinger

NAMES TO KNOW

Hildegard of Bingen
Guido of Arezzo
Song of Roland
Adam de la Halle

Bernart de Ventadorn
Beatriz de Dia
Eleanor of Aquitaine

REVIEW QUESTIONS

1. Make a time-line from 800 to 1600 and locate on it the pieces in NAWM 5–13, their composers, and the Council of Trent and Guido of Arezzo. (The chants in NAWM 3–4 come from many centuries and most cannot be dated accurately, so they cannot be fixed on your time-line.)

2. Why was notation devised, and how was it useful? How would your life as a musician be different if there was no notation?

3. How has the music of chant been shaped by its role in the ceremonies and liturgy of the Roman Church, by the texts, and by the manner in which it has been performed? Use as examples at least two individual chants of varying types, and show in what ways the musical characteristics of each are appropriate for its liturgical role, its text, and its manner of performance.

4. Trace the history of monophonic secular song from the Goliards to the Meistersinger. For each group of poet-composers, note their region, language, place in society, and time of activity, and briefly describe their music.

POLYPHONIC MUSIC FROM ITS BEGINNINGS THROUGH THE THIRTEENTH CENTURY

3

CHAPTER OBJECTIVES

After you complete the reading, study of the music, and study questions for this chapter, you should be able to:

1. name the new trends in eleventh-century music that became distinguishing characteristics of Western music;
2. describe the varieties of polyphony practiced between the ninth and thirteenth centuries and trace their historical development;
3. define important terms and identify the people, works, and schools of composition that played a major role in the development of medieval polyphony; and
4. describe the origins and early evolution of the motet.

CHAPTER OUTLINE

Prelude (CHWM 43–44)

The eleventh and twelfth centuries brought prosperity and a cultural revival to much of western Europe, including the beginning of modern universities. *Polyphony*, music of two or more independent voices, arose in church music and set the stage for the later evolution of Western music. The development of precise notation allowed composers for the first time to fix a work in definitive form and transmit it accurately to others. As a result, written composition began to replace improvisation as a way to create new works. The main types of polyphony in the Middle Ages were *organum*, *conductus*, and *motet*.

I. Early Organum (CHWM 45–48, NAWM 14–15)

Polyphony was probably improvised before it was written down. It was first described in the ninth-century treatise *Musica enchiriadis*. In this early *organum*, an added voice (organal voice or *vox organalis*) appears below a chant melody (principal voice or *vox principalis*), moving either in parallel

26

motion at the interval of a fourth or fifth (*parallel organum*) or in a mixture of parallel and oblique motion (*organum with oblique motion*). In *eleventh-century organum* (also called *note-against-note organum*), the added voice is usually above the chant (though the voices may cross), moving most often in contrary motion to the chant and forming consonant intervals with it (unison, fourth, fifth, and octave). Only those portions of chant that were sung by soloists were set polyphonically, so that in performance sections of polyphony alternate with sections of chant.   **Music: NAWM 14**

1. Florid organum
A new type, *florid organum,* appeared early in the twelfth century in Aquitaine, in southwestern France. The chant is sustained in long notes in the lower voice (called the *tenor*), while the upper voice sings from one to many notes above each note of the tenor.   **Music: NAWM 15**

2. Organum purum and discant
This texture came to be known as *organum, organum duplum* (double organum) or *organum purum* (pure organum). *Organum* (pl. *organa*) was also used to refer to a piece that used this style. A contrasting style in which voices move mainly note against note was called *discant.*

3. Notation of organum purum
Manuscripts for these types of polyphony use *score notation* (one part above the other, with notes that sound together aligned vertically), but do not indicate rhythm or duration.

II. Notre Dame Organum (CHWM 48–54, NAWM 16a–c, 16e, 17)

The first composers of polyphony known to us by name are *Léonin* (ca. 1135–ca. 1201) and *Pérotin* (fl. 1180–ca. 1207). They worked in Paris at Notre Dame Cathedral, the center for a style of music known as *Notre Dame polyphony.* (We know their names because a treatise known as *Anonymous IV* describes their music and names some of their works.)

1. Léonin
Léonin wrote or compiled the *Magnus liber organi* (Great Book of Organum), a cycle of organa for the solo portions of the Graduals, Alleluias, and Office Responsories for the entire church year.

Etude: A Closer Look at the Rhythmic Modes
A notation to indicate patterns of long and short notes was developed during the twelfth and early thirteenth centuries. By about 1250, these patterns were codified as the six *rhythmic modes.* The modes were based on divisions of a three-fold unit called a *perfection.* Each mode was indicated by a different succession of note groupings or *ligatures.*

2. *Alleluia Pascha nostrum*
The Easter chant *Alleluia Pascha nostrum* (NAWM 16) shows several layers of elaboration. The first is Léonin's addition of organa for the solo portions. His organa are in two voices and alternate sections of organum, in which the upper voice may be in free rhythm, with sections in discant style,

in which both voices use the rhythmic modes (the slow fifth mode in the tenor, a faster mode in the upper voice).   **Music: NAWM 16a–c**

3. Clausula

A section in discant is called a *clausula* (pl. *clausulae*). Clausulae are used where there are melismas in the original chant.

4. Pérotin

Pérotin and his contemporaries revised Léonin's work, writing discant clausulae to replace sections of organum and *substitute clausulae* in place of older sections of discant. The tenors in these clausulae often repeat rhythmic patterns and segments of melody.   **Music: NAWM 16c**

5. Triple and quadruple organum

Pérotin also wrote organa in three and four voices, called *organum triplum* and *organum quadruplum* respectively, in which the upper parts are in the rhythmic modes over sustained notes in the tenor. The second voice (reading up from the bottom) was called the *duplum,* the third the *triplum,* and the fourth the *quadruplum.*   **Music: NAWM 17**

III. Polyphonic Conductus (CHWM 54–56, NAWM 18)

The *polyphonic conductus* is a setting of a metrical Latin poem (like the earlier monophonic conductus). The tenor is newly written, not based on chant. The two, three, or four voices move in similar rhythm and declaim the text together, in an almost homorhythmic and syllabic texture known as *conductus style.* Some conductus feature long melismas called *caudae,* especially at the beginning or end. As in organa and discant clausulae, vertical consonances of the fifth and octave are prominent throughout and required at cadences, and the music is written in score notation. Both organum and conductus fell out of favor after 1250.   **Music: NAWM 18**

IV. The Motet (CHWM 56–60, NAWM 16d, 16f–g, 19)

Starting in the early thirteenth century, words were often added to the upper voice or voices of a discant clausula. This produced a new genre, the *motet* (from the French *mot,* for "word"). The duplum of a motet is called the *motetus.* The tenor of a motet, like that of a clausula, consisted of a borrowed chant or *cantus firmus.* Composers created motets by reworking existing clausulae or composing new lines over a given melody. A typical thirteenth-century motet has three voices. Each of the top two voices has its own text, and the tenor could be played or sung. The texts could be in Latin or French, sacred or secular, and were usually on related subjects. A motet is known by a compound title with the first word(s) of each text, including the tenor.   **Music: NAWM 16d, 16f, and 16g**

1. Franconian Motet

In many motets from the second half of the thirteenth century, the upper voice moves more quickly and has a longer text than the middle voice, while the tenor moves more slowly. This type is called the *Franconian*

motet, after the composer and theorist *Franco of Cologne* (fl. ca. 1250–
1280). **Music: NAWM 19**

Etude: Thirteenth-Century Notation

Notation for the rhythmic modes used patterns of ligatures, but the syllabic
text-setting of motets made ligatures impossible. This required a notation
that indicated the duration of each note. *Franconian notation,* codified by
Franco of Cologne in *Ars cantus mensurabilis* (The Art of Measurable
Music, ca. 1280), solved this problem by using different note-shapes for
different relative values. (This same principle underlies modern notation.)
With this more exact notation, polyphonic works no longer had to be written in score and were notated instead in *choirbook format,* in which the
voices all appear on the same or facing pages but are not vertically aligned.

Window: The Motet as Gothic Cathedral (CHWM 58–59)

The voices in a thirteenth-century motet are rhythmically independent yet
coordinated, the higher voices moving faster than the lower ones. This has
parallels in the architecture of the Gothic cathedrals of the time.

STUDY QUESTIONS

Prelude (CHWM 43–44)

1. What important new developments in European music were under way in the
   eleventh century?

Early Organum (CHWM 45–48, NAWM 14–15)

2. In what treatise was polyphony first described? _____

   About when was this treatise written? _____

3. State the rules that govern the composition of Example 3.1 in CHWM, p. 45 (parallel organum in two voices, with a modified cadence).

Music to Study
   NAWM 14: *Alleluia Justus ut palma,* organum from *Ad organum faciendum* (ca. 1100)
      CD 1.30 (Concise 1.10)   Cassette 1.B (Concise 1.A)

4. In the eleventh-century organum *Alleluia Justus ut palma* (NAWM 14), some sections are not set in polyphony. Why not?

   In the sections in two-voice polyphony, which part is the original chant, and which is the added voice? Which of the two is more disjunct (fewer steps, more skips)? Why?

5. If you had to write down the rules for composing organum like this, what would they be? Include mention of the harmonic intervals normally used.

6. In florid organum, which voice has the chant? _____

What is this voice called? _____

Why did it receive this name?

Describe the relationship between the parts in florid organum. What is each voice like?

Music to Study
   NAWM 15: Magister Albertus of Paris, *Congaudeant catholici,* trope on
       Benedicamus Domino (ca. 1146–1177)
   CD 1.31   Cassette 1.B

7. The *Benedicamus Domino* trope *Congaudeant catholici* (NAWM 15) is un-usual for its time in having three voices, the bottom two moving in unison and the top one more melismatic. In what other ways does it differ from the eleventh-century organum *Alleluia Justus ut palma* (NAWM 14)?

Notre Dame Organum (CHWM 48–54, NAWM 16a–c, 16e, 17)

8. Show the rhythmic pattern for each of the six rhythmic modes:

   Mode I   _____

   Mode II   _____

   Mode III   _____

   Mode IV   _____

   Mode V   _____

   Mode VI   _____

9. For which chants of the Mass and Office did Léonin write organa?

   Of these chants, which portions did he set in polyphony?

   What was his collection of organa called? _____

10. According to the treatise called Anonymous IV, what was Léonin best at?

   What was Pérotin noted for?

11. What is a *clausula*?

   What is a *substitute clausula*?

Music to Study
    NAWM 16a–c and e: *Alleluia Pascha nostrum,* plainchant and Léonin's
        setting (late twelfth century), with later anonymous substitutions
      16a: Plainchant   not on recording
      16b: Léonin, organum duplum (pp. 53–54, 56, 58–59)
          CD 1.32–34, 1.36, 1.38–40   Cassette 1.B
      16c: Anonymous discant clausula on "nostrum" (pp. 54–55)
                                 not on recording
      16e: Anonymous substitute clausula on "-la-" (pp. 56–57)
                                 not on recording

      (NAWM 16 can be confusing to follow. See the explanation in NAWM.)

12. The setting of *Alleluia Pascha nostrum* in NAWM 16b, c, and e includes sec-
    tions in both organum duplum and discant style. What are the main features
    of each style?

    organum duplum

    discant style

13. Which sections of *Alleluia Pascha nostrum* use organum style?

    Which sections use discant style? Why is discant used in these passages?

14. Which sections of NAWM 16b use no polyphony? Why are these sections not
    sung polyphonically?

15. In the discant clausula on the word "nostrum" (NAWM 16c), which rhythmic mode predominates in the upper voice? in the lower voice?

   upper voice _____   lower voice _____

   Besides the rhythmic mode itself, what repeated rhythmic pattern is used in the lower voice?

16. In NAWM 16c, how does the lower part compare to the chant melody on "nostrum" in NAWM 16a (other than being a fifth lower)? What happens in the lower voice at m. 19, where the editor has added a double bar and a Roman numeral II?

17. In NAWM 16c, how many times does each of the following vertical sonorities appear on the downbeats?

   octave _____ perfect fifth _____ third _____ unison _____ other _____

18. Using questions 15 and 16 above as guides, describe the use of rhythmic modes and rhythmic and melodic repetition in the discant clausula on "-lu-" in NAWM 16b (pp. 58–59, CD 1.40).

19. What are the names for the various voices in an organum?

   bottom voice   _____

   second voice from the bottom   _____

   third voice from the bottom (if any) _____

   fourth voice from the bottom (if any) _____

   Which voice carries the chant?   _____

Music to Study
   NAWM 17: Pérotin, *Sederunt,* organum quadruplum (late twelfth or early
         thirteenth century), respond only
      CD 1.42–44 (Concise 1.11–13)   Cassette 1.B (Concise 1.A)

20. Compare the organum of Léonin in NAWM 16b with that of Pérotin in
    NAWM 17, an organum quadruplum on *Sederunt.* How is Pérotin's style like
    Léonin's, and how is it different?

21. Which rhythmic mode predominates in each of the following passages of
    Sederunt?

    the top three voices, mm. 2-10   _____

    the top voice, mm. 13-23   _____

    the top voice, mm. 35-40   _____

22. What vertical sonority is used most often at the cadences in *Sederunt?*

Polyphonic Conductus (CHWM 54–56, NAWM 18)

23. How is a polyphonic conductus like a monophonic conductus?

Music to Study
   NAWM 18: *Ave virgo virginum,* conductus (thirteenth century)
      CD 1.45   Cassette 1.B

24. In what ways is *Ave virgo virginum* (NAWM 18) typical of the polyphonic conductus, as described in CHWM?

   How is it different from organum and from discant?

The Motet (CHWM 56–60, NAWM 16d, 16f–g, 19)

25. How did the motet originate, and how did it acquire its name?

26. What is a *cantus firmus,* and what is its role in a motet?

27. What does the title of a motet indicate?

Music to Study
    NAWM 16d: *Gaudeat devotio fidelium,* motet (thirteenth century)
        CD 1.35   Cassette 1.B
    NAWM 16f: *Ave Maria, Fons letitie—Latus,* motet (thirteenth century)
        CD 1.37   Cassette 1.B
    NAWM 16g: *Salve, salus hominum—O radians stella—Nostrum,* bitextual
        motet (thirteenth century)
        CD 1.41   Cassette 1.B
    NAWM 19: *Amours mi font souffrir—En mai—Flos filius eius,* motet in
        Franconian style (late thirteenth century)
        CD 1.46 (Concise 1.14)   Cassette 1.B (Concise 1.A)

28. How are the motets in NAWM 16d, 16f, and 16g related to the discant clausulae on *nostrum* and *-latus* in NAWM 16c and 16e? What has been added, deleted, or changed in creating these new works? What has stayed the same?

29. What makes *Amours mi font souffrir—En mai—Flos filius eius* (NAWM 19) a *Franconian motet,* and how does it differ from earlier motets?

30. When were Franconian motets written? _____

    After whom were they named? _____

    About when was this person active? _____

31. What new notational system was devised to indicate rhythm in motets? How was it different from the notation for the rhythmic modes? Why was this change necessary, and what results did it have?

32. In what major treatise was this notational system codified?

Who wrote it, and when? _____   _____

TERMS TO KNOW

Terms Related to Early Polphony

polyphony
organum
vox principalis, vox organalis
parallel organum
organum with oblique motion
eleventh-century organum (or
   note-against-note organum)

florid organum
tenor (in florid organum, discant,
   and motet)
organum duplum, organum purum
discant
score notation

Terms Related to Notre Dame Polyphony

Notre Dame polyphony
rhythmic modes
perfection (Latin *perfectio*)
ligatures
clausula (pl. clausulae)
substitute clausula

organum triplum, organum
quadruplum
duplum, triplum, quadruplum
polyphonic conductus
cauda (pl. caudae)
conductus style

Terms Related to the 13th-Century Motet

motet	Franconian motet
motetus	Franconian notation
cantus firmus	choirbook format

Names to Know

Musica enchiriadis	*Magnus liber organi*
Winchester Troper	Anonymous IV
Ad organum faciendum	Franco of Cologne
Léonin	*Ars cantus mensurabilis*
Pérotin	

Review Questions

1. Take the time-line you made in chapter 2 and add the pieces in NAWM 14-15, 16b-g, and 17-19, their composers (when known), Franco of Cologne, and the *Ars cantus mensurabilis*.

2. What different forms of polyphony can be found between the ninth century and the first half of the twelfth century? Describe an example of each type.

3. Describe the music of Notre Dame polyphony. Include in your discussion the major composers, the genres they cultivated, the rhythmic and harmonic style of their music, and the way new pieces used, embellished, or substituted for existing music.

4. Trace the development of the motet from its origins through the end of the thirteenth century, using NAWM 16d, 16g, and 19 as examples of three stages in that development.

5. In your view, looking back over chapters 2 and 3, what developments during the period 900–1300 were most significant for the later evolution of music? What styles, practices, techniques, attitudes, or approaches that were new in this time have continued to affect Western music in the last 700 years? In your opinion, which of these have most set music in the Western European tradition apart from music of other cultures?

FRENCH AND ITALIAN MUSIC IN THE FOURTEENTH CENTURY

4

CHAPTER OBJECTIVES

After you complete the reading, study of the music, and study questions for this chapter, you should be able to:

1. explain the increased prominence of secular literature and music in the four-teenth century;
2. describe some of the rhythmic and other stylistic features that characterize the music of the *ars nova, trecento,* and late-fourteenth-century *ars subtilior*;
3. describe isorhythm and its use in fourteenth-century motets and Mass move-ments;
4. name and describe the forms of secular song practiced in France and Italy during the fourteenth century;
5. identify some of the major figures, works, and terms associated with music in the fourteenth century.

CHAPTER OUTLINE

Prelude (CHWM 62–64)

The fourteenth century was an unstable and secular age. Church authority was undermined by the move of the papacy to Avignon (1305–78) and a schism between rival popes (1378–1417). Human reason became an authority in its own sphere, independent of church control, and *humanism* renewed the influence of Greek and Latin literature on Western culture. The reigning musical style in France was the *Ars nova* ("new art"), named after a treatise attributed to *Philippe de Vitry* (1291–1361). (Among the new techniques was the use of duple divisions of the note in addition to triple, which gives fourteenth-century music a rhythm distinct from that of earlier periods.) In Italy, the fourteenth century is known as the *trecento* (from "mille trecento," Italian for 1300).

I. The *ars nova* in France (CHWM 64–70 and 71, NAWM 20–22)

1. *Roman de Fauvel*

The *Roman de Fauvel* (1310–14) is a satirical poem with interpolated music, including 34 motets. By this time, motet texts were usually secular and often referred to contemporary events. Five three-part motets in this work are by Vitry, the outstanding French poet and composer of his day.

2. The isorhythmic motet

The motets of Vitry and other fourteenth-century composers use *isorhythm* ("same rhythm"). The tenor in an *isorhythmic motet* is composed of a repeating series of pitches, called the *color,* and a repeating rhythmic pattern, called the *talea.* One may be longer than the other, and their endings may coincide or overlap. Upper voices may also be isorhythmic in whole or in part, if they feature repeating rhythmic patterns coordinated with repetitions in the tenor. **Music: NAWM 20**

A. *Guillaume de Machaut*

Guillaume de Machaut (ca. 1300–1377) was the leading poet and composer of fourteenth-century France. His isorhythmic motets are longer and more complex than Vitry's and frequently use *hocket.*

1. Mass

The most famous musical work of the fourteenth century is Machaut's *Messe de Notre Dame* (Mass of Our Lady, ca. 1364), a four-part setting of the Mass Ordinary. The Gloria and Credo are syllabic, with all four voices declaiming the text together, and end with isorhythmic Amens. The other movements are isorhythmic, often including isorhythm in all or most voices, and their tenors are drawn from plainchant melodies for the same texts from the Ordinary of the Mass. **Music: NAWM 22**

2. Love songs

Machaut wrote many secular songs (chansons), including monophonic *lais* and *virelais* and polyphonic *virelais, rondeaux,* and *ballades.* The virelai, rondeau, and ballade are called *formes fixes* (fixed forms); each features a particular pattern of rhymes and repeating lines of poetry called *refrains,* and the rhymes and refrains are coordinated with repeating segments of music. The polyphonic songs are for one or two singers and instruments. Unlike the motet, in which the tenor provides structure and was written first, in the secular songs the *cantus,* or top part, is the principal line and was written first. This treble-dominated style of voice and instrumental accompaniment is called *cantilena style.* **Music: NAWM 21**

Etude: Standard Forms of Fourteenth-Century Chansons

The virelai has the form A b b a A, in which A is the refrain and both A and a use the same music. The ballade has the form a a b C and usually has three or four stanzas, each ending with the same line of text (C). Musically, the endings of the a section and the C section may be similar or identical. The rondeau has the form A B a A a b A B, with a refrain in two parts (A and B), the first repeating in the middle of the stanza. The stanza uses the same two sections of music as the refrain, a and b, but with different words.

II. Italian *trecento* Music (CHWM 70–77, NAWM 23–25)

Most fourteenth-century Italian music was monophonic and unwritten, and most sacred polyphony was improvised. Secular polyphony was cultivated among the elite in certain cities in northern Italy, especially Florence, where the *Squarcialupi Codex*, the most important manuscript of four-teenth-century Italian music, was copied.

1. Madrigal
The fourteenth-century *madrigal* (not to be confused with the sixteenth-century form) is for two voices without instruments.   **Music: NAWM 23**

2. Caccia
The *caccia* features two voices in canon at the unison over a free instru-mental part. The texts are often about hunting or other action scenes, with the appropriate sounds imitated in the music.

3. Ballata
The *ballata* evolved from monophonic dance songs with choral refrains (from "ballare," to dance). The polyphonic ballata of the late fourteenth century was a lyrical piece whose form resembles the French virelai.

Etude: Standard Forms of *Trecento* Song
The madrigal has two or three three-line stanzas, all set to the same music, with a closing couplet called the *ritornello,* set to new music in a different meter. The caccia has no set form. In a ballata, a three-line *ripresa* or refrain (A) precedes and follows a seven-line stanza. The stanza's first two pairs of lines, called *piedi,* present a new phrase (b), and the last three lines, the *volta,* use the music of the refrain (a), for an overall form of A b b a A.

4. Francesco Landini
Francesco Landini (ca. 1325–1397) was the leading Italian composer of the fourteenth century. He is best known for his ballate and wrote no sacred works. Landini has lent his name to the *"Landini" cadence,* in which the usual cadence formula of a sixth expanding to an octave between cantus and tenor is decorated by the upper voice descending a step before resolving to the octave.   **Music: NAWM 24**

5. French influence and the later fourteenth century
In the late fourteenth century, Italian composers began to absorb aspects of the French style. Composers at Avignon and other courts in southern France developed a style that was both refined and complex, especially in rhythm and notation.   **Music: NAWM 25**

Window: The *ars subtilior* (The Subtler Art) (CHWM 78–79)

The complex late-fourteenth-century style has been called the *ars subtilior* ("the subtler art") because of its intricate rhythms and notation.

III. Theory and Practice in Fourteenth-Century Music (CHWM 77–81)

Performers often altered notes chromatically, a practice known as *musica ficta.* In cadences in which a minor sixth expanded to an octave, the top note was often raised to make a major sixth, so that the top line resolved upward by half step, like a leading tone. A three-voice cadence in which both octave and fifth are approached from a half step below is called a *double leading-tone cadence*. Other chromatic alterations were made to avoid tritones or to create smooth lines. Composers and scribes tended not to notate these changes, leaving it to performers to judge where they were needed. Modern editors often suggest where changes should be made by indicating accidentals above or below the affected notes.

Etude: Fourteenth-Century Notation

In *ars nova* notation, the long, breve, and semibreve could each be divided into either two or three of the next smaller note value. These divisions were called *mode, time,* and *prolation* respectively; triple divisions were *perfect* and duple *imperfect* (*major* and *minor* respectively for prolation). Combining time and prolation produced four possible meters, equivalent to 9/8, 6/8, 3/4, and 2/4. The *minim* and *semiminim* were introduced for notes smaller than a semibreve. About 1425, note-heads began to be left open instead of being filled in. The resulting note-shapes evolved into modern notation (whole note, half note, and so on).

IV. Instruments (CHWM 81–82)

Music manuscripts of the fourteenth century do not specify which parts are vocal and which are instrumental, for each piece could be performed in a variety of ways. Polyphonic music was probably most often performed with one voice or instrument on a part. Instruments were classified as loud (*haut* or "high") or soft (*bas* or "low"). Loud instruments such as *shawms, cornetts,* slide trumpets, and *sackbuts* were often used outdoors; soft instruments such as the harp, vielle, lute, psaltery, portative organ, transverse flute, and recorder were used indoors, and percussion was used in both environments. Larger organs were used in churches.

STUDY QUESTIONS

Prelude (CHWM 62–64)

1. What currents in religion, philosophy, and literature helped to make the fourteenth century a secular age?

2. With what nation and what century is each of the following styles associated?

   ars nova   _____   _____

   trecento   _____   _____

   Who wrote *Ars nova*, and when? _____   _____

   What does the phrase "ars nova" mean? _____

   From what does the term "trecento" derive?

The *ars nova* in France (CHWM 64–70, NAWM 20–22)

3. What is the *Roman de Fauvel*? When was it written? What music does it contain?

4. How is the tenor of an isorhythmic motet constructed? What are the names of the elements that repeat?

Music to Study
   NAWM 20: Philippe de Vitry, *Garrit gallus—In nova fert—Neuma*, motet
      from *Roman de Fauvel* (ca. 1314)
      CD 1.47–52   Cassette 1.B

5. What are the texts of Vitry's motet *Garrit gallus—In nova fert—Neuma* (NAWM 20) about? How is this typical of the subject matter and function of the motet at this time?

6. Write out the color of Vitry's motet *Garrit gallus—In nova fert—Neuma* as a series of note names (that is, F, G, A, and so on).

   How many notes does the color contain? _____

   How many times is the color stated in the motet? _____

7. Write out the talea of this motet as a series of durations. Include the rests. To make it easier to follow the rhythm, reduce the value of each note or rest to a third of its value, so that a dotted whole note becomes a half note, a dotted half note becomes a quarter note, and so on. In this notation, the first note would be a dotted half note, the second a quarter note, and so on.

   How many notes does the talea contain? _____

   How many times is the talea stated in the motet? _____

   In this motet, how are the talea and color coordinated?

8. How does the tenor of this piece compare in its structure with those of the motets in NAWM 16d and 16f? In what ways is it structured according to similar ideas, and in what ways is it more complex?

9. Briefly describe Guillaume de Machaut's career. Where did he live, whom did he serve, and what did he do?

Music to Study
> **NAWM 22:** Guillaume de Machaut, *Messe de Notre Dame*, Mass, excerpt:
> Agnus Dei (ca. 1364)
> CD 1.56–58 (Concise 1.18–22)   Cassette 1.B (Concise 1.A)

10. What is the *Messe de Notre Dame*? What is special about it?

    Which movements are isorhythmic? _____

    What other style is used, and in what movements? Why is it appropriate for these movements?

11. In the Agnus Dei, the isorhythm begins with the words "qui tollis" after each "Agnus Dei." Each time, the color is stated only once, the talea more than once. The last note of each section follows the last statement of the talea.
    (Note that in certain cases, some repetitions of an isorhythmic pattern will subdivide a few notes. For example, compare mm. 15–17 in all four voices with mm. 8–10. For each voice, the rhythm is virtually the same in both passages, but in the top three voices there is a half note in one passage that is divided into smaller note values in the other. This kind of small difference varies but does not negate the basic isorhythmic structure.)

    Write out the talea for the first "qui tollis." _____

    How many measures long (in this modern transcription) is this talea? _____

    How many times is it stated? _____

    To what extent are the other three voices isorhythmic?

    Write out the talea for the second "qui tollis." _____

    How many measures long (in this modern transcription) is this talea? _____

    How many times is it stated? _____

    To what extent are the other three voices isorhythmic?

12. Diagram the form of the three *formes fixes*, using letters to indicate musical repetitions and capital letters to show the refrains.

    virelai   _____   ballade   _____

    rondeau   _____

13. How does the fourteenth-century rondeau resemble *Robins m'aime* (NAWM 8) by the thirteenth-century trouvère Adam de la Halle?

Music to Study
> **NAWM 21:** Guillaume de Machaut, *Rose, liz, printemps, verdure*, rondeau
>   (mid-fourteenth century)
>   CD 1.53–55 (Concise 1.15–17)   Cassette 1.B (Concise 1.A)

14. Copy the rondeau form from your answer to question 12. _____

    Which measures in the music of *Rose, liz, printemps, verdure* (NAWM 21) correspond to each letter of your diagram?

    How do the rhymes in the poetry coordinate with this form?

    What relation does the music in mm. 32-37 have to music heard previously?

    How do cadences help delineate the form?

15. Describe the melodic and rhythmic style of the two upper parts, the triplum and the cantus. How do these compare to the upper parts of the motets in NAWM 19 and 20? Describe what is distinctive about Machaut's style, as compared with melodies of the late thirteenth and early fourteenth centuries.

Italian *trecento* Music (CHWM 70–77, NAWM 23–25)

16. Define and describe the fourteenth-century *caccia*.

Music to Study
  NAWM 23: Jacopo da Bologna, *Fenice fù*, madrigal (mid-1300s)
    CD 2.1   Cassette 2.A
  NAWM 24: Francesco Landini, *Non avrà ma' pietà*, ballata (second half of
      fourteenth century)
    CD 2.2–4 (Concise 1.21–23)   Cassette 2.A (Concise 1.A)

17. How does Jacopo da Bologna's *Fenice fù* fit the definition of a fourteenth-century madrigal as given in CHWM (pp. 72 and 75), including the type of poetry used, the poetic form, the form of the piece, and the melodic style?

18. In a ballata, what is the *ripresa*? What measures of Landini's *Non avrà ma' pietà* (NAWM 24) correspond to this part of the form?

What are the *piedi* and *volta*? Where do these appear in Landini's ballata?

How does the form of a ballata resemble that of a virelai? How is it different?

19. What is a "Landini cadence"? Where do Landini cadences appear in Landini's ballata?

20. Compare Landini's melodic, rhythmic, and harmonic style to that of Machaut's rondeau (NAWM 21). Where do melismas occur in each one, and how is their practice similar or different in this respect? What other similarities and differences do you observe?

Music to Study
  NAWM 25: Baude Cordier, *Belle, bonne, sage,* rondeau (early 1400s)
    CD 2.5   Cassette 2.A

21. How does Baude Cordier's *Belle, bonne, sage* (NAWM 25) resemble Machaut's rondeau (NAWM 21), and how is it different in style? What aspects of the Cordier link it to the *ars subtilior*?

22. In what shape is Cordier's rondeau presented in the manuscript, and why?

Theory and Practice in Fourteenth-Century Music (CHWM 77–81)

23. What is *musica ficta*? Under what circumstances is it used, and why?

24. Briefly describe fourteenth-century French notation. What are the divisions of the long, breve, and semibreve called? What are the four prolations, and how do they correspond to modern meters?

Instruments (CHWM 81–82)

25. What types of instruments were in use during the fourteenth century? What are *haut* ("high") and *bas* ("low") instruments? How were instruments used in vocal music?

TERMS TO KNOW

Terms Related to Ars Nova Music

humanism	virelai
Ars nova	rondeau
isorhythm	ballade
isorhythmic motet	formes fixes
color	refrain
talea	cantus
hocket	cantilena style
lai	

Terms Related to Trecento and Late-Fourteenth-Century French Music

trecento	ritornello (in fourteenth-century
madrigal (fourteenth-century)	madrigal)
caccia	ripresa, piedi, volta
ballata	ars subtilior

Terms Related to Music Theory and Instruments

Landini cadence	minim, semiminim
musica ficta	haut and bas instruments
double leading-tone cadence	shawm
mode, time, prolation	cornett
perfect and imperfect time	sackbut
major and minor prolation	

NAMES TO KNOW

Ars nova	*La Messe de Notre Dame*
Philippe de Vitry	*Squarcialupi Codex*
Roman de Fauvel	Francesco Landini
Guillaume de Machaut	

REVIEW QUESTIONS

1. Make a time-line for the pieces, composers, and treatises discussed in this chapter.

2. What is new about the *ars nova*? How does it compare to thirteenth-century music? How does late-fourteenth-century French music (the *ars subtilior*) extend the ideas of the ars nova?

3. Describe isorhythm as practiced in Vitry's motets and Machaut's Mass.

4. Name and describe the forms of secular song practiced in France and Italy during the fourteenth century. How are French and Italian music similar? How do they differ?

5. Describe the melodic, rhythmic, and harmonic style of Machaut. How do the works of Vitry, Jacopo da Bologna, Landini, and Cordier resemble or differ from those of Machaut in melodic, rhythmic, and harmonic style? What features do they all share?

ENGLAND AND THE BURGUNDIAN LANDS IN THE FIFTEENTH CENTURY: THE BEGINNINGS OF AN INTERNATIONAL STYLE

5

CHAPTER OBJECTIVES

After you complete the reading, study of the music, and study questions for this chapter, you should be able to:

1. describe the traits of English music that distinguished it from French and Italian styles and influenced music on the Continent in the fifteenth century;
2. describe fauxbourdon, chant paraphrase, and cantus firmus techniques;
3. explain how an international musical style developed in the mid-fifteenth century and the historical circumstances that placed Burgundian composers at the center of these developments;
4. describe the music of Burgundian composers, particularly Dufay, and explain the differences between their musical practices and those of the fourteenth century; and
5. describe the cantus firmus Mass.

CHAPTER OUTLINE

Prelude (CHWM 83–86)

English music made important contributions to the development of an international style in the first half of the fifteenth century. The influence of English style on Continental composers was celebrated in a poem of about 1440 that praised the *"contenance angloise"* (English guise) of "lively consonance." The new style, which blended French, Italian, and English traits, was nurtured particularly by composers from the duchy of *Burgundy,* where the dukes maintained a large *chapel* of singers and composers and employed numerous instrumentalists. Due to the dukes' lavish patronage, most of the leading composers of the fifteenth and early sixteenth centuries came from Burgundian lands, mainly from modern-day Belgium and northeastern France. Musicians traveled with their patrons or moved to new posts in other regions, and their interactions with musicians from all over Europe aided the development of an international style.

53

I. English Music and Its Influence (CHWM 86–90, NAWM 26–27, 29)

English music favored the major mode, homophony, use of imperfect consonances, and fullness of sound. A frequent occurrence in English music is parallel motion in thirds and sixths, often in combination (that is, parallel sixths between the outer voices and parallel thirds between the bottom and middle voices, resolving to an octave and fifth respectively at cadences). A distinctive English form is the *carol*.   **Music: NAWM 27**

1. Fauxbourdon

The parallel sixths and thirds of English music may have inspired the Continental technique of *fauxbourdon,* prominent ca. 1420–50. This led to a new style in which the voices move in similar rhythms and are almost equally important and the music is suffused with imperfect consonances.

Etude: A Closer Look at Fauxbourdon

In a fauxbourdon, two notated voices (usually a paraphrased chant in the cantus and a tenor below it) move mostly in parallel sixths, resolving to an octave at cadences, and a third unwritten part is sung a fourth below the cantus, producing parallel thirds with the tenor.   **Music: NAWM 29**

2. Dunstable

John Dunstable (ca. 1390–1453) was the leading English composer of the first half of the fifteenth century. He served for a time in the English possessions in France, which helped bring his music to the Continent. He wrote in all the prevailing genres and styles of polyphony.

3. Dunstable's motets

Dunstable is best known for his three-voice sacred works. They use a variety of techniques, including an ornamented chant melody in the top voice, a cantus firmus in the tenor, and free counterpoint not based on chant. In the fifteenth century, the isorhythmic motet waned in popularity, and the term *motet* came to be applied to any polyphonic setting of a Latin text other than part of the Mass Ordinary.   **Music: NAWM 26**

II. Music in the Burgundian Lands (CHWM 91–97, NAWM 28–30)

1. Guillaume Dufay

Guillaume Dufay (c. 1400–1474) was educated at Cambrai in the duchy of Burgundy, served several patrons in Italy and Savoy in the 1420s and 1430s, returned to Cambrai, went back to Savoy in the 1450s, and finished his career at Cambrai, making him a truly international composer.

2. Gilles Binchois

Gilles Binchois (c. 1400–1460) served the Burgundian court chapel for most of his career. He was best known for his chansons.

3. Genres and style

The main genres of the period were Masses, Magnificats, motets, and French secular chansons. The chansons continued the three-voice treble-dominated texture of the fourteenth century, but the melodic style was smoother and the harmony more consonant.

4. Burgundian chansons

In the fifteenth century, *chanson* (song) was the term for any polyphonic setting of a French secular text. Most chansons were in the form of a rondeau or (less often) a ballade.   **Music: NAWM 28**

5. Burgundian motets

Motets in this period were often written in the style of the chanson, with the main melody (often paraphrased from chant) in the treble, supported by the tenor, with a contratenor to fill out the harmony. Isorhythmic motets were still sometimes composed for special occasions.   **Music: NAWM 29**

6. Masses

After about 1420, composers regularly set the Mass Ordinary as a unified cycle, creating the genre of the *polyphonic Mass cycle*. Some Masses were unified simply by musical style or liturgical association, others by opening each movement with the same material, called a *head motive* or *motto*.

7. Tenor Mass

The most important form was the *cantus firmus Mass* or *tenor Mass*, which used the same cantus firmus in every movement. This form was developed by English composers and became predominant throughout Europe by 1450. The cantus firmus was usually placed in the tenor in long notes and treated in isorhythmic fashion. Below it was a *contratenor bassus* (low contratenor) or *bassus* (bass) to provide a harmonic foundation; above it was the *contratenor altus* (high contratenor) or *altus* (alto); the top part was called *cantus* (melody), *discantus* (discant), or *superius* (highest part). The cantus firmus could be taken from a chant, a secular song, or the tenor of a chanson, and the Mass was named after the borrowed tune. Although cantus firmus Masses used learned devices such as isorhythm, they conformed to the style that prevailed after 1430, with careful control of dissonance, emphasis on consonance, four-voice texture, and some use of imitation.   **Music: NAWM 30**

STUDY QUESTIONS

Prelude (CHWM 83–86)

1. What political factors facilitated the development of an international musical style in the fifteenth century? Why were Burgundian composers at the center of these developments?

English Music and Its Influence (CHWM 86–90, NAWM 26–27, 29)

2. What characteristics of English music set it apart from music on the Continent in the thirteenth through early fifteenth centuries? How did the Continental style change as it absorbed the influence of English music in the first half of the fifteenth century?

3. Describe the relationship between the Dunstable melody and the plainchant melody it paraphrases in Example 5.2 on p. 89 of CHWM. How does Dunstable embellish the chant?

Music to Study
   NAWM 26: John Dunstable, *Quam pulchra es*, motet (first half, fifteenth century)
      CD 2.6 (Concise 1.24)   Cassette 2.A (Concise 1.A)
   NAWM 27: *Salve, sancta parens*, carol (fifteenth century)
      CD 2.7   Cassette 2.A
   NAWM 29: Guillaume Dufay, *Conditor alme siderum*, motet (hymn paraphrase) in alternation with chant (middle third of fifteenth century)
      CD 2.11–12   Cassette 2.A

4. In what sense is *Quam pulchra es* (NAWM 26) a motet? Which part, if any, has the chant? How are the parts related to each other? How had the definition of "motet" changed by the early 15th century to include a piece such as this?

---

5. How does Dunstable shape the music of *Quam pulchra es* to reflect the divisions of the text and the rhythms of the words?

6. Where are there passages in *Quam pulchra es* that feature parallel thirds, sixths, or tenths? (Note that the middle voice is to be performed an octave lower than written, so that all three parts begin on middle C.)

About how often during the work are imperfect consonances sounding?

7. How often in *Quam pulchra es* do harmonic dissonances appear? How often do parallel unisons, fifths, or octaves occur? How does this compare with the thirteenth-century conductus *Ave virgo virginum* (NAWM 18) and with Machaut's fourteenth-century Agnus Dei (NAWM 22)?

8. Compare the melodic style of the top voice in Dunstable's motet to that of the top lines in Machaut's *Rose, liz, printemps, verdure* (NAWM 21) and Landini's *Non avrà ma' pietà* (NAWM 24). What are the main differences between the English style of the first half of the fifteenth century and these fourteenth-century styles?

9. Now do the same for the melodic style of the tenors, and for the relationship between the top part and the tenor.

10. Where are there parallel sixths, thirds, or tenths between the outer voices in the carol *Salve, sancta parens* (NAWM 27)? In the three-voice Burden II, where is there a texture in which the outer voices move in parallel sixths and the bottom two voices in parallel thirds? (Note: Sometimes the rhythm of the parts is slightly different, while the voices still essentially move in parallel.)

11. Where are there Landini cadences in the following works?

    Salve, sancta parens (NAWM 27) _____

    Dunstable, *Quam pulchra es* (NAWM 26) _____

12. In Dufay's polyphonic setting of the even-numbered verses of the plainchant hymn *Conditor alme siderum* (NAWM 29), how is the chant melody embellished? Where in the phrase do embellishments occur? (Note that the chant melody itself is notated here in longs and breves, producing a pattern like the first rhythmic mode.)

13. How does this piece fit the description of *fauxbourdon* in CHWM, p. 88?

    How does this compare to the use of parallel sixth-third sonorities in the English carol *Salve, sancta parens* (NAWM 27)? Which piece is more varied in its texture?

Music in the Burgundian Lands (CHWM 91–97, NAWM 28–30)

14. Briefly summarize Dufay's career. How was it typical of musicians at the time? How did such a career facilitate the creation of an international style?

15. How does the fifteenth-century cadence formula described on p. 92 of CHWM resemble fourteenth-century cadences, and how is it like cadences in common-practice tonality?

Music to Study
NAWM 28: Guillaume Dufay, *Resvellies vous et faites chiere lye*, ballade (1423)
    CD 2.8-10   Cassette 2.A

16. In Dufay's *Resvellies vous et faites chiere lye* (NAWM 45), which parts of the upper line seem to suggest instrumental performance? Why?

17. *Resvellies vous* was composed in 1423 when Dufay was working in Italy, and it shows a strong influence from fourteenth-century French and Italian music. What elements in this piece resemble Machaut's rondeau (NAWM 21)? Which elements suggest the mannered, rhythmically complex late-four-teenth-century *ars subtilior* style? How does the melodic line in the texted portions suggest Italian rather than French influence?

---

18. What is a *cantus firmus Mass* or *tenor Mass*?

    What kinds of borrowed melodies were used in cantus firmus Masses?

    In what voice of the four-part texture does the cantus firmus normally occur in a Mass?

Music to Study
 NAWM 30a: Guillaume Dufay, *Se la face ay pale,* ballade (1430s)
  CD 2.13 (Concise 1.25)   Cassette 2.A (Concise 1.B)
 NAWM 30b: Guillaume Dufay, *Missa Se la face ay pale,* Mass, excerpt:
  Gloria (ca. 1450s)
  CD 2.14–19 (Concise 1.26–31)   Cassette 2.A (Concise 1.B)

19. How does Dufay use the tenor of his chanson *Se la face ay pale* (NAWM 30a) in the tenor of the Gloria from his *Missa Se la face ay pale* (NAWM 30b)? How is this like isorhythm? How does it provide a form for the Gloria movement?

20. Where in the Gloria does Dufay borrow material from the other two voices of his chanson? What purpose might this borrowing serve?

21. How do the four voices of the Gloria differ from each other in function and style?

22. Examine the upper voices in the Gloria. How often do two successive measures have the same rhythm? How often do the top two voices move in the same rhythm at the same time? What does this suggest about Dufay's use of rhythm?

23. In the isorhythmic works of Vitry and Machaut, we can find parallel fifths and octaves and double leading-tone cadences. Can any of these be found in Dufay's Mass movement? How would you describe the harmony?

TERMS TO KNOW

"contenance angloise"
chapel
carol
fauxbourdon
motet (fifteenth-century and later)
chanson

polyphonic Mass cycle
head motive or motto
cantus firmus Mass or tenor Mass
bassus (contratenor bassus)
altus (contratenor altus)
cantus, discantus, superius

NAMES TO KNOW

Burgundy
John Dunstable

Guillaume Dufay
Gilles Binchois

REVIEW QUESTIONS

1. Make a time-line for the pieces and composers discussed in this chapter. Include dates for the poem that mentions the "contenance angloise"; dates for the end of the duchy of Burgundy and the reigns of Philip the Good and Charles the Bold; the dates and places of Dufay's birth, death, and employment; and dates for any historical events listed on p. 86 of CHWM with which you are familiar, to help orient you to the fifteenth century.

2. What new ways of using and reworking Gregorian chant developed during the fifteenth century?

3. What special role did the duchy of Burgundy and Burgundian composers play in the development of music during the fifteenth century?

4. Describe the music of Dufay and explain how he synthesizes elements from France, Italy, and England in a cosmopolitan style.

5. Describe the cantus firmus Mass as composed in the fifteenth century, and compare Dufay's *Missa Se la face ay pale* (a cantus firmus Mass) to Machaut's *Messe de Notre Dame*.

The Age of the Renaissance: Music of the Low Countries

6

Chapter Objectives

After you complete the reading, study of the music, and study questions for this chapter, you should be able to:

1. describe some aspects of the influence of humanism on the culture and music of the fifteenth and sixteenth centuries;
2. name some of the most significant theorists and treatises of the time;
3. describe the beginnings of music printing and its effects on musical life;
4. describe the music and briefly describe the careers of some of the major composers active at the end of the fifteenth century and the beginning of the sixteenth century.

Chapter Outline

Prelude (CHWM 99–100)

The Renaissance was not a musical style, but a period of history marked by the rediscovery and renewed influence of ancient Greek and Roman culture. Although no ancient music was known, ancient writings on music became available during the fifteenth century. Greek and Roman writers' descriptions of the emotional effects of music caused some in the Renaissance to criticize the lack of such effects in the music of their own time. Most prominent composers in the period 1450–1550 came from France, Flanders, or the Netherlands, and they served at courts in Italy and across western Europe. The greatest composer of the era was *Josquin des Prez* (ca. 1440–1521).

I. The Musical Culture of the Renaissance (CHWM 101–5)

1. Humanism

Humanism, the recovery of ancient culture, was an influence on music as on the other arts. During the fifteenth century, all the major Greek writings on music were translated into Latin. *Franchino Gaffurio* (1451–1522) incorporated ancient Greek theory into his treatises, the most influential of his time. *Dodekachordon* (The Twelve-String Lyre, 1547) by *Heinrich Glareanus* (1488–1563) added four new modes (authentic and plagal modes on A and C, akin to later minor and major modes) to the eight earlier modes.

2. Tuning
New tuning systems were introduced that allowed imperfect consonances to sound well, and triads began to appear at cadences.

3. Consonance and dissonance
Strict rules for controlling dissonance were followed by composers and codified in treatises such as *Liber de arte contrapuncti* (A Book on the Art of Counterpoint, 1477) by *Johannes Tinctoris* (ca. 1435–ca. 1511) and *Le istitutioni harmoniche* (The Harmonic Foundations, 1558) by Gioseffo Zarlino.

4. Music and words
Humanism encouraged composers to pay increasing attention to the meaning, sound, form, and rhythm of the texts they set. Whereas text underlay had often been left to the singers, sixteenth-century composers sought to fix it precisely, for good accentuation.

5. Music printing
Printing allowed wider distribution of writings on music and of music itself at a lower cost, with greater accuracy and less time spent recopying by hand. *Ottaviano de' Petrucci* (1466–1539) of Venice was the first to print polyphonic music from movable type in 1501.

6. Why Italy?
Humanism and the arts thrived particularly in Italy, where rulers of small city-states and principalities sought to outdo each other in their patronage of literature and the arts. Many of the composers they employed were from France, Flanders, and the Netherlands, particularly from the formerly Burgundian lands.

II. Northern Composers and Their Music (CHWM 105–11, NAWM 31)

1. Ockeghem
Johannes Ockeghem (ca. 1420–1497) was born in the north and spent most of his career in the service of the kings of France. He was famous as a composer and as a teacher of many of the leading composers of the next generation. He wrote 13 Masses, 10 motets, and about 20 chansons. He extended the range of the bassus down to low F, giving a fuller and darker sound, and all four voices tend to be equally active. His melodic lines are long and sinuous, with few pauses, varied rhythms, and many changes of direction as they wind to their goal.

2. Masses
Ockeghem wrote cantus firmus Masses and others not based on a cantus firmus. He often creates contrasts of light and dark by varying the texture, setting some passages for only two or three voices and sometimes alternat-

ing between high and low pairs of voices. Ockeghem seldom uses imitation but does use *canon,* which at this time meant a procedure for deriving more than one voice from a notated voice.

Etude: Mensuration Canons in an Ockeghem Mass
Ockeghem's *Missa prolationum* uses *mensuration canons,* in which one notated line generates two voices through a different mensuration sign.

3. Ockeghem's chansons
Ockeghem's chansons continue to follow the formes fixes, especially the rondeau, but feature smoother lines and more use of imitation. Chansons of the period were freely altered, arranged, and transcribed for instruments, and some became very popular. **Music: NAWM 31**

Window: The "Gutenberg Bible" of Music Printing (CHWM 106–7)

Petrucci used three impressions (for the staff lines, for the notes, and for the text) to print beautiful and clear collections of chansons, motets, or Masses. Most works were published as *partbooks,* one book for each voice or instrumental part. Printing made music widely available and created the first real market for music as a commodity.

III. Josquin and His Contemporaries (CHWM 111–18, NAWM 32–34)

1. Ockeghem's pupils
Many composers of the next generation were taught or influenced by Ockeghem. The three greatest were *Jacob Obrecht* (ca. 1452–1505), *Heinrich Isaac* (ca. 1450–1517), and Josquin. All were trained in the Low Countries and worked in Italy and elsewhere, and their music blends northern polyphony, intricacy, and subtly flowing rhythms with the Italian preferences for homophony, simplicity, and clearly articulated phrases.

2. *Odhecaton*
The first volume of polyphony printed from movable type was Petrucci's *Harmonice musices odhecaton A* (1501), an anthology of chansons from ca. 1470–1500 in both older and newer styles. The newer style favored a four-voice texture instead of three voices; more imitation between the voices; greater equality of the voices; and a clearer harmonic structure.

3. Chansons
By the early sixteenth century, Josquin and others abandoned the formes fixes for more varied poetic and musical forms. The voices are no longer independent layers around the cantus and tenor, but all are equal in a flexible texture that includes imitation and dialogue between voices. (This change of style apparently motivated a change of compositional practice; instead of writing the tenor or cantus first and adding lines one by one, composers worked out all the parts simultaneously.) **Music: NAWM 32**

A. *Josquin des Prez*

1. Career
Josquin des Prez (ca. 1440–1521) was considered the best composer of his time and is one of the greatest of all time. He was born in northern France

and served patrons in Italy and France. His works, which include about 18 Masses, 100 motets, and 70 secular vocal works, were published and recopied more widely than any other composer of his day.

2. Motets

The influence of humanism and of Italian popular songs (which were mostly syllabic) led Josquin and others to match the music more carefully to the accents and rhythms of the words. One Italian technique was *falsobordone*, in which root-position triads harmonize a recitation formula in the top voice; some of Josquin's early motets use this texture. In his late motets, Josquin also sought to depict the meaning of the words. His music may be the first to be expressive of the emotions suggested by its text. In a Josquin motet, each phrase of text receives its own musical figure, which is usually treated in a point of imitation.   **Music: NAWM 33–34**

3. Masses

Most of Josquin's Masses use a secular tune as a cantus firmus. One Mass honors his patron, the duke of Ferrara, by using a theme derived from his name as rendered in solmization syllables. An *imitation Mass* (also called *parody Mass*) borrows, not a single line, but the entire multi-voice texture of a polyphonic work, and reworks it to create something new in each movement of the Mass.

STUDY QUESTIONS

The Musical Culture of the Renaissance (CHWM 101–5)

1. What is *humanism*? What was its role in Renaissance intellectual life? What aspects of music did it influence?

2. How did humanism influence the relation between music and text in vocal pieces? How did the new understanding of text setting relate to ancient Greek ideas?

3. Why did Italy provide an ideal ground for Renaissance humanism as a movement and for the development of the international musical styles of the late fifteenth and sixteenth centuries?

4. When did printing of polyphonic music from movable type begin? _____

   Who was the first printer to use this technique, and where was he active?

   _____   _____

   What was the name of his first publication? _____

   What kind of music did it contain? _____

   What impact did printing have on the dissemination of musical works?

Northern Composers and Their Music (CHWM 105–11, NAWM 31)

5. Summarize Ockeghem's career and reputation.

6. What is a *mensuration canon,* and how does it work in Ockeghem's *Missa prolationum?*

Music to Study

> **NAWM 31:** Johannes Ockeghem, *D'ung aultre amer*, chanson (second half of the fifteenth century)
>
> CD 2.20 (Concise 1.32)   Cassette 2.A (Concise 1.B)

7. Compare the frequency of the cadences in this rondeau by Ockeghem to the frequency of cadences in Dufay's ballade *Se la face ay pale* (NAWM 30a). Which composer seems more concerned with writing short, clear phrases?

   Which one is more interested in long, overlapping phrases, for an effect of seamless continuity?

   Compare the top lines, tenors, and contratenors of the two chansons. Which composer is more interested in achieving a smooth, singable line in all three parts of the chanson?

   Summarize your observations (these and others) in a brief description of the differences between the chanson styles of Dufay and of Ockeghem.

8. The motive in mm. 1–2 of the contratenor (here, the bottom voice) of *D'ung aultre amer* is imitated in mm. 3–4 of the superius. Where else does this motive appear in the chanson?

   Where else does Ockeghem use imitation between the voices?

   How does this use of imitation relate to the relative equality between the voices?

Josquin and His Contemporaries (CHWM 111–18, NAWM 32–34)

Music to Study
> **NAWM 32a:** Josquin des Prez, *Mille regretz*, chanson (ca. 1520)
> > CD 2.21 (Concise 1.33)   Cassette 2.A (Concise 1.B)
> **NAWM 32b:** Luis de Narváez, Arrangement for vihuela of Josquin des
> > Prez's *Mille regretz*, chanson arrangement (ca. 1538)
> > CD 2.22 (Concise 1.34)   Cassette 2.A (Concise 1.B)

9. One could sing the superius of Ockeghem's *D'ung aultre amer* (NAWM 31),
   and it would make sense as a monophonic song. One could perform the
   superius and tenor together, without the contratenor, and it would sound well
   in two-part counterpoint. (Try doing this, to convince yourself this is true.)
      Neither is possible in Josquin's chanson *Mille regretz* (NAWM 32a): no
   voice alone makes sense as a song, and no two voices form satisfactory
   cadences with each other. Why not? Why are all four voices essential?

10. How does *Mille regretz* differ from Ockeghem's *D'ung aultre amer* or
    Dufay's ballade *Se la face ay pale* (NAWM 30a) in the following respects?
    All of these are typical of the difference between fifteenth-century chansons
    and early-sixteenth-century chansons.

    the number of voices

    the intended performance medium of each part

    the setting of the text

    the musical and poetic form

    the final sonority at the end of the piece

11. What changes did Luis de Narváez make in arranging *Mille regretz* for vihuela (NAWM 32b)? How do these changes reflect the change of medium, from voices to plucked strings? (The vihuela is a plucked string instrument akin to the guitar.)

12. Where and when did Josquin live and work? In what genres did he compose? How was he regarded by his contemporaries?

Music to Study

NAWM 33: Josquin des Prez, *Tu solus, qui facis mirabilis,* motet (late fifteenth century)
CD 2.23–26 (Concise 1.35–38)   Cassette 2.B (Concise 1.B)
NAWM 34: Josquin des Prez, *De profundis clamavi ad te,* motet (first or second decade of the sixteenth century)
CD 2.27–30   Cassette 2.B

13. What is *falsobordone*? Where in Josquin's motet *Tu solus, qui facis mirabilis* (NAWM 32) does he use a similar technique?

14. Where and how does *Tu solus, qui facis mirabilis* use borrowed material? Why is it used?

15. Where do cadences occur in Josquin's motet *De profundis clamavi ad te* (NAWM 34)? How does the location of cadences relate to the structure of the text?

16. How does Josquin's music reflect the meaning of the opening words of *De profundis clamavi ad te*?

    How does the music reflect the natural accentuation of the words elsewhere in the motet?

17. A motet of Josquin's generation is made up of a series of phrases. Each segment of the text is given its own musical phrase, which is usually treated in a point of imitation or is presented homophonically. Most phrases are marked off with cadences, although some points of imitation overlap. One of Josquin's trademarks is his alternation of voices in pairs with each other and with the full four-voice texture. These changes of texture, along with the frequent cadences, help to make the structure clear.

    In Josquin's motet *De profundis clamavi ad te*, where do phrases begin with a point of imitation? List each instance, including the measure number it begins, the first words of the phrase of text, and the number of voices that participate in the point of imitation.

TERMS TO KNOW

humanism
partbooks
canon

mensuration canon
falsobordone
imitation Mass (or parody Mass)

NAMES TO KNOW

Josquin des Prez
Franchino Gaffurio
Dodekachordon, by Heinrich
  Glareanus
Liber de arte contrapuncti, by
  Johannes Tinctoris
Le istitutioni harmoniche, by
  Gioseffo Zarlino

Ottaviano de' Petrucci
Johannes Ockeghem
Missa prolationum
Jacob Obrecht
Heinrich Isaac
Harmonice musices odhecaton A

REVIEW QUESTIONS

1. Make a time-line for the pieces, composers, treatises, and theorists discussed in this chapter.

2. Define humanism as a movement in the Renaissance, and explain how it was reflected in the culture and music of the time.

3. Trace the development of the motet in the fifteenth and early sixteenth centuries from Dunstable to Josquin, using the motets in NAWM as examples.

4. What are the major changes in the style of secular vocal music from Ockeghem's generation to that of Josquin?

5. Describe Ottaviano de' Petrucci's method of music printing and the effects music printing had on musical life.

6. Compare the careers and music of any two of the following composers: Machaut, Dufay, Ockeghem, Josquin.

THE AGE OF THE RENAISSANCE: NEW CURRENTS IN THE SIXTEENTH CENTURY

7

CHAPTER OBJECTIVES

After you complete the reading, study of the music, and study questions for this chapter, you should be able to:

1. describe the principal styles and genres of sixteenth-century secular vocal music and instrumental music;
2. describe the relation of music and words in sixteenth-century vocal music and contrast it with earlier practices of setting texts;
3. identify some of the major composers of sixteenth-century music; and
4. identify the characteristics of national schools of composition in the sixteenth century.

CHAPTER OUTLINE

Prelude (CHWM 120–21)

The years 1520–1550 saw a growing diversity of styles, genres, and forms, including the growth of national styles, the madrigal, the emergence of Italy as the musical center of Europe, and the rise of instrumental music.

I. The Generation after Josquin (1520–1550) (CHWM 121–24)

Church composers after Josquin used a similar smooth polyphonic style but increasingly wrote for five or six voices rather than four. Chants were often paraphrased in all voices rather than set apart as a cantus firmus.

A. *Adrian Willaert*

Adrian Willaert (ca. 1490-1562) was among the most important composers of his generation. Director of music at St. Mark's Church in Venice for the second half of his life, he exercised a great influence through his teaching, his compositions, and his ideas for the treatment of text. He specified which syllable was to be sung to each note and sought to ensure that the text was correctly accented and punctuated. He marked major breaks in the

73

text with full cadences and lesser breaks with weak or evaded cadences. His melodic lines and cadences convey the mode by emphasizing the final and other important notes in the mode.

II. The Rise of National Styles: Italy (CHWM 124–25, NAWM 36)

1. Frottola and lauda
The *frottola,* an Italian genre common in the late fifteenth and early sixteenth centuries, was a strophic secular song with an amorous or satirical text set in a simple, syllabic, and homophonic style. The polyphonic *lauda* was a religious song, not used in the liturgy. Later Italian composers used other light genres of secular vocal music, such as the *villanella, canzonetta,* and *balletto.* **Music: NAWM 36**

2. Petrarchan movement
The rise of the madrigal was closely connected to renewed interest in the poetry and ideals of fourteenth-century Italian poet *Francesco Petrarch* (1304–1374), whose poems reflect the mood or imagery of the words in the sound of the language itself. Early madrigalists often set his poetry, especially his sonnets, and later composers set poets influenced by him.

III. The Italian Madrigal (CHWM 125–35, NAWM 37–41)

Unlike the frottola or fourteenth-century madrigal, the sixteenth-century *madrigal* did not use a refrain or set form, but was a through-composed work that sought to capture the ideas and feelings in the words through a series of changing musical textures and images. The poems used were serious or artful and were often by a major poet. Madrigals were sung in courtly gatherings and academies, usually by amateurs for their own enjoyment. They were also sung in plays and theatrical productions, and after about 1570 some patrons employed professional singers to perform madrigals, such as the *concerto delle donne* (women's ensemble) at Ferrara. Madrigals were perhaps the first commercial popular music, with over 2000 collections published and sold by 1600. Madrigals of 1520–50 are usually for four voices and later ones for five or more, with one singer to a part, sometimes doubled or replaced by an instrument.

1. Arcadelt
Jacob Arcadelt (ca. 1505–ca. 1568) and Willaert were northerners skilled in composing church music, and they brought into the madrigal the imitative counterpoint, changing textures, overlapping cadences, and novel harmonic effects of the motet. Arcadelt's style was simpler than Willaert's and closer to the homophony of the frottola. **Music: NAWM 37–38**

2. Rore
Cipriano de Rore (1516–1565), a student of Willaert's, was the leading madrigalist of his generation. His music was famed for its vivid expression of the feelings in the text. Zarlino described the musical means for representing certain contrasting moods in his treatise *Le istitutioni harmoniche.* **Music: NAWM 39**

3. Other composers

Among the important madrigal composers of the late sixteenth century were both northern composers and native Italians, most notably *Luca Marenzio* (1553–1599). In his writings and music, *Nicola Vicentino* (1511–ca. 1576) explored chromaticism to an unprecedented degree, inspired by the ancient Greek chromatic and enharmonic genera.

4. Gesualdo

Carlo Gesualdo (ca. 1561–1613) is known for using chromaticism. His vertical sonorities are mostly consonant, but the motion through successive sonorities can be quite unpredictable. The contrast between chromatic and diatonic sections to convey the changing moods of the text is also a hallmark of his style.   **Music: NAWM 40**

5. Monteverdi

Claudio Monteverdi (1567–1643) was the most important Italian composer of the late sixteenth and early seventeenth centuries. He was born in Cremona, worked in Mantua, and was choirmaster at St. Mark's in Venice for the last 30 years of his life. His several books of madrigals show a variety of techniques, including increased use of unprepared dissonance, declamatory passages, and other methods of conveying the feeling of the text. He defended his unorthodox use of dissonance as a "second practice" (as distinguished from the "first practice" taught by Zarlino) in which the music was the servant of the poetry.   **Music: NAWM 41**

Window: Caravaggio Paints a Performer (CHWM 127)

Caravaggio's picture of a musician playing the lute and singing a madrigal by Arcadelt can reveal much about musical culture in the 1590s.

IV. The Rise of National Styles: Secular Song outside Italy (CHWM 135–40, NAWM 42–45)

1. French chanson

Composers centered in Paris in the first half of the sixteenth century cultivated the *Parisian chanson*. These were strophic songs in a light, fast style, mostly syllabic and homophonic, with the melody in the upper voice, occasional brief points of imitation, and short repeated sections. The main publisher of Parisian chansons was *Pierre Attaingnant* (ca. 1494–ca. 1551), and the principal composers were *Claudin de Sermisy* (ca. 1490–1562) and *Clément Janequin* (ca. 1485–ca. 1560), who was renowned for his descriptive chansons. Outside of Paris, northern composers continued the older, more contrapuntal chanson tradition. Late in the century, poets wrote French verse that imitated the long and short syllables of ancient Greek poetry, and *Claude Le Jeune* (1528–1600) and other composers set these to music.   **Music: NAWM 42–43**

2. English madrigal

Nicholas Yonge's publication in 1588 of *Musica transalpina,* a collection of Italian madrigals in English translation, launched a fashion for madrigal singing and composition in England. The leading composers included

Thomas Morley (1557–1602) and *Thomas Weelkes* (ca. 1575–1623). Morley was particularly skilled in lighter forms such as the *ballett* and *canzonet* (related to the Italian balletto and canzonetta). Madrigals were aimed at amateurs and often sung at social gatherings.   **Music: NAWM 44**

3. English lute songs

Solo songs with lute accompaniment, known as *lute songs,* became popular in England after about 1600, especially the songs or *airs* of *John Dowland* (1562–1626). These feature less text-painting than the madrigal but care-fully follow the natural declamation of the text.   **Music: NAWM 45**

4. German lied

Secular polyphony came late to Germany, where the monophony of the Meistersinger continued through the sixteenth century. The polyphonic *Lied* wove Franco-Flemish counterpoint around a familiar German tune. Later lieder were influenced by the Italian madrigal, as are the Lieder of *Orlando di Lasso* (1532–1594), who also wrote madrigals and chansons.

V. The Rise of Instrumental Music (CHWM 140–43)

The period 1450–1550 saw an increase in instrumental music and the beginnings of independent styles and forms of writing for instruments. Two main trends can be seen: (1) the use of styles and genres idiomatic to instruments and independent of vocal music, and (2) instrumental music adapted from vocal music or inspired by vocal genres.

Etude: Instruments Used during the Renaissance

Renaissance instruments were built in *families,* with each type of instrument built in different sizes and registers from bass to soprano. A complete set of a single type of instrument was called a *chest* or *consort.*

1. Wind instruments included recorders, shawms, capped-reed instru-ments, transverse flutes, cornetts, trumpets, and sackbuts.
2. The main type of bowed string instrument was the *viol,* which had frets, six strings, and a delicate tone.
3. The *lute* was the most popular household instrument. Its music was notated in *tablature,* which showed not the pitches to play but which string to pluck and where to stop the string to produce the correct pitch. (For examples of tablature, see CHWM, pp. 138 and 200, and NAWM 45 and 66a.)
4. Keyboard instruments included the organ, the *clavichord,* and the *harpsichord.*

VI. Categories of Instrumental Music (CHWM 143–48, NAWM 46–47)

There are five main categories of Renaissance instrumental music, which continue into the seventeenth century: (1) dance, (2) improvisatory pieces, (3) contrapuntal works, (4) canzona and sonata, and (5) variation.

A. *Dance Music*

Social dancing was important to Renaissance society, and thus much of the instrumental music of the time was written for dancing or based on dance forms. In stylized dance pieces, an instrumental style independent of vocal models could develop. An important theatrical dance form was the *ballet*. Dances were often grouped in pairs or in threes, usually a slow dance in duple meter followed by a fast one in triple meter. **Music: NAWM 46**

B. *Improvisatory Pieces*

Renaissance musicians were trained in improvisation, both in embellishing a given line and in adding contrapuntal lines to a given melody. Players of keyboards and lutes improvised polyphonic pieces, and works in the same general style were written down under names such as *prelude, fantasia,* and *ricercare*. Preludes and fantasias often served to establish the mode for a following vocal piece. The chief keyboard genre in improvisatory style in the second half of the sixteenth century was the *toccata* (from the Italian word for "touched").

C. *Contrapuntal Genres*

The *ricercare* or *ricercar* evolved from an early improvisatory form into a work for ensemble or solo instrument based on a series of subjects treated in imitation, like an instrumental relative of the motet.

D. *Canzona or Sonata*

1. Canzona

The Italian instrumental *canzona* originated as a work in the same style as a Parisian chanson, with a typical opening figure of a note followed by two notes of half its value (e.g., a half note and two quarter notes). Early canzonas were for organ; ensemble canzonas were written after 1580 and evolved into the seventeenth-century sonata da chiesa. Canzonas were often based on a series of different figures, most of them treated in imitation. The result was a piece in a series of sections.

2. Sonata

Sonata is a term with many different meanings throughout music history. It was first used for a piece of purely instrumental music. The Venetian sonata of the late sixteenth century was more serious than the canzona. Among the most important Venetian composers of sonatas and canzonas was *Giovanni Gabrieli* (ca. 1557–1612). His *Sonata pian' e forte,* for two instrumental choirs, was among the first instrumental ensemble pieces to designate specific instruments and dynamic markings.

E. *Variations*

Written sets of *variations* first appear in the early sixteenth century. There are both variations on tunes and variations over *ostinatos* in the bass. In the late sixteenth and early seventeenth centuries, *the English virginalists—*composers of music for virginals, or harpsichord—wrote many variations and other keyboard works. The most prominent of these composers was *William Byrd* (1543–1623), and the most important manuscript collection is the *Fitzwilliam Virginal Book*. **Music: NAWM 47**

STUDY QUESTIONS

The Generation after Josquin (1520–1550) (CHWM 121–24)

1. What principles did Willaert follow in setting words to music?

2. In his motet *O crux, splendidior cunctis astris* (excerpted in CHWM, pp. 123–24), how does Willaert project the transposed Dorian mode?

The Rise of National Styles: Italy (CHWM 124–25, NAWM 36)

Music to Study
> **NAWM 36:** Marco Cara, *Io non compro più speranza*, frottola (ca. 1500)
> CD 2.32–38   Cassette 2.B

3. What is a *frottola*? Where and when was it popular? What traits of the genre are exemplified in Cara's *Io non compro più speranza* (NAWM 36)?

---

4. Who was Francesco Petrarch? When did he live? What was his importance for the sixteenth-century madrigal?

The Italian Madrigal (CHWM 125–35, NAWM 37–41)

5. How does the sixteenth-century *madrigal* differ from the fourteenth-century madrigal? How does it differ from the frottola?

6. In what circumstances were madrigals performed, and by whom?

Music to Study

NAWM 37: Jacob Arcadelt, *Ahimè, dov'è 'l bel viso,* madrigal (ca. 1538)
   CD 2.39–41 (Concise 1.39–41)   Cassette 2.B (Concise 1.B)
NAWM 38: Adrian Willaert, *Aspro core e selvaggio e cruda voglia,* madrigal
   (ca. 1540s)
   CD 2.42–46   Cassette 2.B
NAWM 39: Cipriano de Rore, *Datemi pace, o duri miei pensieri,* madrigal
   (ca. 1557)
   CD 2.47–50 (Concise 1.42–45)   Cassette 2.B (Concise 1.B)
NAWM 40: Carlo Gesualdo, *"Io parto" e non più dissi,* madrigal (ca. 1600)
   CD 2.51–53   Cassette 2.B

7. In what ways does Arcadelt's madrigal *Ahimè, dov'è 'l bel viso* (NAWM 37) resemble a frottola, such as Cara's *Io non compro più speranza* (NAWM 36)?

In what ways is it different from a frottola?

8. In what ways does Arcadelt reflect in his music the feelings or the imagery of the text?

9. In what ways is Willaert's *Aspro core* (NAWM 38) like a motet of the sixteenth century, such as Josquin's *De profundis clamavi ad te* (NAWM 34)?

10. What suggestions for setting a text does Zarlino (who was Willaert's student) make in the passage on p. 131 of **CHWM**? How does this reflect Willaert's practice in the opening passage of *Aspro core*?

11. In Rore's *Datemi pace* (NAWM 39), how does the music reflect the meaning of the words?

How does the music reflect the accentuation and rhythm of the words?

How does the music reflect the structure of the poetry?

12. How does Gesualdo use chromaticism, contrasting diatonic sections, and rhythm to reflect the emotional sense of the words in *"Io parto" e non più dissi* (NAWM 40)?

13. Briefly outline Monteverdi's career, including his date and place of birth, his early training, and his employment, including place, position, and dates of service.

Music to Study
   NAWM 41: Claudio Monteverdi, *Cruda Amarilli*, madrigal (ca. 1600)
      CD 2.54–58 (Concise 1.46–50)   Cassette 2.B (Concise 1.B)

14. How does Monteverdi use dissonant harmonies, and particularly unprepared dissonances, to convey the meaning of the text in *Cruda Amarilli* (NAWM 41)?

The Rise of National Styles: Secular Song outside Italy (CHWM 135–40, NAWM 42–45)

15. Who was the major publisher of the Parisian chanson in the early sixteenth century?

    Who were the principal composers of these chansons?

    What evidence is there for the popularity of this type of chanson?

Music to Study
   NAWM 42: Claudin de Sermisy, *Tant que vivray*, chanson (second quarter
      of the sixteenth century)
      CD 2.59–60 (Concise 1.51–52)   Cassette 2.B (Concise 1.B)
   NAWM 43: Claude Le Jeune, *Revecy venir du printans*, chanson (late
      sixteenth century)
      CD 2.61–69   Cassette 2.B

16. How does the "new" Parisian chanson, exemplified by Sermisy's *Tant que vivray* (NAWM 42), differ from the older Franco-Flemish chanson, exemplified by Josquin's *Milles regretz* (NAWM 32a)?

17. How does the Parisian chanson resemble the Italian frottola? Use Sermisy's *Tant que vivray* and Cara's frottola *Io non compro più speranza* (NAWM 36) as examples for your comparison.

---

18. How does Le Jeune's *Revecy venir du printans* (NAWM 43) reflect the rhythm of the text?

19. In this strophic song with refrain, how does Le Jeune vary the verses? How does this give shape to the whole work?

20. What was *Musica transalpina,* and when did it appear? What effect did it have on the development of the English madrigal?

Music to Study
    NAWM 44: Thomas Weelkes, *O Care, thou wilt despatch me,* madrigal (ca. 1600)
        CD 3.1–4 (Concise 1.53–56)   Cassette 3.A (Concise 1.B)
    NAWM 45: John Dowland, *Flow my tears,* air (ca. 1600)
        CD 3.5–7 (Concise 1.57–59)   Cassette 3.A (Concise 1.B)

21. In Weelkes's madrigal *O Care, thou wilt despatch me* (NAWM 44), how are the images and feelings in the text conveyed in the music?

22. Locate where the following unusual vertical sonorities occur in Weelkes's madrigal. (Some occur more than once.)

    a diminished seventh   _____

    an augmented triad   _____

    a diminished octave   _____

    What purposes do these dissonances serve? How can you explain their presence?

23. Comparing Weelkes's madrigal to the madrigals in NAWM 37–41, what similarities and what differences do you notice between English and Italian madrigals?

24. What are the characteristics of an English lute song ca. 1600, as exemplified by Dowland's *Flow, my tears* (NAWM 45)? How is it like a madrigal, and how is it different?

The Rise of Instrumental Music (CHWM 140–43)

25. Why do we have so little instrumental music from before 1450? How and why did this change after about 1450? What evidence is there for a rising interest in instrumental music during the Renaissance?

26. What is an *instrument family*? Why is it significant that instruments were built in families?

27. Which were the principal instrument families in the sixteenth century? How do they relate to their medieval ancestors, and how do they relate to their modern relatives?

28. What is *tablature*? What does it convey to the performer?

29. What are the main kinds of instrumental pieces in the sixteenth century?

Music to Study
    NAWM 46: Pierre Attaingnant (editor and printer), Basse danse and Branle
        gay from *Danseries a 4 Parties*, second book (published 1547)
        CD 3.8–9 (Concise 1.60–61)   Cassette 3.A (Concise 1.B)

30. How do the Basse danse and Branle gay from Pierre Attaingnant's *Danseries
a 4 Parties*, second book (NAWM 46), exemplify the characteristics of
Renaissance dance music?

---

31. What role did improvisation play in sixteenth-century music performance
and education?

32. What is a *toccata*? On which instruments was it performed? What are its main
musical characteristics, and how are they exemplified in the toccata by Claudio Merulo excerpted on p. 145 of CHWM?

33. What was a *ricercare* (or *ricercar*) in the sixteenth century? What were its
main characteristics? What vocal genre did the late-sixteenth-century ricercare resemble?

34. What is an instrumental *canzona*? What vocal form was it related to, and what
did it develop into?

35. What did the term *sonata* mean in the sixteenth century?

36. What is special about Giovanni Gabrieli's *Sonata pian' e forte*?

37. What types of variations were written in the sixteenth century? In the music of the English virginalists, what kinds of tunes were used as themes for variations, and how were they treated in the variations?

Music to Study
   NAWM 47: William Byrd, *Pavana Lachrymae,* keyboard variations on
        NAWM 45, Dowland's *Flow my tears* (early seventeenth century)
   CD 3.10–12 (Concise 2.1–3)   Cassette 3.A (Concise 2.A)

38. How is Dowland's *Flow my tears* (NAWM 45) treated in Byrd's *Pavana Lachrymae* (NAWM 47)?

TERMS TO KNOW

Terms Related to Sixteenth-Century Vocal Music

frottola	Parisian chanson
lauda	ballett and canzonet
villanella	lute song
canzonetta	air
balletto	lied
madrigal (sixteenth-century)	

Terms Related to Sixteenth-Century Instrumental Music

instrument family
chest or consort of viols
viol
lute
tablature
clavichord
harpsichord
prelude

fantasia
toccata
ricercare
canzona
sonata (sixteenth-century)
variations
ostinato
the English virginalists

NAMES TO KNOW

Adrian Willaert
Francesco Petrarch
the *concerto delle donne* of
 Ferrara
Jacob Arcadelt
Cipriano de Rore
Luca Marenzio
Nicola Vicentino
Carlo Gesualdo
Claudio Monteverdi
Pierre Attaingnant
Claudin de Sermisy

Clément Janequin
Claude Le Jeune
Musica transalpina
Thomas Morley
Thomas Weelkes
John Dowland
Orlando di Lasso
Giovanni Gabrieli
Sonata pian' e forte
William Byrd
The Fitzwilliam Virginal Book

REVIEW QUESTIONS

1. Make a time-line for the sixteenth century and place on it the pieces, composers, and treatises discussed in this chapter. (You will add to this time-line in the next chapter.)

2. Trace the development of secular vocal music in Italy from the frottola to the madrigals of Gesualdo and Monteverdi. In what ways did humanism and the revival of ancient Greek ideas about music influence this development?

3. Describe the varieties of secular vocal music practiced in France, England, and Germany during the sixteenth century. Which of these forms were influenced by the Italian madrigal, and in what ways?

4. Describe the relation of music and words in the various forms of sixteenth-century vocal music and contrast it with earlier practices of setting texts.

5. Name and describe the various types of notated instrumental music in the sixteenth century. Which ones were related to vocal models, to dancing, or to improvisation?

Church Music of the Late Renaissance and Reformation

8

Chapter Objectives

After you complete the reading, study of the music, and study questions for this chapter, you should be able to:

1. describe the attitudes toward and uses of music in Protestant churches in the sixteenth century and the genres they used;
2. recount the effect of the Counter-Reformation on sixteenth-century Catholic music and describe the styles of Palestrina, Victoria, and Lasso; and
3. identify some of the most important composers and terms associated with these trends.

Chapter Outline

Prelude (CHWM 150–51)

> The *Reformation* brought new Protestant sects with their own liturgies and music, particularly in northern Europe. In reaction, the Catholic Church undertook its own internal program of reform, the *Counter-Reformation,* which likewise had important effects on church music.

I. The Music of the Reformation in Germany (CHWM 151–53)

1. Lutheran church music
Martin Luther (1483–1546), the leader of the Reformation in Germany, loved music and gave it a central position in the Lutheran Church, including congregational singing. Lutheran services used parts of the Roman liturgy in Latin, parts in translation, or Luther's German version of the Mass liturgy, the *Deudsche Messe* (1526). The music used was also a mixture of plainsong, Latin polyphony, and German hymns.

2. The Lutheran chorale
The *chorale* was a strophic hymn sung by the congregation in unison. Luther wrote many chorale texts and perhaps some of the tunes. Besides

newly written melodies, chorale tunes were often adapted from Gregorian chant or German sacred or secular songs.

3. Contrafacta

Many chorales were adapted from secular songs by revising the text to give it a spiritual meaning or by replacing it with a new sacred text. The new works that resulted are called *contrafacta.*

4. Polyphonic chorale settings

Composers soon began to arrange the monophonic chorales in polyphonic settings for choirs to perform, using a variety of styles from cantus firmus style or imitative motet style to simple chordal style. By the late sixteenth century, Protestant composers began to write *chorale motets,* free polyphonic elaborations of a chorale.

II. Reformation Church Music outside Germany (CHWM 153–58, NAWM 52)

1. Calvinism

Reformation movements in France, the Low Countries, and Switzerland, led by *Jean Calvin* (1509–1564) and others, rejected the Catholic liturgy, musical artistry, and nonbiblical texts in favor of rhymed translations of the Psalms. These were published in *Psalters* and sung in unison to simple melodies. The main French Psalter used tunes composed or adapted by *Loys Bourgeois* (ca. 1510–ca. 1561), whose melodies were often borrowed by churches in other lands, including the New England colonies. Psalm tunes were sometimes set polyphonically or in simple chordal style.

2. England

For reasons of war and politics, England was again relatively isolated in the second half of the fifteenth and first half of the sixteenth centuries. The leading English composer of this period was *John Taverner* (ca. 1490–1545), renowned for his Masses and Magnificats. The most important mid-century English composer was *Thomas Tallis* (ca. 1505–1585), known for his music for both the Catholic and Anglican liturgies.

Etude: More About Anglican Church Music

The Church of England separated from the Roman Catholic Church in 1534, largely for political reasons (Henry VIII wanted an annulment of his marriage, and the pope refused to grant it). A new liturgy in English was printed in *The Book of Common Prayer* (1549), and composers wrote church music in English. The two main genres were the *service* and the *anthem.*

1. A *service* consisted of music for Morning and Evening Prayer and for Holy Communion, and could be either a *Great Service* (contrapuntal and melismatic) or a *Short Service* (chordal and syllabic).
2. An *anthem* was equivalent to a motet. There were two types: the *full anthem,* sung by choir throughout, and the *verse anthem,* for solo voice or voices with organ or viol accompaniment, with brief passages for chorus.

Among the most important composers of Anglican music was William Byrd (mentioned in chapter 7), a Catholic who also wrote Latin motets and Masses. **Music: NAWM 52**

Window: Music as a Symbol for Human Frailty (CHWM 154–55)

In a Dutch painting on the transience of life, a violin and bow represent the impermanence of music and the tenuous pleasures it offers.

III. The Counter-Reformation (CHWM 158–68, NAWM 49–51)

1. Council of Trent
The *Council of Trent* met periodically between 1545 and 1563 to reform the Catholic Church. Music was only one factor that was considered, and the Council urged very general reforms designed to ensure that the words of the liturgy were clear and the music religious in tone.

A. *Palestrina*

There is a legend, apparently untrue, that *Giovanni Pierluigi da Palestrina* (1525 or 1526–1594) convinced the Council not to abolish polyphony by writing the *Pope Marcellus Mass*. Palestrina spent his entire career in Rome as a church musician. Most of his music was sacred, including 104 Masses and about 250 motets. He also supervised the revision of Gregorian chant to conform to the edicts of the Council of Trent.

1. Style
Palestrina's style became a model for later composers of polyphonic church music. His Masses use techniques ranging from cantus firmus to imitation Masses and from paraphrase to canon. His vocal lines move mostly by step in a smooth, flexible arch. He avoids chromaticism, stresses the important notes in the mode, and declaims the text clearly. **Music: NAWM 49**

Etude: Palestrina's Counterpoint
Palestrina's counterpoint is smooth and mostly consonant, with dissonance restricted to *suspensions,* passing notes, and *cambiatas.* The voices move independently within a regular harmonic rhythm. He uses different spacings to create variety in sonority.

B. *Palestrina's contemporaries*

Tomás Luis de Victoria (1548–1611) was a Spanish composer active in Rome and in Spain whose music is more intense than Palestrina's in its expression of the text and use of accidentals. Orlando di Lasso (mentioned in chapter 7) is as important for his motets as Palestrina is for his Masses. His motets often use pictorial, rhetorical, and dramatic devices and are written in a variety of styles. William Byrd (mentioned in chapter 7 and above) wrote three Masses and numerous motets, in addition to secular music and music for the Anglican church. **Music: NAWM 50a, 50b, and 51**

STUDY QUESTIONS

The Music of the Reformation in Germany (CHWM 151–53)

1. What is a *chorale*? How were they sung, and by whom?

2. What are the chief sources of tunes for chorales? What are *contrafacta*?

3. In what ways did chorales receive polyphonic treatment in the sixteenth and early seventeenth centuries? How were these polyphonic settings performed?

Reformation Church Music outside Germany (CHWM 153–58)

4. How was music used in the Calvinist churches outside Germany? How does this differ from the Lutheran Church?

5. What is a *Psalter*, and what does it contain?

6. What are the principal forms of Anglican church music? How does a *full anthem* differ from a *verse anthem*? How does a *Great Service* differ from a *Short Service*?

Music to Study
    NAWM 52: William Byrd, *Sing joyfully unto God,* full anthem (late sixteenth
        century)
      CD 3.29–41 (Concise 2.9–12)   Cassette 3.B (Concise 2.A)

7. How does Byrd illustrate the text in *Sing joyfully unto God* (NAWM 52)?
   How does he highlight the accentuation and phrasing of the text?

The Counter-Reformation (CHWM 158–68, NAWM 49–51)

8. What was the Council of Trent? When was it held, and what was its purpose?
   What matters relating to music were discussed, and what actions relating to
   music did the Council take?

9. Briefly summarize Palestrina's career. Why was his music important for later
   composers?

10. How many Masses did Palestrina write? _____

What compositional techniques did he use in his Masses?

Music to Study
    NAWM 49: Giovanni da Palestrina, *Pope Marcellus Mass*, excerpts (1562–
        63)
        49a: Credo   CD 3.14–18   Cassette 3.A
        49b: Agnus Dei I   CD 3.19 (Concise 2.4)   Cassette 3.A (Concise 2.A)

11. Describe Palestrina's style in terms of melody, harmony, counterpoint and
    dissonance treatment, sonority, and rhythm, using examples from the Credo
    and first Agnus Dei of the *Pope Marcellus Mass* (NAWM 49a and 49b).

    melody:

    harmony:

    counterpoint and dissonance treatment:

    sonority:

    rhythm:

Music to Study
>   **NAWM 50a:** Tomás Luis de Victoria, *O magnum mysterium*, motet (published 1572)
>   CD 3.20–22   Cassette 3.A
>   **NAWM 50b:** Tomás Luis de Victoria, *Missa O magnum mysterium*, Mass, excerpt: Kyrie (published 1592)
>   CD 3.23–24   Cassette 3.A

12. How is each phrase of text treated in Victoria's motet *O magnum mysterium* (NAWM 50a)? How does the placement of cadences help to give shape to the piece and make clear the divisions of the text?

13. Compare the Kyrie of Victoria's *Missa O magnum mysterium* (NAWM 50b) to the motet on which it is based (NAWM 50a). What has Victoria borrowed from his earlier motet, and how has he varied it?

14. What is an *imitation Mass* or *parody Mass* (see the definition in CHWM, p. 118)? How does Victoria's *Missa O magnum mysterium* exemplify this kind of Mass?

15. How do Orlando di Lasso's career, music, and musical output contrast with those of Palestrina? (Note: There is additional information on Lasso in chapter 7 of CHWM.)

Music to Study
NAWM 51: Orlando di Lasso, *Tristis est anima mea,* motet (published 1565)
CD 3.25–28 (Concise 2.5–8)   Cassette 3.B (Concise 2.A)

16. How does Lasso use pictorial, rhetorical, or dramatic devices to convey the meaning of the words in his motet *Tristis est anima mea* (NAWM 51)?

17. Briefly recount William Byrd's career. What kinds of music did he write? How did the situation of religion in England affect his career and compositional output? (You may wish to refer back to parts of chapter 7 of HWM in answering this question.)

TERMS TO KNOW

Reformation
Counter-Reformation
chorale
contrafacta
chorale motet

Psalter
service: Great Service, Short Service
anthem: full anthem, verse anthem
suspension
cambiata

NAMES TO KNOW

Martin Luther
Deudsche Messe
Jean Calvin
Loys Bourgeois
John Taverner
Thomas Tallis

The Book of Common Prayer
Council of Trent
Giovanni Pierluigi da Palestrina
Pope Marcellus Mass
Tomás Luis de Victoria

REVIEW QUESTIONS

1. Add to the time-line you made for the sixteenth century in chapter 7 the pieces, composers, and events discussed in this chapter.

2. How was music regarded, how was it used, and what musical genres were cultivated in the Lutheran church and in Calvinist churches during the sixteenth century?

3. How did the Counter-Reformation affect music for the Catholic church?

4. Describe Palestrina's style in his Masses.

5. How did composers of church music in the later sixteenth century treat the words they set? What are some of the approaches to setting or expressing a text, as exemplified by the pieces treated in this chapter?

MUSIC OF THE EARLY BAROQUE PERIOD

9

CHAPTER OBJECTIVES

After you complete the reading, study of the music, and study questions for this chapter, you should be able to:

1. describe the characteristics that distinguish Baroque music from music of earlier periods;
2. relate music of the Baroque period to the culture and art of the time;
3. describe the various styles of music that flourished and competed in the first half of the seventeenth century;
4. trace the evolution of opera in Italy from its forerunners through the middle of the seventeenth century;
5. describe the genres and styles of secular and sacred vocal music practiced in the early seventeenth century;
6. explain what is distinctive about Venice and Venetian music in the late sixteenth and early seventeenth centuries; and
7. name and briefly describe the most important genres and styles of instrumental music in the early Baroque period.

CHAPTER OUTLINE

Prelude (CHWM 170–72)

The *Baroque period* of about 1600–1750 embraced a variety of musical styles that share some general conventions and ideals, including the belief that music should move the emotions of the listener. Many rulers supported music, as did the church, many cities, and independent academies. Italy remained the most influential region, with important centers at Florence, Rome, Venice, Naples, and Bologna. New vocal genres developed, from opera and cantata to sacred concerto and oratorio, and for the first time instrumental music became as important as vocal music. Literature and art flourished throughout Europe, from the poetry of Milton to the paintings of Rembrandt. New developments in philosophy and science were particularly spectacular, as Bacon, Descartes, Galileo,

98

Kepler, Newton, and others helped lay the foundations of modern thought. Musicians around 1600 sought to give expression to a wider range of emotions and ideas than before. Their search for new methods led to the codification of a new musical language by the middle of the century.

I. General Characteristics of Baroque Music (CHWM 172–76)

1. Two practices

Writing in 1605, Monteverdi contrasted the *prima pratica* (first practice), in which a composer follows the rules of dissonance treatment codified by Zarlino, with the *seconda pratica* (second practice), in which those rules could be violated in order to express better the feelings in the text.

2. Idiomatic writing

The growing importance of soloists led seventeenth-century composers to write with a specific medium in mind. As a result, distinctive idiomatic styles developed for the voice and various instruments.

3. Affections

Baroque composers sought to write music that was expressive of *the affections,* or states of the soul. These are not the composer's own emotions but generalized states of feeling.

4. Rhythm

Music before the seventeenth century was conceived primarily in terms of durations, but Baroque and later composers thought in terms of strong and weak beats grouped in *measures.* On the other hand, free and irregular rhythms were used in vocal recitative and instrumental preludes and toccatas. Some standard forms paired a relatively free section with a strictly metered section, such as a recitative and aria or a toccata and fugue.

5. Basso continuo

Renaissance polyphony used a texture of equal voices, but in Baroque music the melody and bass were the two essential lines. In the notational system called *thorough bass* or *basso continuo,* the accompaniment was not fully written out; instead, *continuo instruments* such as harpsichord, organ, or lute would play the notated bass line and fill in the appropriate chords above it, while often a sustaining instrument like a viola da gamba or bassoon would reinforce the bass. Accidentals, nonharmonic tones, and chords other than root-position triads could be indicated by numbers and other figures; a part notated this way is called a *figured bass.* A basso continuo part can be *realized* by the performer(s) in various ways from simple chords to elaborate improvisations.

6. The new counterpoint

A new kind of counterpoint evolved in which the lines had to fit the chords of the basso continuo, so that the counterpoint was governed by harmony.

7. Dissonance

The new importance of harmony led to a conception of dissonance as a note outside a chord, rather than an interval between two voices, and to an increased role for dissonance in defining the tonal direction of a piece.

8. Chromaticism

Chromaticism was used in the early seventeenth century for expression of extreme emotions or to give harmonic interest to improvisations. Later in the century, it also gained a role in defining tonal direction.

9. Major-minor tonalities

These and other developments led by the last third of the seventeenth century to *tonality*, the system of major and minor keys organized around a tonic triad, which replaced the older system of modes.

II. Early Opera (CHWM 176–86, NAWM 53–58)

1. Forerunners

An *opera* is a staged drama set to continuous (or nearly continuous) music. The first operas were written around 1600, but many earlier forms of theater used music, including Greek tragedies, liturgical dramas, religious plays, Renaissance theater, and *intermedi* or *intermezzi*, theatrical interludes between acts of a play.   **Music: NAWM 53**

2. Florentine Camerata

Girolamo Mei (1519–1594) argued that the ancient Greek tragedies were sung throughout and that the Greeks achieved powerful emotional effects through solo melody that followed the inflections and rhythms of the human voice. His views influenced the *Florentine Camerata,* an informal group that met in Florence during the 1570s and 1580s. Following Mei, *Vincenzo Galilei* (d. 1591) attacked counterpoint and argued that only *monody,* a solo vocal melody with instrumental accompaniment, could express the feelings of poetry.

3. Earliest Operas

The first surviving opera was *Euridice* (Florence, 1600) by poet *Ottaviano Rinuccini* (1562–1621) and singer-composer *Jacopo Peri* (1561–1633); that same year, *Giulio Caccini* (1551–1618) also set Rinuccini's *Euridice.* Both composers wrote monody and sought a style between speech and song that conveyed the text clearly, expressively, and naturally.

4. Caccini

Caccini's song collection *Le nuove musiche* (The New Music, 1602) contains strophic *airs* and through-composed *solo madrigals,* with vocal ornaments written out rather than left to the singer.   **Music: NAWM 54**

5. Recitative Style

In *stile recitativo* or *recitative style,* Peri sought to imitate speech by harmonizing the syllables that were naturally stressed or intoned in speech, letting the bass follow these main syllables rather than making the voice "dance to the movement of the bass," and setting the syllables in between to notes that might be either consonant or dissonant with the bass, thus resembling the continuous motions of speech. He used this and other types of monody in *Euridice* to represent the actions and emotions of the drama. **Music: NAWM 55**

6. Monteverdi's *Orfeo*

Monteverdi's opera *Orfeo* (Mantua, 1607), to a libretto by Alessandro Striggio, is on the same subject as Peri's *Euridice* and uses more contrast of styles. The recitative is more continuous and tonally organized; there are more airs and madrigals; repeating ritornellos and choruses create large-scale form; and the orchestra is large and varied. **Music: NAWM 56**

7. Francesca Caccini

Only a few more operas were staged through the 1620s. The Florentine court preferred ballets and intermedi, such as *La liberazione di Ruggiero* (1625), an opera-like blend of ballet and intermedio by *Francesca Caccini* (1587–ca. 1640). The daughter of Giulio Caccini, she was known as both a singer and a composer and was the highest-paid musician at court.

8. Rome

Opera became established in Rome in the 1620s. There the comic opera became established as a separate genre. Solo singing separated into two distinct types, *recitative* and *aria*. By mid-century, operas often included comic episodes, scenic spectacle, extraneous characters, and other elements that were entertaining as theater but no longer conformed to the Florentine ideal of a unified drama akin to that of ancient Greece.

9. Venetian opera

Opera was introduced to Venice in 1637 in a public theater; this marked the first time opera was staged for a paying public.

Etude: Opera in Seventeenth-Century Venice

Venice was ideal for opera, with many visitors in Carnival season (from the day after Christmas to the day before Lent), wealthy backers, and a steady audience. Plots were drawn from mythology, epics, and Roman history.

10. Monteverdi's *Poppea*

Monteverdi's last two operas, *Il ritorno d'Ulisse* (The Return of Ulysses, 1641) and *L'incoronazione di Poppea* (The Coronation of Poppea, 1642), were written for Venice. They alternate passages of recitative, aria, and *arioso* (a style between recitative and aria) as appropriate to convey the drama. **Music: NAWM 57**

11. Cavalli and Cesti

Pier Francesco Cavalli (1602–1676) and *Antonio Cesti* (1623–1669) were important composers of opera in Venice. Their arias are fully developed and use a new vocal idiom later known as *bel canto* (beautiful singing), with smooth diatonic lines and easy rhythms. **Music: NAWM 58**

12. Characteristics of opera

By the mid-seventeenth century Italian opera was characterized by a focus on solo singing, with little ensemble or instrumental music; a separation of recitative and aria; and the use of distinctive types of aria.

III. Vocal Chamber Music (CHWM 186–92, NAWM 59–60)

Most secular vocal music was chamber music. Like opera, chamber works used monody and basso continuo. *Strophic arias* used the same music for each strophe or stanza; *strophic variations* used the same harmonic and melodic plan for each stanza, but varied the melodic details.

Etude: Baroque Ostinato Patterns

Composers often based works on the *romanesca* and other standard patterns for singing poetry in *ottave rime* (stanzas of eight 11-syllable lines) or on a repeating bass figure called a *ground bass* or *basso ostinato*. The *chaconne* and *passacaglia* both feature a repeating bass figure in a slow triple meter.   **Music: NAWM 59**

1. The concertato medium

The seventeenth-century *concerto* brought together contrasting sounds into a harmonious whole, in what is called the *concertato medium*. A *concertato madrigal* uses instruments as well as voices; a *sacred concerto* likewise joins instruments with a vocal setting of a sacred text; and an *instrumental concerto* pits groups of instruments against each other, usually soloists against a larger group. Monteverdi's later books of madrigals include a number of concertato madrigals.

Etude: Monteverdi's Eighth Book of Madrigals

Monteverdi's Book 8, *Madrigali guerrieri et amorosi* (Madrigals of War and Love, 1638), includes a variety of concerted pieces, along with two staged ballets and *Il Combattimento di Tancredi e Clorinda* (The Combat of Tancred and Clorinda), a theatrical piece of 1624. The latter uses pictorial music to suggest the action and introduces a new style, *stile concitato* (excited style), to suggest warlike feelings and actions.

2. Genres of vocal solo music

Monodies were very popular in early-seventeenth-century Italy and were published in large number. The *cantata* was a work for solo voice and continuo; later ones, such as those by *Barbara Strozzi* (1619–after 1664) alternated recitatives and arias, like an operatic scene.   **Music: NAWM 60**

3. Church music

Monody, the basso continuo, and the concertato medium were used in church music as well as in secular music. But Renaissance polyphony was not abandoned; the counterpoint of Palestrina became the model for the elevated church style, known as *stile antico* (old style).

Window: Barbara Strozzi, Renaissance Woman (CHWM 190–91)

Barbara Strozzi (1619–after 1664) won fame as a singer and composer of cantatas and other vocal works focused on the theme of love.

IV. The Venetian School (CHWM 192–93, NAWM 61)

Venice was an independent city-state and a major trading center with the East. *Saint Mark's Church* was a center of music and pageantry, and many great composers served as choirmaster (such as Willaert, Rore, Zarlino, and Monteverdi) or organist (including *Giovanni Gabrieli*, ca. 1553–1612). Venetian music was often homophonic, richly textured, and varied in sonority. Many works of the late 1500s and early 1600s used two or more choirs, each accompanied by instruments or organ and placed apart from the others. In motets for *cori spezzati* (divided choirs), called *polychoral motets*, the choirs sing alone, answer each other in antiphony, and join together for large climaxes. The Venetian style influenced composers throughout Europe, and the use of contrasting sonorities became an important element of Baroque music. **Music: NAWM 61**

V. Genres of Sacred Music: Catholic and Lutheran (CHWM 193–98, NAWM 62–65)

1. Grand concerto
A *grand concerto* was a large work for singers and instruments, often arranged in two or more separate choirs.

2. Concerto for few voices
More common were concertos for one to three voices with organ continuo. *Lodovico Viadana* (1560–1627) was among the first to use this medium, in his 1602 collection *Cento concerti ecclesiastici* (One Hundred Sacred Concertos). *Alessandro Grandi* (ca. 1575/80–1630) was noted for his sacred works in the new style. **Music: NAWM 62–63**

3. Oratorio
An *oratorio* was a sacred drama like an opera, sung throughout with recitatives, arias, ensembles, and instrumental preludes and ritornellos, but performed in a church hall without staging or costumes. Oratorios often featured a narrator, and the chorus was much more prominent than in opera. *Giacomo Carissimi* (1605–1674) was the leading Italian composer of oratorios in the mid-seventeenth century. **Music: NAWM 64**

4. Lutheran church music
Lutheran composers in Germany in the seventeenth century also wrote grand concertos and concertos for few voices, along with chorale motets. An important collection of small sacred concertos was *Opella nova* (1618 and 1626) by *Johann Hermann Schein* (1586–1630).

5. Heinrich Schütz
Heinrich Schütz (1585–1672) was the leading German composer of his time. He studied in Venice and was chapelmaster for the elector of Saxony at Dresden for over half a century. He is renowned for his church music; he apparently wrote no independent instrumental music, and most of his secular vocal music is lost. His sacred music includes polychoral works, small sacred concertos, and concertato motets. **Music: NAWM 65**

Window: The Ecstasy of Saint Teresa (CHWM 196–97)

Bernini's sculpture *The Ecstasy of Saint Teresa* is typical of Baroque art in being theatrical, representing action and seeking to move our emotions.

VI. Instrumental Music (CHWM 198–207, NAWM 66–68)

Over the first half of the seventeenth century, instrumental music gradually became the equal of vocal music in quantity and content.

A. *Dance Music*

Dances and other types of pieces often used dance rhythms. German composers cultivated the *dance suite,* a series of dances of varied character that often were melodically related. French composers arranged dances for lute, playing chords one note at a time (the *style brisé,* or broken style) and using ornaments called *agréments* to highlight or prolong a note. These features were adapted to the harpsichord and became characteristic of French style. *Johann Jakob Froberger* (1616–1667) took the French style to Germany and standardized the dances in the suite as *allemande, courante, sarabande,* and *gigue.*   **Music: NAWM 66a, 66b, and 67**

B. *Improvisatory Compositions*

Among the best-known early Baroque toccatas are those by *Girolamo Frescobaldi* (1583–1643), organist at St. Peter's in Rome, and Froberger. Frescobaldi's feature a series of overlapping sections, and Froberger alternates free improvisation with imitative sections.   **Music: NAWM 68**

C. *Contrapuntal or Fugal Genres in Continuous (Non-Sectional) Imitative Counterpoint*

Most seventeenth-century *ricercares* are short, serious pieces for keyboard that treat a single subject in imitation throughout. Frescobaldi is well known for his ricercares. A longer imitative work on a single subject was usually called a *fantasia.* English composers wrote imitative fantasias or *fancies* for viol consort.

D. *Canzona or Sonata*

1. Canzona

Canzonas featured a series of sections, most in imitative counterpoint. A *variation canzona* uses variants of the same subject in each section.

2. Sonata

In the seventeenth century, *sonata* came to refer to works for one or two instruments with basso continuo. The solo writing was often idiomatic and expressive, as in solo vocal works. Sonatas tend to be sectional, with contrasting mood and figuration in each section. In violin sonatas, the idiomatic violin style includes runs, trills, double stops, and improvised embellishments. A common scoring for a sonata was two treble instruments and continuo, called a *trio sonata.*

E. *Variations*

Variations were common in the seventeenth century, sometimes under titles such as *partite* (divisions). There were several types:
1. In *cantus firmus variations,* the melody was largely unchanged and was surrounded by other contrapuntal lines.
2. In another type, the melody was in the top voice and was embellished differently in each variation.
3. Other types of variations are based on a bass or harmonic plan rather than on a melody.

German composers wrote variations on chorale melodies.

STUDY QUESTIONS

Prelude (CHWM 170–72)

1. Which famous artists, writers, philosophers, and scientists were active in the seventeenth century? How does music show a similar intellectual ferment?

General Characteristics of Baroque Music (CHWM 172–76)

2. What is the *seconda pratica*? How does it differ from the *prima pratica*?

   How is the *seconda pratica* reflected in Monteverdi's madrigal *Cruda Amarilli* (NAWM 41)? (Hint: Review the discussion of this piece in NAWM, pp. 174–75, and CHWM, pp. 134–35, Monteverdi's comment on p. 133 of CHWM, and your answer to question 14 in chapter 7.)

3. How did the Renaissance ideal of writing music that could be performed by any combination of voices and instruments change in the seventeenth century? What was the effect on composition?

4. What are the *affections*? How does the representation of affections in music differ from the later idea of expressing an individual artist's feelings?

5. What is new about rhythm in seventeenth-century music, in contrast to earlier music?

6. Define the following terms, and explain the significance of each concept.

   basso continuo or thorough bass

   figured bass

   continuo instruments

7. Compare the opening of Giulio Caccini's *Perfidissimo volto* as it appears in NAWM 54 with the original publication, shown in CHWM, p. 173. (In the latter, note that the vocal line is notated in tenor clef.) What notes are present in the NAWM edition that are not present in the original publication?

   How are these notes differentiated from the others on the page?

   Why are they present in the NAWM edition? Why are they absent in the original publication?

   What is the practice of supplying these notes called? _____

8. How did the emphasis on the bass and the use of basso continuo change how counterpoint was conceived and written and how dissonance was defined?

9. Why was figured bass important in the development of *major-minor tonality* as a replacement for the older system of modes?

Early Opera (CHWM 176–86, NAWM 53–58)

10. In what sense was ancient Greek tragedy a model for opera? Who were Girolamo Mei and Vincenzo Galilei, and what did each one do to promote the revival of Greek ideals that ultimately led to opera?

11. What were the roles of Ottavio Rinuccini, Jacopo Peri, and Giulio Caccini in the creation of the first operas?

12. What does the term *monody* mean? What different types of monody did Peri and Caccini use in their vocal music?

Music to Study

NAWM 53: Emilio de' Cavalieri, *Dalle più alte sfere*, madrigal for voice and instruments (1589)

    CD 3.33–34   Cassette 3.B

NAWM 54: Giulio Caccini, *Perfidissimo volto*, madrigal for voice and continuo (ca. 1600)

    CD 3.35–36   Cassette 3.B

NAWM 55: Jacopo Peri, *Le musiche sopra l'Euridice*, opera, excerpts (1600)

  55a: Prologue, *Io, che d'alti sospir*, strophic air with ritornello

    CD 3.37   Cassette 3.B

  55b: *Nel pur ardor*, canzonet (dance-song) with ritornello

    CD 3.38   Cassette 3.B

  55c: *Per quel vago boschetto*, recitative

    CD 3.39–41   Cassette 3.B

NAWM 56: Claudio Monteverdi, *L'Orfeo*, opera, excerpts (1607)

  56a: Prologue, *Dal mio Permesso amato*, strophic variations

    CD 3.42–47   Cassette 3.B

  56b: *Vi ricorda o boschi ombrosi*, strophic canzonet (excerpt)

    CD 3.48–49 (Concise 2.13–14)   Cassette 3.B (Concise 2.A)

  56c: *In un fiorito prato*, recitative; *Tu se' morta*, expressive recitative; and *Ahi caso acerbo*, chorus (madrigal)

    CD 3.50–56 (Concise 2.13–21)   Cassette 3.B (Concise 2.A)

13. How do Cavalieri's madrigal *Dalle più alte sfere* (NAWM 53) and Caccini's madrigal *Perfidissimo volto* (NAWM 54) differ from other madrigals we have seen?

What traits do they share with other sixteenth-century Italian madrigals? Why are they madrigals, and not airs?

14. What kinds of embellishments are used to decorate the vocal lines of *Dalle più alte sfere* and *Perfidissimo volto*?

15. What is the *stile recitativo* or *recitative style*? How does Peri describe it in the preface to *Euridice* (excerpted in CHWM, p. 180)? How does the dialogue from his setting of *Euridice* (NAWM 55c) reflect his conception?

16. How does Peri use harmony, dissonance, and rhythm in Orfeo's response to the death of Euridice (mm. 63–87) to convey the meaning of the words and the feelings they reflect?

17. What style of monody does Peri use in the other excerpts from *Euridice* (NAWM 55a and 55b)? How does this style differ from recitative style?

18. Compare and contrast Monteverdi's *Orfeo* with Peri's *Euridice*, including the excerpts in NAWM 56 and 55 respectively and the description of each in CHWM. In what ways is the Monteverdi similar and different?

19. Monteverdi's prologue (NAWM 56a) is a *strophic variation,* in which the harmony and general melodic contour are the same for each strophe of the text, but details in the music are changed to fit the new text. How are the first two strophes different? Note the changes Monteverdi has made.

   How does the last strophe differ from the others in the way it ends, and how does that illustrate the text? (Hint: Look at the melody, the harmony, and the last few words of the text.)

20. How does Monteverdi convey the meaning of the text and the feelings it reflects in Orfeo's recitative *Tu se' morta* (NAWM 56c, mm. 43–64)?

21. In *Orfeo,* Monteverdi uses particular musical forms and styles to convey the changing dramatic situation and the feelings of the characters. What characteristics make each of the following forms and styles appropriate for the scene in which it is used?

   56a: La Musica, strophic variation with ritornello

   56b: Orfeo, strophic canzonet with ritornello

   56c: Messenger, recitative

      Orfeo, expressive recitative

      Chorus, choral madrigal

22. Who was Francesca Caccini, when and where did she live and work, and for what was she renowned?

23. When and where was opera first made available to the paying public?

What made this city ideal for opera?

Music to Study

NAWM 57: Claudio Monteverdi, *L'incoronazione di Poppea*, opera, excerpt: Act I, Scene 3 (1642)

    CD 4.1–5   Cassette 4.A

NAWM 58: Antonio Cesti, *Orontea*, opera, excerpt: *Intorno all' idol mio*, aria from Act II, Scene 17 (ca. 1649)

    CD 4.6–7   Cassette 4.A

24. Compare and contrast the scene from Monteverdi's *L'incoronazione di Poppea* in NAWM 57 with the scene from *Orfeo* in NAWM 56c. What devices does Monteverdi use in each case to depict the text and portray the dramatic situation?

25. In this scéne from *L'incoronazione di Poppea,* the music shifts back and forth often between recitative and aria styles. Why does Monteverdi set Poppea's "Deh non dir di partir" (mm. 280–87) as recitative, and her words "Vanne, vanne ben mio" (mm. 303–9) as a brief aria? (Hint: Do not be fooled by the notation of the latter; it is in a fast triple time.)

26. Contrast the aria from Cesti's *Orontea* (ca. 1649) in NAWM 58 with the airs from Peri's *Euridice* (1600) in NAWM 55a and 55b. How has the style of operatic song changed from the beginning to the middle of the seventeenth century?

27. How does the aria from *Orontea* exemplify the *bel canto* style?

28. What important operatic conventions took shape in Italy by the middle of the seventeenth century? How did opera in Rome and Venice at mid-century differ from Florentine operas of about 1600?

Vocal Chamber Music (CHWM 186–92, NAWM 59–60)

29. Define the following terms:

ground bass or basso ostinato

concertato medium

concertato madrigal

sacred concerto

instrumental concerto (in the 17th century)

Music to Study
NAWM 59: Claudio Monteverdi, *Ohimè dov' è il mio ben,* madrigal (1610s)
    CD 4.8–11   Cassette 4.A

30. What is the *romanesca*? How is each of the four parts of Monteverdi's madrigal *Ohimè dov' è il mio ben* (NAWM 59) a variant of the romanesca?

31. In what senses is this work a strophic variation?

In what senses is this a madrigal, and how does it compare with sixteenth-century madrigals?

32. What is the *stile concitato*? Who first used it? When, and in what piece?

33. What is a *cantata* in the seventeenth century? How does it resemble opera, and how is it different?

Music to Study
NAWM 60: Barbara Strozzi, *Lagrime mie,* cantata (published 1659)
    CD 4.12–16   Cassette 4.A

34. In her cantata *Lagrime mie* (NAWM 60), Strozzi uses sections of recitative, aria, and arioso (a style between recitative and aria, usually more metric than recitative). Where is each kind of monody used? (Indicate by measure numbers.)

    recitative   _____

    aria   _____

    arioso   _____

    In what ways are the sections of text set as aria particularly appropriate for that style of music?

35. What musical devices does Strozzi use to represent the following words and the feelings or actions behind them?

    "lagrime" (tears)

    "respiro" (breath)

    "tormenti" (torments)

The Venetian School (CHWM 192–93, NAWM 61)

Music to Study
    NAWM 61: Giovanni Gabrieli, *In ecclesiis*, motet (published 1615)
        CD 4.17–22   Cassette 4.A

36. What are *cori spezzati*? What is a *polychoral motet*? How does Gabrieli's
    motet *In ecclesiis* (NAWM 61) exemplify the characteristics of the genre?

**Genres of Sacred Music: Catholic and Lutheran (CHWM 193–98, NAWM 62–
    65)**

37. What varieties of sacred concerto were written in the seventeenth century? For
    what circumstances and occasions was each type suited?

38. What is an *oratorio*? From what does its name derive? How is it like opera,
    and how does it differ?

Music to Study
> **NAWM 62:** Lodovico Viadana, *O Domine Jesu Christe*, sacred concerto (ca. 1602)
> CD 4.23   Cassette 4.A
> **NAWM 63:** Alessandro Grandi, *O quam tu pulchra es*, motet (1625)
> CD 4.24–26   Cassette 4.A
> **NAWM 64:** Giacomo Carissimi, *Historia di Jephte*, oratorio, excerpt (ca. 1650)
>   64a: *Plorate colles*, expressive recitative
>   CD 4.27   Cassette 4.B
>   64b: *Plorate filii Israel*, chorus
>   CD 4.28   Cassette 4.B
> **NAWM 65:** Heinrich Schütz, *Saul, was verfolgst du mich* (SWV 415), grand concerto (ca. 1650)
>   CD 4.29–30 (Concise 2.22–23)   Cassette 4.B (Concise 2.A)

39. How is Viadana's *O Domine Jesu Christe* (NAWM 62) like a sixteenth-century motet, such as Victoria's *O magnum mysterium* (NAWM 50), and how is it different?

40. How is Viadana's sacred concerto like secular monody of around the same time, such as Caccini's *Perfidissimo volto* (NAWM 54), and how is it different?

41. How is Grandi's *O quam tu pulchra es* (NAWM 63) like a sixteenth-century motet, and how is it different?

42. How does Grandi's motet compare to the alternation of recitative and aria styles in the scene from Monteverdi's *L'incoronazione di Poppea* in NAWM 57? How does each work respond to its text?

43. Compare the excerpt from Carissimi's *Historia di Jephte* in NAWM 64 with the scene from Monteverdi's *Orfeo* in NAWM 56c. What elements does each use?

How do Monteverdi and Carissimi use harmony to convey emotions?

How does each use the chorus?

44. How does Schütz use changes of texture and other musical effects to depict the events and text of *Saul, was verfolgst du mich* (NAWM 65)? What types of style and texture does he use?

Instrumental Music (CHWM 198–207, NAWM 66–68)

45. What is a dance *suite*? What dances typically appear in a suite by Froberger?

46. What is *style brisé* (broken style)?

What are *agréments*?

On what instrument did *style brisé* and *agréments* originate? _____

Why were they necessary or useful on that instrument?

To what instrument were they later adapted? _____

Music to Study

> **NAWM 66a:** Ennemond Gaultier, *La Poste,* gigue for lute (early to mid-
> seventeenth century)
>
> CD 4.31   Cassette 4.B
>
> **NAWM 66b:** Anonymous arrangement for harpsichord of Ennemond Gaul-
> tier's *La Poste* (seventeenth century)
>
> CD 4.32   Cassette 4.B
>
> **NAWM 67:** Johann Jakob Froberger, *Lamentation on the Death of Emperor
> Ferdinand III* (1657)
>
> CD 4.33–34   Cassette 4.B
>
> **NAWM 68:** Girolamo Frescobaldi, Toccata No. 3 (1628)
>
> CD 4.35 (Concise 2.24)   Cassette 4.B (Concise 2.A)

47. Compare Gaultier's gigue for lute (NAWM 66a) with its arrangement for
harpsichord (NAWM 66b). How does the keyboard version imitate the style
of the lute?

48. What features of Froberger's *Lamentation on the Death of Emperor Ferdinand III* (NAWM 67) mark it as a piece in French style?

   What features are particularly appropriate to its subject?

49. How is Frescobaldi's Toccata No. 3 (NAWM 68) divided into sections? Where does the style or figuration change?

50. In the first half of the seventeenth century, what is the difference between a ricercare and a fantasia?

   What is the difference between a canzona and a sonata?

51. What kinds of variations were written in the seventeenth century? In each type, what stayed the same in each variation, and what changed?

TERMS TO KNOW

Terms Related to the Baroque Period

Baroque period	basso continuo
prima pratica, seconda pratica	continuo instruments
the affections	figured bass
measures	realization of a figured bass
thorough bass	tonality (major-minor tonality)

Terms Related to Early Opera

opera
intermedi or intermezzi
monody
air
solo madrigal

stile recitativo (recitative style)
recitative
aria
arioso
bel canto

Terms Related to Vocal Music

strophic aria
strophic variation
romanesca
ottave rime
ground bass or basso ostinato
chaconne
passacaglia
concerto (seventeenth-century)
concertato medium
concertato madrigal

sacred concerto
instrumental concerto
stile concitato
cantata (seventeenth century)
stile antico
cori spezzati
polychoral motet
grand concerto
oratorio

Terms Related to Instrumental Music

dance suite
style brisé
agréments
allemande, courante, sarabande,
    gigue
ricercare (seventeenth-century)
fantasia (seventeenth-century)

fancy
canzona (seventeenth-century)
variation canzona
sonata (seventeenth-century)
trio sonata
partita (or partite)
cantus firmus variations

NAMES TO KNOW

Names Related to Early Opera

Girolamo Mei
Florentine Camerata
Vincenzo Galilei
Euridice
Ottaviano Rinuccini
Jacopo Peri
Giulio Caccini
Le nuove musiche

Orfeo
Francesca Caccini
La liberazione di Ruggiero
Il ritorno d' Ulisse
L'incoronazione di Poppea
Pier Francesco Cavalli
Antonio Cesti

Names Related to Vocal Music

Madrigali guerrieri et amorosi
*Il Combattimento di Tancredi e
    Clorinda*
Barbara Strozzi
Saint Mark's Church
Giovanni Gabrieli
Lodovico Viadana

Cento concerti ecclesiastici
Alessandro Grandi
Giacomo Carissimi
Opella nova
    Johann Hermann Schein
Heinrich Schütz

Names Related to Instrumental Music

Johann Jakob Froberger   Girolamo Frescobaldi

REVIEW QUESTIONS

1. Make a time-line for the pieces, composers, treatises, and theorists discussed in this chapter.

2. What are the principal characteristics that distinguish music of the Baroque period from music of the Renaissance?

3. What new concepts or procedures were developed in the period 1600–1650 as composers sought to find ways to capture human emotions in music?

4. Trace the development of opera in Italy from its origins to 1650. Include in your answer changes of aesthetic aims and ideas as well as changes of style and procedure.

5. What connections do you see between Monteverdi's madrigals and his operas? What effects did his experience as a madrigal composer have on his operas?

6. What new forms and styles of secular vocal music were introduced in the first half of the seventeenth century?

7. How was sacred music affected by the new developments in secular music in the first half of the seventeenth century? What new forms or styles of sacred music emerged during this time?

8. What was the concertato medium, and where was it used?

9. What types of instrumental music were practiced during the early seventeenth century? Which of these genres and styles were new, and which continued trends from the sixteenth century? Of the latter, how were the older genres or styles changed in the seventeenth century?

10. What are some elements that distinguish French from Italian instrumental style in the early Baroque?

OPERA AND VOCAL MUSIC IN THE LATE SEVENTEENTH CENTURY

10

CHAPTER OBJECTIVES

After you complete the reading, study of the music, and study questions for this chapter, you should be able to:

1. describe developments in Italian opera in the second half of the seventeenth century and the beginning of the eighteenth century;
2. trace the origins and development of musical theater in France, England, and Germany during the seventeenth and early eighteenth centuries and explain what makes each national tradition distinctive;
3. describe the cantata and other secular vocal genres in the late seventeenth century;
4. describe the varieties of sacred music being composed in the late seventeenth and early eighteenth centuries; and
5. define and use the most important terms and identify some of the composers and works associated with opera and vocal music in the late seventeenth and early eighteenth centuries.

CHAPTER OUTLINE

Prelude (CHWM 208)

> In the second half of the seventeenth century, opera spread across Italy and Europe, and its styles influenced vocal chamber and sacred music.

I. Opera (CHWM 209–18, NAWM 69–72)

A. *Venice*

> Singers were the stars of opera, often commanding much higher fees than composers. There were many types of aria, including strophic, two-part, and three-part forms, and arias over ostinato basses or in dance rhythms. Many Italian composers made careers writing Italian operas in Germany.

Etude: An Aria by Agostino Steffani

A typical Italian aria of the time included coloratura passages and mood or text painting. Many arias featured a *motto,* in which the singer states the opening motive (the motto), the instruments interrupt, and then the singer begins again. Also common was a running-bass accompaniment.

B. *Naples*

A new operatic style that emphasized elegant melodies over dramatic effect developed in Naples and became dominant in the early eighteenth century. There were two types of recitative, later called *recitativo semplice* or *secco* (simple or dry recitative, with basso continuo), for dialogue or monologue, and *recitativo obbligato* or *accompagnato* (accompanied recitative, with orchestra), for dramatic situations. The principal aria type was the *da capo aria,* in which the first section (with or without the opening ritornello) is repeated after a contrasting middle section. *Alessandro Scarlatti* (1660–1725) was a leading composer of this kind of opera. **Music: NAWM 69**

C. *France*

A distinctive style of opera developed in France in the 1670s under the patronage of Louis XIV. *Jean-Baptiste Lully* (1632–1687) drew on two strong French traditions, court ballet and classical French tragedy, to create the *tragédie lyrique.* His librettos by *Jean-Phillippe Quinault* featured mythological plots often interrupted by *divertissements,* long interludes of choral singing and dancing. Lully's recitative is a new style, matched to the rhythms and inflections of French, with two types: *récitatif simple,* in freely shifting meter, and *récitatif mesuré,* in a more songlike, measured style. Lully codified the *ouverture,* or *French overture,* as an introduction to a ballet, opera, suite, or other large work. A French overture usually has two parts, the first slow, stately, homophonic, and marked by dotted rhythms, and the second fast and imitative, often closing with a return to the slower first tempo. **Music: NAWM 70a and 70b**

D. *England*

Musical theater in seventeenth-century England included the *masque,* akin to the French court ballet; plays with extensive incidental music, called *semi-operas*; and only two full operas. *Henry Purcell* (1659–1695) is considered the greatest English composer of the Baroque era. He wrote a large amount of music for chorus, voice, chamber ensembles, and keyboard, and incidental music for forty-nine plays. His opera *Dido and Aeneas* (1689) combined French overture, dance, and choral styles with Italian and English vocal styles. **Music: NAWM 71–72**

E. *Germany*

While German courts supported Italian opera, some German cities, notably Hamburg, supported opera in German, called *Singspiel* (play with music). These usually used spoken dialogue instead of recitative. *Reinhard Keiser* (1674–1739) was the foremost composer of German opera in the early eighteenth century, unifying German and Italian traits.

II. Vocal Music for Chamber and Church (CHWM 218–25)

1. Italian cantata

   In the second half of the seventeenth century, the Italian cantata was a dramatic narrative or soliloquy for voice and continuo laid out as a series of two or three recitative-aria pairs. It was like a scene from an opera, but performed in a chamber setting and without staging. Many opera composers wrote cantatas; Alessandro Scarlatti wrote over 600.

2. France, Germany, and England

   French and German composers also wrote cantatas, following Italian models. English composers wrote songs in a native style; *catches*, unaccompanied humorous canons; and *odes*, large works for soloists, chorus, and orchestra celebrating state occasions and holidays.

3. Church music

   Catholic church music mixed old and new styles. Oratorios were written in the same style as operas and substituted for opera during Lent and other seasons when theaters were closed.

4. French church music

   Marc-Antoine Charpentier (1634–1704) brought the Latin oratorio to France, combining Italian and French traits. At Louis XIV's chapel, the leading genres were the motet for solo voice and continuo and the *grand motet* (large motet) for soloists, choruses, and orchestra.

5. Lutheran church music

   Lutheran music reached its height in the period 1650–1750. Among important composers of Lutheran concerted church music were *Dietrich Buxtehude* (ca. 1637–1707)' and *Johann Pachelbel* (1653–1706). Orthodoxy was challenged by *Pietism,* which emphasized individual freedom and simple, direct expression of feelings in music.

6. The Lutheran church cantata

   The *Lutheran church cantata* was devised around 1700 by *Erdmann Neumeister* (1671–1756) as a series of recitatives and arias meditating on a biblical text and closing with a chorale. Neumeister blended orthodoxy with Pietism, and composers setting his cantata texts to music blended elements of chorale settings, solo song, the sacred concerto, and opera.

Etude: The Passion

   The *historia* was a German genre setting a Bible story to music. The most important type was the *Passion,* telling the story of the suffering and death of Jesus. In the late seventeenth century a new type appeared that resembled an oratorio and is known as the *oratorio Passion.* Beyond relating the Bible story, Passions came to include chorales sung by the choir or congregation and poetic texts set as solo arias.

STUDY QUESTIONS

Opera (CHWM 209–18, NAWM 69–72)

1. What were the most important elements of Italian opera in the late seventeenth and early eighteenth centuries? How did drama and music relate in Italian opera of this period, and how did this compare with the ideals of the Florentine Camerata?

2. Describe each of the following. In what circumstances was each used?

    recitativo semplice or secco

    recitativo obbligato or accompagnato

Music to Study
> **NAWM 69:** Alessandro Scarlatti, *Griselda,* opera, excerpt: *Mi rivedi, o selva ombrosa* (1721)
>
> CD 4.36–38   Cassette 4.B

3. What type of aria is Scarlatti's *Mi rivedi, o selva ombrosa* (NAWM 69)? Chart the form of this aria as it would be performed.

4. Look at the words of this aria in translation. What emotions is Griselda experiencing?

   How does Scarlatti's music convey Griselda's feelings? How does the musical form help to capture the conflicting emotions Griselda feels?

5. On what two French traditions did French opera draw?

   _____   _____

   Name the composer and librettist who founded the French opera tradition.

   _____   _____

Music to Study
   NAWM 70: Jean-Baptiste Lully, *Armide,* opera, excerpts (1686)
      70a: Ouverture
         CD 4.39–41   Cassette 4.B
      70b: Act II, Scene 5: *Enfin il est en ma puissance*
         CD 4.42–44   Cassette 4.B

6. What characteristics of the overture to *Armide*(NAWM 70a) mark it as a French overture?

7. How does the musical setting of Armide's recitative *Enfin il est en ma puissance* (NAWM 70b) reflect the form and accentuation of the text?

8. How does the musical setting reflect the dramatic situation and the emotional conflict Armide is feeling?

9. How does this scene from Armide differ from the recitative and aria of Italian opera?

10. What are the characteristics of these genres of musical theater? What nation is each from, and how does it differ from Italian opera?

   masque

   semi-opera

   Singspiel

Music to Study

    NAWM 71: Henry Purcell, *Dido and Aeneas,* opera, excerpt from Act III
       (1689)
    Recitative: *Thy hand, Belinda*
      CD 5.1 (Concise 2.25)   Cassette 5.A (Concise 2.A)
    Aria: *When I am laid in earth*
      CD 5.2–3 (Concise 2.26–27)   Cassette 5.A (Concise 2.A)
    Chorus: *With drooping winds*
      CD 5.4   Cassette 5.A
    NAWM 72: Henry Purcell, *The Fairy Queen,* semi-opera, excerpt: *Hark!*
       The ech'ing air (1692)
      CD 5.5   Cassette 5.A

11. Compare Purcell's recitative *Thy hand, Belinda* (in NAWM 71) to Lully's recitative from *Armide* (in NAWM 70b) and Peri's recitative in *L'Euridice* (in NAWM 55c). How does Purcell's music follow the accentuation of the English text? How does the music convey Dido's emotions?

12. Laments in Italian operas were often written over a descending ground bass, and Purcell's aria *When I am laid in earth* (in NAWM 71) follows this tradition. Part of the expressivity comes from dissonances or conflicts in phrasing between the ostinato bass and the vocal line. Where do these dissonances or conflicts in phrasing occur?

Besides these conventions, what other devices does Purcell use to give this music the feeling of a lament?

13. How does the air from Purcell's *The Fairy Queen* (NAWM 72) compare to the aria from Scarlatti's *Griselda* (NAWM 69) and the air from Lully's *Armide* (in NAWM 70b)? Would you say this Purcell air is more Italian or more French in style?

Vocal Music for Chamber and Church (CHWM 218–25)

14. Describe the form and style of the secular Italian cantata in the late seventeenth and early eighteenth centuries. How does it compare to opera?

15. Describe the Lutheran church cantata. Who devised it, and when? What was the text like? What was the music like, and from which traditions did it draw?

TERMS TO KNOW

Terms Related to Opera

motto (motto beginning)
recitativo semplice or secco
recitativo obbligato or
  accompagnato
da capo aria
tragédie lyrique
divertissement

récitatif simple
récitatif mesuré
French overture (ouverture)
masque
semi-opera
Singspiel

Terms Related to Other Vocal Music

catch
ode
grand motet
Pietism

Lutheran church cantata
historia
Passion
oratorio Passion

NAMES TO KNOW

Alessandro Scarlatti
Jean-Baptiste Lully
Jean-Phillippe Quinault
Henry Purcell
Dido and Aeneas

Marc-Antoine Charpentier
Reinhard Keiser
Dietrich Buxtehude
Johann Pachelbel
Erdmann Neumeister

REVIEW QUESTIONS

1. Make a time-line for the pieces, composers, librettists, and theorists discussed in this chapter.

2. How did Italian opera develop and change during the seventeenth and early eighteenth centuries, from Monteverdi through Scarlatti?

3. Trace the development of musical theater in France during the seventeenth century and explain what distinguishes it from Italian opera.

4. What factors influenced the development of English musical theater in the seventeenth century? What genres did the English use? What did the English borrow from the French and Italian traditions?

5. Describe the secular Italian cantata of the late seventeenth century, using Scarlatti's *Lascia, deh lascia* as an example (see CHWM, pp. 218–19).

6. Describe the varieties of Lutheran sacred music being composed in the late seventeenth and early eighteenth centuries.

INSTRUMENTAL MUSIC IN THE LATE BAROQUE PERIOD

11

CHAPTER OBJECTIVES

After you complete the reading, study of the music, and study questions for this chapter, you should be able to:

1. name and describe the genres of instrumental music composed in the second half of the seventeenth century and the early eighteenth century;
2. trace the development of keyboard music in this period and describe the styles of various regions and individual composers; and
3. trace the development of ensemble music and orchestral music in this period and describe the style of Corelli.

CHAPTER OUTLINE

Prelude (CHWM 227–28)

In the latter seventeenth and early eighteenth centuries, the medium for which instrumental music was intended helped to determine how it was composed. There are two main categories, keyboard and ensemble music. The principal genres of keyboard music are these:

1. Toccata, prelude, or fantasia and fugue;
2. Settings of chorales or chants, such as a chorale prelude;
3. Variations;
4. Passacaglia and chaconne;
5. Suite; and
6. Sonata (after 1700).

The principal genres of ensemble music are these:

1. Sonata (sonata da chiesa), sinfonia, and related forms;
2. Suite (sonata da camera) and related forms; and
3. Concerto.

This was a golden age of instrument making and composition for the church organ, especially in Germany; for the harpsichord, especially in France; and for strings, especially in Italy.

I. Music for Organ (CHWM 228–33, NAWM 73–74)

Baroque organs could achieve a variety of timbres, with many different stops or registers. Much organ music was written for Protestant services, where it served as a prelude to part of the service.

1. Toccata
The seventeenth-century German toccata or prelude includes both sections in improvisatory style and sections in imitative counterpoint, like fugues between toccata passages. From this contrast evolved the eighteenth-century form of toccata (or prelude) and fugue.   **Music: NAWM 73**

2. Fugue
The ricercare was gradually replaced by the *fugue,* which was composed as an independent piece or as part of a prelude. A fugue opens with an *exposition,* in which the *subject* in the tonic is imitated by the *answer* in the dominant and the other voices alternate subject and answer. Later appearances of the subject are also called expositions and alternate with *episodes* where the subject is absent and modulation may occur.

Etude: Key Cycles and Equal Temperament
Lute players could play in all 24 major and minor keys because their frets were equally spaced, giving *equal temperament,* and keyboard players gradually adopted this system.

3. Chorale compositions
Lutheran chorales were used in several types of organ composition. Chorales could be accompanied with harmonizations or counterpoint; varied in *chorale variations* (also called *chorale partita*); fragmented and developed in a *chorale fantasia*; or presented in embellished form. A *chorale prelude* presents a chorale once, varied melodically or given a contrapuntal setting.   **Music: NAWM 74**

II. Music for Harpsichord and Clavichord (CHWM 233–37, NAWM 75)

The main genres for stringed keyboard instruments were the *theme and variations* and the *suite.* Composers often wrote variations on an original melody rather than an existing tune. The German suite (or *partita*) always contained an allemande, courante, sarabande, and gigue, and might also contain an introductory prelude or one or more dances added after one of the last three standard dances. The French *clavecinists* (harpsichordists), such as *Elisabeth-Claude Jacquet de la Guerre* (1665–1729) and *François Couperin* (1668–1733), wrote suites that include a wider variety of dance types. Couperin's *ordres* contain any number of short movements, most of them in dance rhythms and most with evocative titles. The passacaglia and chaconne often appeared in suites or as independent works. Couperin's treatise *L'Art de toucher le clavecin* (The Art of Playing the Harpsichord, 1716) detailed how to play the harpsichord, including fingering and performing the agréments (French ornaments).   **Music: NAWM 75**

Etude: Characteristic Dances of the German Suite

The allemande, probably a German dance, moves in continuous eighth or sixteenth notes in a moderately fast duple meter, with a short upbeat. The French courante is in moderate 6/4 or 3/2 meter. The Mexican-Spanish sarabande is in a slow triple meter with an emphasis on the second beat, and is the most homophonic. The Anglo-Irish gigue is usually in a fast compound triple meter and often features imitative counterpoint.

III. Ensemble Music (CHWM 237–47, NAWM 76–77)

1. Ensemble sonatas

The sonata was a work in several contrasting sections or movements for a small number of instruments with basso continuo. After about 1660, there were two main types: *sonata da camera* (chamber sonata), a suite of stylized dances, often opening with a prelude, and *sonata da chiesa* (church sonata), a series of mostly abstract movements, often ending with a dance. A *trio sonata* is a sonata (of either type) for two treble instruments (usually violins) and basso continuo. This is the most common instrumentation for a sonata, followed by the *solo sonata* for one treble instrument and continuo.   **Music: NAWM 76**

Etude: Emergence of the Baroque Sonata

The Baroque sonata gradually evolved from the canzona, as the contrasting sections lengthened and separated into independent movements.

A. *Arcangelo Corelli*

Arcangelo Corelli (1653–1713) was the greatest master of seventeenth-century instrumental music. After studies at Bologna, he lived in Rome. He published two sets each of trio sonatas da chiesa and da camera, a set of solo violin sonatas, and a set of concerti grossi, with twelve works per set.

1. Trio sonatas

Corelli's trio sonatas feature lyrical violin lines within a limited range of technique. Suspensions and *sequences* drive the music forward and help create the directed harmonic motion characteristic of common-practice tonality (which was new in Corelli's generation). His church sonatas most often include four movements in the pattern slow-fast-slow-fast, with a majestic prelude, a fugue, a slow aria or duet, and a fast binary dance, such as a gigue. His chamber sonatas typically begin with a prelude and include two or three dance movements. Each movement presents and develops a single melodic idea, as is typical of the late Baroque.   **Music: NAWM 77**

2. Solo sonatas

Corelli's violin sonatas use the same format as his trio sonatas but demand more virtuosity from the violin.

Etude: Baroque Ornamentation

Performers were expected to embellish written melodies, whether with small figures such as trills, turns, appoggiaturas, and mordents or with freer embellishment such as scales, runs, and arpeggios. Ornamentation was not only decorative but added interest and helped to convey the affections.

Performers could also omit movements or sections and add instruments as desired. (In sum, pieces were seen as opportunities for performance, not as hallowed works that were only to be performed as the composer intended.)

3. Influence outside Italy

Purcell, Handel, and other composers wrote trio sonatas influenced by Corelli. François Couperin sought a union of French and Italian styles.

B. *Larger Ensembles*

Sonatas, dance suites, and concertos were also written for larger ensembles. In Germany, many towns had a *collegium musicum,* a group that played and sang music for their own pleasure, and a town band, the *Stadtpfeifer.*

1. Orchestral music

In the late seventeenth century, musicians began to distinguish between *chamber music* for one player on a part and *orchestral music.* The German *orchestral suite* (also called *ouverture,* after the opening movement) was modeled on Lully's suites from his operas and ballets.

2. The concerto

The instrumental concerto was a new genre that emerged in the late seventeenth century and became the most important Baroque orchestral genre. The *concerto grosso* contrasted a small ensemble (or *concertino*) with a large ensemble (or *concerto grosso*), and the *solo concerto* set a solo instrument with continuo against the orchestra. In both, the full orchestra was called *tutti* (all) or *ripieno* (full). Corelli's concerti grossi were like sonatas punctuated by changes of texture.

3. Giuseppe Torelli

Giuseppe Torelli (1658–1709) helped to codify the concerto as a work in three movements in the pattern fast-slow-fast. The fast movements are in *ritornello form,* in which the full orchestra states a *ritornello* in the tonic at the beginning; the soloist or soloists contribute an episode, which usually modulates; the large group states the ritornello (or a part of it) in the new key; this alternation of episode and ritornello continues for some time; and the movement ends with the reappearance of the ritornello in the tonic.

Window: Queen Christina of Sweden and Her Circle (CHWM 244–45)

Queen Christina of Sweden (1626–1689) abdicated her throne and settled in Rome in 1655 as a patron of intellectual life and the arts. Corelli dedicated his first publication to her and later served her as a musician.

STUDY QUESTIONS

Prelude (CHWM 227–28)

1. What are the main types of keyboard music in the later Baroque period? How do these compare to the types of keyboard music practiced in the sixteenth century and in the early seventeenth century?

2. What are the main types of ensemble music in the later Baroque period? How do these compare to the main types of instrumental ensemble music practiced in the sixteenth century and in the early seventeenth century?

Music for Organ (CHWM 228–33, NAWM 73–74)

> *Music to Study*
> **NAWM 73:** Dietrich Buxtehude, Praeludium in E, BuxWV 141, prelude for organ (late seventeenth century)
> CD 5.6–10   Cassette 5.A

3. How does Buxtehude's Praeludium in E (NAWM 73) fit the definition of a late-seventeenth-century toccata or prelude given in CHWM, pp. 228–30? What types of texture and figuration does it use? How does it fall into sections?

4. What types of organ composition in the late seventeenth and early eighteenth centuries were based on chorales? In each type, how was the chorale treated?

Music to Study
> **NAWM 74:** Dietrich Buxtehude, *Danket dem Herrn*, BuxWV 181, chorale variations (late seventeenth century)
>
> CD 5.11–13   Cassette 5.A

5. How does Buxtehude treat the chorale melody in his variations on *Danket dem Herrn* (NAWM 74)?

Music for Harpsichord and Clavichord (CHWM 233–37, NAWM 75)

6. What four dances are typically part of the German keyboard suite, and in what order? What is the meter, relative speed, nation of origin, and character of each?

dance	meter	speed	nation of origin	other characteristics
_____	_____	_____	_____	_____
_____	_____	_____	_____	_____
_____	_____	_____	_____	_____
_____	_____	_____	_____	_____

What other movements might be part of a German suite?

Music to Study
   NAWM 75: François Couperin, *Vingt-cinquième ordre* (Twenty-fifth Order), keyboard suite (1730)
   75a: *La Visionaire* (The Dreamer)
      CD 5.14–15 (Concise 2.28–29)   Cassette 5.A (Concise 2.A)
   75b: *La Misterieuse* (The Mysterious One)
      CD 5.16 (Concise 2.30)   Cassette 5.A (Concise 2.A)
   75c: *La Monflambert*
      CD 5.17   Cassette 5.A
   75d: *La Muse victorieuse* (The Victorious Muse)
      CD 5.18   Cassette 5.A
   75e: *Les Ombres errantes* (The Roving Shadows)
      CD 5.19   Cassette 5.A

7. In what sense is *La Visionaire* (NAWM 75a) "a French overture," as it is described in CHWM, p. 236?

8. What elements of *La Misterieuse* (NAWM 75b) suggest that it is an allemande?

9. What are the names of the following *agréments* in the upper melody of *La Misterieuse* (NAWM 75b), and how is each one played? (Hint: See CHWM, pp. 370–71.)

   first measure, second note (E)

   first measure, notes 6–7 (A–B)

   measure 25, fifth note (A)

Ensemble Music (CHWM 237–47, NAWM 76–77)

10. What two main types of sonata began to be distinguished after about 1660? Describe each type as practiced by Corelli.

11. What was the most common instrumentation for sonatas in the late seventeenth century? What was a sonata in this instrumentation called?

Music to Study
  NAWM 76: Giovanni Legrenzi, *La Raspona,* trio sonata (published 1655)
      CD 5.20–21   Cassette 5.B
  NAWM 77: Arcangelo Corelli, Trio Sonata in D Major, Op. 3, No. 2 (published 1689)
      1. Grave   CD 5.22   Cassette 5.B
      2. Allegro CD 5.23   Cassette 5.B
      3. Adagio   CD 5.24 (Concise 2.31)   Cassette 5.B (Concise 2.B)
      4. Allegro CD 5.25–26 (Concise 2.32–33)   Cassette 5.B (Concise 2.B)

12. In what ways are the violin melodies in Legrenzi's *La Raspona* (NAWM 76) idiomatic for instruments and unlike vocal style?

13. Is Corelli's Op. 3, No. 2 (NAWM 77) a church sonata or a chamber sonata? What traits mark it as this type of sonata?

---

14. Corelli's trio sonatas are marked by sequences and by suspensions, especially chains of suspensions in sequence. For each of these techniques, find two passages in which it is prominent.

	location of passage 1	location of passage 2
sequences	_____	_____
chain of suspensions	_____	_____

How do these techniques help to give these passages a sense of forward momentum toward the next cadence?

15. In what ways are Corelli's solo violin sonatas like his trio sonatas, and in what ways are they different?

16. How did Baroque musicians regard ornamentation of written melodies?

17. Describe the two main ways of ornamenting a melody in the Baroque period.

18. Why did Couperin seek to unite the French and Italian styles of instrumental music? Which composers did he invoke as representative of each style?

19. What is the difference between *chamber music* and *orchestral music*? In the seventeenth century, what kinds of pieces might have been played by either type of ensemble?

20. Name and describe the two main types of *concertos* composed around 1700. How were Baroque principles of contrast embodied in each of them?

21. How many movements does a typical concerto by Giuseppe Torelli have, and what is the relative tempo of each movement?

22. Describe *ritornello form* as used by Torelli. How does ritornello form embody the Baroque interest in contrast, and how does it draw contrasting parts into a unified whole?

TERMS TO KNOW

Terms Related to Keyboard Music

fugue
fugue subject, answer, exposition, episode
equal temperament
chorale variations (chorale partita)
chorale fantasia

chorale prelude
theme and variations
suite (or partita)
clavecinist
ordre

Terms Related to Ensemble Music

sonata da chiesa
sonata da camera
trio sonata
solo sonata
sequences (in Baroque music)
collegium musicum
Stadtpfeifer
chamber music, orchestral music

orchestral suite (or ouverture)
concerto grosso
solo concerto
concertino and concerto grosso
tutti, ripieno
ritornello
ritornello form

NAMES TO KNOW

Elisabeth-Claude Jacquet de la
  Guerre
François Couperin
L'Art de toucher le clavecin

Arcangelo Corelli
Giuseppe Torelli
Queen Christina of Sweden

REVIEW QUESTIONS

1. Make a time-line for the pieces, composers, treatises, and theorists discussed in this chapter.

2. Name the varieties of keyboard music being composed in the late seventeenth and early eighteenth centuries. Name and briefly describe an example for as many of these genres as you can.

3. What functions did keyboard music serve in the late seventeenth and early eighteenth centuries? Name the functions for as many genres as you can.

4. As a review of this and previous chapters, trace the evolution of keyboard music from ca. 1500 to ca. 1700.

5. Name the varieties of ensemble music composed in the late seventeenth and early eighteenth centuries. Name and briefly describe an example for as many of these varieties as you can.

6. As a review of this and previous chapters, trace the development of music for instrumental chamber ensemble from ca. 1500 to ca. 1700.

7. What did Corelli and Torelli contribute to the development of instrumental ensemble music?

Music in the Early Eighteenth Century

12

Chapter Objectives

After you complete the reading, study of the music, and study questions for this chapter, you should be able to:

1. summarize the careers, describe the musical styles, and name and describe some of the most significant works by each of four major composers of the early eighteenth century: Antonio Vivaldi, Jean-Philippe Rameau, Johann Sebastian Bach, and George Frideric Handel;
2. compare the music of each to that of his predecessors and contemporaries; and
3. explain the historical significance of each of these composers.

Chapter Outline

Prelude (CHWM 249–50)

In the decades between 1720 and 1750, music of the high Baroque competed with a simpler, more songful style. Antonio Vivaldi, Jean-Philippe Rameau, Johann Sebastian Bach, and George Frideric Handel were the most eminent composers of the early eighteenth century, and each created a unique idiom within the established Baroque genres.

I. Antonio Vivaldi (CHWM 250–55, NAWM 78–79)

Antonio Vivaldi (1678–1741) was trained as a musican and priest. He was music director, teacher, conductor, and composer at the *Pio Ospedale della Pietà* in Venice, a home and school for orphaned or abandoned girls. Music was an important part of the curriculum, and the concerts at the Pietà were well attended. At this time, there were no musical "classics," and audiences expected new music each season. Vivaldi composed quickly and always for a specific occasion, writing concertos and church music for the Pietà and 49 operas for theaters in Venice and other cities. About 500 of his concertos survive, along with about 90 sonatas and many operas and religious works.

1. Vocal works
Vivaldi is best known today as an instrumental composer, but was also successful and prolific as a composer of church music and of opera.

2. Concertos
Most Vivaldi concertos are for solo (usually violin) and orchestra; others feature two soloists or a concertino group of which one or two members are the main soloists. Most of his concertos are in three movements, with fast outer movements in ritornello form and a slow aria-like middle movement in a closely related key. In Vivaldi's hands ritornello form is infinitely variable, not at all a rigid scheme. The soloist in the fast movements is a real virtuoso, standing apart from the orchestra as a singer does in an opera. Vivaldi's sinfonias mark him as a founder of the Classic-era symphony. **Music: NAWM 78–79**

II. Jean-Philippe Rameau (CHWM 255–60, NAWM 80)

Jean-Philippe Rameau (1683–1764), the foremost eighteenth-century French composer, became known first as a theorist and only later as a composer, writing his major works late in life. His early training and positions were as an organist. In 1722 he published his *Traité de l'harmonie* (Treatise on Harmony), which made his reputation as a theorist. From the 1730s, Rameau wrote operas and opera-ballets which were produced in Paris with the backing of a wealthy patron.

1. Rameau's theoretical works
Rameau sought to put music theory on a solid acoustical basis. He founded the theory of tonal music (or functional harmony), as opposed to modal music, and all later tonal theory is derived from his work.

Etude: A Synopsis of Rameau's Most Important Musical Theories
Rameau posited the chord as the basic unit in music, derived from the overtone series and built in thirds; suggested that chords maintain their identity and original roots when inverted, and that root progressions determine successions of chords; and established the tonic, dominant, and subdominant chords as the pillars of harmony and related all other chords to them.

2. Musical style
Rameau's operas are like Lully's in alternating realistically declaimed recitatives with airs, choruses, instrumental interludes, and long divertissements. But his style is quite different. Rameau believed that melody was rooted in harmony; his melodies are often triadic and make clear their underlying harmony, and much of his expressivity comes from harmonic dissonance and modulation. His airs, like those of other French composers, are restrained in comparison to Italian arias, while his choruses are effective and his instrumental interludes remarkable in their ability to depict scenes. **Music: NAWM 80**

III. Johann Sebastian Bach (CHWM 260–76, NAWM 81–84)

Johann Sebastian Bach (1685–1750) was not the most famous composer of his time but has become so in the last two centuries. He was born in Eisenach into a family of professional musicians and was trained by his father and elder brother. He blended German, French, and Italian styles, which he learned by copying and arranging music by leading composers of each region. He served as church organist at Arnstadt (1703–7) and Mühlhausen (1707–8), organist and concertmaster for the duke of *Weimar* (1708–17), music director for a prince in *Cöthen* (1717–23), and cantor of *St. Thomas Church* and school in *Leipzig* (1723–50), writing music for his immediate use in each post.

A. *Organ Works*

Bach's first positions were as an organist, and his first major works were for the organ. His early works were influenced by Buxtehude. At Weimar, he arranged Vivaldi concertos for keyboard, learned the Italian style, and adopted many Vivaldi traits in his own works. From Italian, French, and German elements he forged his own style.

1. Toccatas and fugues

Some of Bach's organ toccatas intersperse fugue and toccata sections, but more common are works with separate fugues. Most of Bach's important organ preludes and fugues date from his Weimar years, and many use elements from the Italian concerto.   **Music: NAWM 81**

2. *Orgelbüchlein* and chorale preludes

Bach wrote about 170 chorale settings for organ, using all current types of setting. His *Orgelbüchlein* (Little Organ Book) contains short chorale preludes that state the chorale once, usually in the soprano, accompanied with counterpoint or embellished.   **Music: NAWM 82**

B. *Harpsichord and Clavichord Music*

Bach wrote in all keyboard genres of his time. Most of these works were written at Cöthen and Leipzig, and they show the intermingling of Italian, French, and German elements in Bach's style.

1. *The Well-Tempered Keyboard*

Bach's best-known keyboard work is *The Well-Tempered Keyboard* [or *Clavier*], two cycles of 24 preludes and fugues in all twelve major and minor keys. Book I (ca. 1722) is a teaching manual in offering the player diverse technical challenges, exemplifying numerous genres in the preludes, and using a variety of approaches in the fugues. Book II (ca. 1740) includes pieces from many periods in Bach's life.

2. Suites

Bach wrote three sets of six suites each, the English Suites (ca. 1715), the French Suites (1722–25), and the six Partitas (1726–31). All contain the standard four dances with additions, and the English Suites begin with preludes.

3. *Goldberg Variations*

The *Goldberg Variations* (published 1741 or 1742) is a set of thirty variations on a sarabande. Every third variation is a canon; the interval of imitation grows from a unison in variation 3 to a ninth in variation 27. The last variation is a quodlibet, followed by a reprise of the theme. The noncanonic variations are of many types.

C. *Solo and Ensemble Music*

Bach's sonatas, partitas, and suites for unaccompanied violin, cello, and flute suggest a polyphonic texture by using multiple stops or jumping back and forth between implied independent lines. Most of his sonatas for violin, viola da gamba, or flute and harpsichord have four movements, slow-fast-slow-fast, like a sonata da chiesa, and are like trio sonatas, with the right hand of the harpsichord acting as the other solo instrument while the left hand supplies the continuo.

1. Concertos and suites

Bach's six concertos for the Margrave of Brandenburg (1721) follow Italian models, but expand the form. He was perhaps the first to write or arrange concertos for one or more harpsichords and orchestra. His orchestral suites (or ouvertures) are sprightly and appealing.

2. *A Musical Offering* and *The Art of Fugue*

Two works are surveys of musical possibilities. *A Musical Offering* (1747) presents a trio sonata, two ricercares, and ten canons based on a theme by King Frederick the Great of Prussia, on which Bach improvised while visiting the king. *The Art of Fugue* (1749–50) sums up the fugue in a series of eighteen canons and fugues of increasing complexity, all based on the same subject.

D. *Bach at Leipzig: Vocal Music*

As cantor in Leipzig, Bach oversaw the music at St. Thomas and St. Nicholas churches and taught Latin and music in the St. Thomas school. Each Sunday, Bach directed a cantata, alternating between the two churches. The service also included a motet, a Lutheran Mass (Kyrie and Gloria), and chorales, using a choir of at least twelve singers (three for each part). The cantata followed the Gospel reading in the liturgy and often was related in subject. Bach composed four complete cycles of cantatas for the church year (1723–29), plus cantatas for various occasions such as weddings. About 200 cantatas survive, representing a variety of forms and approaches.

1. Neumeister cantatas

Bach set five cantata texts by Erdmann Neumeister and was influenced by his combination of chorale verses, Bible passages, and new poetry. In his cantatas, Bach frequently combined secular genres such as French overture, recitative, and da capo aria with chorale settings.

2. Chorale cantatas

Bach's cantatas use chorales in various ways. Bach often based the opening chorus on a chorale and ended with the same chorale in simple four-part harmony, with independent solos and duets and an occasional chorale setting in between.   **Music: NAWM 83**

3. Secular cantatas

Bach also wrote secular cantatas for various occasions. In some he experimented with the newer operatic style.

4. Passions

Bach's *St. John Passion* (1724) and *St. Matthew Passion* (1727) were performed during Good Friday services. In both, the Bible story is narrated by the tenor soloist, with characters played by other soloists and the crowd by the chorus, and chorales, recitatives, and arias are interpolated as commentary on the story.

5. Mass in B Minor

Bach's Mass in B Minor was assembled in 1747–49 from existing and some newly composed movements. It includes styles from stile antico and cantus firmus to the modern galant style. Bach may have intended it as a universal statement of religious feeling.   **Music: NAWM 84**

E. *Reception History*

Even before his death, Bach's music was viewed as old-fashioned in comparison to the newer, more tuneful style of contemporary Italian opera. His music was known to some in the latter eighteenth century, then revived and popularized in the nineteenth century. His blend of styles, genres, and forms and the balance in his music among melody, harmony, and counterpoint and between expression and technique have made Bach seem in retrospect the greatest musician of his age.

IV. George Frideric Handel (CHWM 276–85, NAWM 85-86)

George Frideric Handel (1685–1759) was a truly international composer. He was the first composer to be remembered by all later generations and to have his music performed in a continuous tradition down to the present.

1. Handel's life

Handel was born in Halle and studied organ and composition. In 1703 he moved to Hamburg, where he wrote his first opera. In 1706 he went to Italy, where he met the leading patrons and composers, including Corelli and Alessandro Scarlatti. In 1710 he was named music director for the elector of Hanover, later crowned King George I of England in 1714. Handel preceded his patron to London and soon established himself as a composer of Italian opera. During the 1720s, Handel composed operas for the *Royal Academy of Music*; after that company failed, he formed his own opera company. When rising costs and falling interest made opera no longer viable, Handel turned to oratorios in English, which were less costly and attracted a broader audience. The oratorios gave him a great and enduring popularity in England.

2. Instrumental music

Handel's most significant instrumental works are the orchestral suites *Water Music* (1717) and *Music for the Royal Fireworks* (1749) and twelve concerti grossi, Op. 6, in a style indebted to Corelli.

3. Operas

Handel's operas were among the most successful of his time. The plots are freely adapted from history and literature, and the music consists mainly of recitatives to forward the action and arias that reflect on the characters' feelings, using a variety of aria types.   **Music: NAWM 85**

4. Oratorios

Handel's oratorios blend operatic recitative and aria with elements from the English masque and choral anthem, the German *historia*, and French and ancient Greek drama. The oratorios were in English and often used Old Testament stories. The prominence of the chorus in his oratorios is indebted to choral music in both Germany and England. The chorus often comments on the action, as in a Greek drama, or participates in the action. Handel often uses musical figures to depict images in the text or convey a feeling.   **Music: NAWM 86**

5. Handel's borrowings

Handel often borrowed and reworked material from his own music and from other composers. Borrowing, transcribing, and reworking were universally accepted practices. When Handel borrowed, he "repaid with interest," using the borrowed material in new and more ingenious ways.

Window: Farinelli, the Adored Castrato (CHWM 280–81)

Castratos were males castrated before puberty to preserve their soprano or contralto voices. Castratos sang in church and took leading roles (playing male characters) in operas. Their voices were prized for their strength, agility, and thrilling sound. Leading castratos, such as *Farinelli* (1705–1782), were adored by listeners and commanded enormous fees.

STUDY QUESTIONS

Antonio Vivaldi (CHWM 250–55, NAWM 78–79)

1. For what institution did Vivaldi work for most of his career? Describe the institution's purpose, the role of music in it, and Vivaldi's role.

2. What was the eighteenth-century attitude toward new music? How did this attitude affect Vivaldi?

3. In Vivaldi's concertos, which instruments does he favor as soloists?

4. What is the typical pattern of movements in Vivaldi's concertos, including the number of movements and their tempo, forms, and key relationships?

Music to Study
   NAWM 78: Antonio Vivaldi, Concerto Grosso in G minor, Op. 3, No. 2 (published 1712), excerpts
   78a: First movement, Adagio e spiccato
      CD 5.27   Cassette 5.B
   78b: Second movement, Allegro
      CD 5.28–34 (Concise 2.34–40)   Cassette 5.B (Concise 2.B)
   NAWM 79: Antonio Vivaldi, Concerto for Violin and Orchestra, Op. 9, No. 2 (published 1728), second movement
      CD 5.35   Cassette 5.B

5. How does Vivaldi treat texture and contrasts of texture in his concertos? How is this exemplified in the concerto movements in NAWM 78 and 79?

6. Chart the form of the second movement of Vivaldi's Op. 3, No. 2 (NAWM 78b) by completing the table below. Use the abbreviations "Rit" for ritornello, "Solo" for the solo episodes, and letters for the melodic material of the ritornello as it returns. (See the discussion of ritornello form in chapter 11 if needed.)

Before you begin, what is the relationship between b and c in the table below?

Beginning measure	Section	Tutti or soloists	Melodic material	Key
14	Rit	Tutti	a	g minor
17	↓	↓	b	↓
20	↓	↓	c	↓
23	Solo	Soloists		↓

Jean-Philippe Rameau (CHWM 255–60, NAWM 80)

7. Briefly trace Rameau's career. What were his various occupations? How did he earn a living? What (and who) made it possible for him to write operas and opera-ballets?

8. What were Rameau's contributions to the theory of music?

Music to Study
    NAWM 80: Jean-Philippe Rameau, *Hippolyte et Aricie,* opera (1733), ex-
        cerpt: *Ah! faut-il* (Act IV, Scene 1)
    CD 5.36 (Concise 2.41)   Cassette 5.B (Concise 2.B)

9. At the opening of Act IV of Rameau's *Hippolyte et Aricie,* the noble young
man Hippolyte is alone in the woods, banished from home, and despairing.
How does Rameau use harmony, melody, rhythm, and choice of instrument
in the instrumental prelude (NAWM 80, mm. 1-13) to convey his situation
and mood? In particular, what suggests that he is in despair? in a rural setting? alone?

10. Diagram the form of this excerpt. Use letters to designate the melodic material of the orchestral introduction (A starting in m. 1, B in m. 4, C in m. 9, D
in m. 11) and "Recit" to indicate passages in recitative.

How would you describe this form? How does it reflect Hippolyte's emotions?

11. How does this excerpt compare with the scene from Lully's *Armide* in NAWM 75b? How are Rameau's approach and style similar to Lully's, and how are they different? What is the role of dissonance in each excerpt?

Johann Sebastian Bach (CHWM 260–76, NAWM 81–84)

12. How did Bach learn music? How did he absorb the Italian style?

13. Where did Bach work, and when? What were his duties in each position? How did his employment affect the music he composed?

Music to Study
> **NAWM 81:** Johann Sebastian Bach, Praeludium et Fuga in A minor for organ, BWV 543 (1710s?)
> 81a: Praeludium (Prelude)
>> CD 5.37 (Concise 2.42)   Cassette 5.B (Concise 2.B)
> 81b: Fuga (Fugue)
>> CD 5.38 (Concise 2.43)   Cassette 5.B (Concise 2.B)

14. How do the melodies in Bach's prelude and fugue (NAWM 81) show the influence of Italian violin style? Use the solo violin portions of Vivaldi's Concerto Grosso in G minor, Op. 3, No. 2, second movement (NAWM 78b) for comparison.

15. Bach's fugue alternates between statements of the subject (first presented in mm. 1-5) with episodes of other figuration, often moving in sequence. How does this format resemble the ritornello form of Vivaldi's concertos?

16. How does this Bach fugue compare to the first fugal section of Buxtehude's Praeludium in E (NAWM 73) in form and in other respects?

17. Based on the comparisons you have made above, write a brief summary of how Bach's prelude and fugue blends North German and Italian influences.

Music to Study
   NAWM 82: Johann Sebastian Bach, *Durch Adams Fall*, BWV 637, cho-
      rale prelude from the *Orgelbüchlein* (ca. 1716–23)
   82a: Chorale melody   not on recordings
   82b: Bach setting
      CD 5.39   Cassette 5.B

18. How does Bach employ musical imagery in his chorale prelude on *Durch Adams Fall* (NAWM 82b) to convey the images in the chorale text?

---

19. What does *The Well-Tempered Keyboard* contain? When was it written?

20. What types of chamber music and orchestral music did Bach write?

21. What were Bach's duties as Cantor of St. Thomas and Music Director of Leipzig?

Music to Study

NAWM 83: Johann Sebastian Bach, *Wachet auf, ruft uns die Stimme* [Cantata No. 140], BWV 140 (1731)

1a: Philipp Nicolai, *Wachet auf, ruft uns die Stimme,* chorale (source for movements 1, 4, and 7)   not on recordings

1b: Chorus, *Wachet auf, ruft uns die Stimme*
CD 6.1–5 (Concise 2.44–48)   Cassette 6.A (Concise 2.B)

2: Tenor recitative, *Er kommt, er kommt*
CD 6.6   Cassette 6.A

3: Duet for soprano and bass, *Wann kömmst du, mein Heil?*
CD 6.7   Cassette 6.A

4: Tenor chorale verse, *Zion hört die Wächter singen*
CD 6.8   Cassette 6.A

5: Bass recitative, *So geh' herein zu mir*
CD 6.9   Cassette 6.A

6: Duet for soprano and bass, *Mein Freund ist mein!*
CD 6.10–11   Cassette 6.A

7: Chorale, *Gloria sei dir gesungen*
CD 6.12   Cassette 6.A

NAWM 84: Johann Sebastian Bach, Mass in B Minor, BWV 232 (1747-49), excerpts from the Credo (*Symbolum Nicenum*)

84a: Bass Aria, *Et in Spiritum sanctum Dominum*
CD 6.13–14   Cassette 6.B

84b: Chorus, *Confiteor*
CD 6.15–17   Cassette 6.B

84c: Chorus, *Et expecto resurrectionem*
CD 6.18–19   Cassette 6.B

22. For which day of the church calendar did Bach write the cantata *Wachet auf, ruft uns die Stimme* (NAWM 83)? Where in the liturgy was the cantata performed? How do the words of the chorale Bach uses and of the added texts relate to the Gospel reading for the day?

23. How are the words and images of the text reflected in the music for the opening chorus (1b) and the two duets (3 and 6)?

24. How is the chorale tune *Wachet auf, ruft uns die Stimme* used in the first movement (1b)?

    In the fourth movement (4)?

    In the final movement (7)?

25. What Italian forms and textures, adapted from opera, concerto, and sonata, are used in this cantata, and in which movements? What other Italian traits do you notice?

26. In what ways does the music of *Et in Spiritum sanctum Dominum* from Bach's Mass in B Minor (NAWM 84a) show traces of an up-to-date style?

27. Where and in which voices does the cantus firmus appear in the chorus Confiteor (NAWM 84b)? How is it treated?

28. In addition to cantus firmus technique, what other Renaissance traits can you find in the *Confiteor*? What Baroque traits make clear that this is a Baroque composition in *stile antico,* not a work from the Renaissance?

29. How does Bach use changes of musical style and texture to convey the sense of the words "and I await the resurrection of the dead"? (Note that these words are set twice, in two different styles, to bring out two different aspects of their meaning.)

George Frideric Handel (CHWM 276–85, NAWM 85-86)

30. By the age of 25, where had Handel lived, studied, and worked? What genres had he tried? What influences had he absorbed? What made his music "international" in style?

31. In which genre was Handel first successful in England? Why and when did his success fade? Which new genre supplanted the first and allowed Handel to continue his career?

32. In Act III, Scene 4, of *Giulio Cesare* (NAWM 85), Handel rearranges the
    expected order of events for expressive reasons. We might expect to hear a
    recitative, then a da capo aria with an opening ritornello, first section, con-
    trasting middle section, and reprise of the first section. Instead of this, what is
    the order of events in this scene? How does this order of events in the music
    work to set the scene and convey Caesar's feelings? When the first section is
    finally repeated, how have Caesar's words gained in intensity by what has
    intervened?

33. What national styles and genres did Handel combine in his oratorios?

34. What language is used in Handel's oratorios? How did the language and the
    subject matter influence the success of his oratorios? Where were they per-
    formed, and for whom?

35. How did Handel use the chorus in his oratorios? How does this differ from the practice of Italian composers? What traditions influenced Handel in this regard?

Music to Study
   NAWM 86: George Frideric Handel, *Jephtha*, oratorio (1752), excerpt: Chorus, *How dark, O Lord, are Thy decrees!*

Largo, *How dark, O Lord, are thy decrees!*	CD 6.7	Cassette 6.B
Larghetto, *All our joys to sorrow turning*	CD 6.8	Cassette 6.B
A tempo ordinario, *No certain bliss*	CD 6.9	Cassette 6.B
Larghetto, *Yet on this maxim still obey*	CD 6.10	Cassette 6.B

36. In the chorus "How dark, O Lord, are Thy decrees!" from *Jephtha* (NAWM 86), how does Handel use contrasts between contrapuntal and homophonic writing to delineate the form and to convey the meaning of the text?

37. How does Handel's choral writing in this work differ from that of Bach in the choral movements from his cantata *Wachet auf* (NAWM 83) and Mass in B Minor (NAWM 84), and how is it similar?

NAMES TO KNOW

Antonio Vivaldi
Pio Ospedale della Pietà
Jean-Philippe Rameau
Traité de l'harmonie
Johann Sebastian Bach
Weimar
Cöthen
Leipzig
St. Thomas Church
Orgelbüchlein
The Well-Tempered Keyboard

Goldberg Variations
A Musical Offering
The Art of Fugue
St. John and *St. Matthew Passions*
Mass in B Minor
George Frideric Handel
Royal Academy of Music
Water Music
Music for the Royal Fireworks
Farinelli

REVIEW QUESTIONS

1. Add to the time-line you made for the previous chapter the *Traité de l'harmonie* and the composers and pieces discussed in this chapter.

2. Describe the career and music of Vivaldi. How did the circumstances of his employment relate to the music he wrote? How are his concertos similar to those of Corelli and Torelli, and how are they different?

3. How do the operas and opera-ballets of Rameau continue the tradition of Lully, and how do they differ?

4. Trace Bach's career and explain how the circumstances of his training and employment influenced the types of music he wrote and the styles he drew upon.

5. What did Bach's instrumental music draw from German sources? What did he draw from Italian models and from French models? Describe a piece by Bach that blends at least two of these national traditions, and explain how Bach combined elements from different nations into a coherent idiom.

6. Adopting the aesthetic position of Johann Adolph Scheibe (as quoted on p. 275 of CHWM), describe what is wrong with Bach's Praeludium et Fuga in A minor (NAWM 81) and the opening chorus of his cantata *Wachet auf, ruft uns die Stimme* (NAWM 83).

7. Trace Handel's career and explain how his experiences as a composer influenced the types of music he wrote and the styles he drew upon.

8. Compare and contrast the musical ideals and styles of Bach and Handel, focusing particularly on their vocal music.

9. What was the historical significance of Vivaldi, Rameau, Bach, and Handel? What trends did each absorb, what influence did each have on later music, and in what respects did each achieve a unique musical idiom?

THE EARLY CLASSIC PERIOD: OPERA AND INSTRUMENTAL MUSIC IN THE EIGHTEENTH CENTURY

13

CHAPTER OBJECTIVES

After you complete the reading, study of the music, and study questions for this chapter, you should be able to:

1. briefly describe the intellectual, cultural, and aesthetic background to music in the Classic period;
2. name and describe the principal musical styles, genres, and forms current in the second half of the eighteenth century; and
3. name some of the composers of the period, describe their individual styles, and identify some of their works.

CHAPTER OUTLINE

Prelude (CHWM 287–91)

> The music of Haydn and Mozart was later called *classic,* and the term is now applied to the entire period 1720–1800. The term *galant* (elegant) was used in the eighteenth century for the new style that featured melody in clearly demarked phrases over light accompaniment. *Empfindsamkeit* (sentimentality) was a related style that added surprising harmonies, chromaticism, nervous rhythms, and speech-like melody. All were influenced by *Enlightenment* ideals of reason, knowledge, naturalness, and humanitarianism. Politics, culture, and the arts were cosmopolitan. The flutist and composer *Johann Joachim Quantz* held that the best music combined features of many nations and thus was universally pleasing. A growing middle-class public pursued learning and the arts and supported the new institution of the public concert. The latter eighteenth century preferred music that was universal in appeal, both noble and entertaining, expressive yet tasteful, natural, simple, and immediately pleasing.

Etude: Cosmopolitan Vienna
> Musicians from across western Europe were active in Vienna, enabling a mixing of styles and the synthesis of the "Viennese" classical style.

I. General Characteristics of the New Style (CHWM 291–94)

In contrast to the constant spinning-out of Baroque music, the new styles were *periodic,* divided into short phrases that combine into periods and larger sections, like the phrases, sentences, and paragraphs of a speech. Harmonic change slowed down. To compensate, the texture was animated through devices such as the *Alberti bass.* Composers no longer sought to express one single affection in a movement, as in the Baroque, and instead presented contrasting styles and feelings within a single movement.

II. Opera Buffa (CHWM 294–98, NAWM 87 and 89–90)

Many style elements of the Classic era derive from Italian opera, especially comic opera. An *opera buffa* was a full-length comic opera with both comic and serious characters. An *intermezzo* was a series of short comic scenes performed between acts of a serious opera or play. The best-known intermezzo is *La serva padrona* (The Maid as Mistress, 1733), by *Giovanni Battista Pergolesi* (1710–1736). Both opera buffa and intermezzo were sung throughout, the dialogue in rapid *recitative* with keyboard accompaniment and the *arias* in short tuneful phrases over simple harmonies. Comic opera grew in importance after 1760. Each nation or region had its own type, using the national language and musical styles. Comic opera exercised an important influence on later music, in its style, its preference for naturalness, and its use of national characteristics.   **Music: NAWM 87**

1. France

French *opéra comique* began as a show with *vaudevilles* or other simple tunes. The 1752 visit of an Italian comic opera troupe to Paris inspired French composers to write comic operas in a mixed style with original airs called *ariettes.* One of the first was *Le Devin du village* (The Village Soothsayer, 1752) by *Jean-Jacques Rousseau.* Although the Italians set dialogue as recitative, the French and other national comic opera traditions used spoken dialogue. Later in the century, opéra comique was also used for serious subjects.   **Music: NAWM 89**

2. English ballad opera

Ballad opera became popular in England after *John Gay*'s success with *The Beggar's Opera* (1728), a mostly spoken play which sets new words to popular tunes and parodies operatic conventions.   **Music: NAWM 90**

3. German Singspiel

The success of ballad opera inspired a revival of *Singspiel* in Germany. Some Singspiel tunes became so popular that they have virtually become folksongs. In the north, Singspiel merged with native opera in the early nineteenth century; in the south, it was influenced by Italian comic opera.

III. Opera Seria (CHWM 298–302, NAWM 88)

An *opera seria* was a serious opera on a heroic classical subject without comic interludes. The form was codified by the librettist *Pietro Metastasio* (1698–1782), whose librettos were set hundreds of times. His plots show a conflict of passions that is resolved through heroism or renunciation, and his aim was to promote morality and to show examples of enlightened rulers. The action proceeds in recitative, and characters comment on the situation in arias.

1. The aria

The standard aria form was the *da capo aria,* featuring a large A section with two vocal statements surrounded by orchestral ritornellos, a shorter contrasting B section with a new text and in a related key, and a reprise of the A section. This format was sometimes shortened by omitting the first ritornello on the reprise of A. The form evolved over time, as composers introduced a greater variety of moods and figuration and borrowed formal ideas from the sonata and concerto.

2. Hasse and Bordoni

Johann Adolph Hasse (1699–1783), music director at the Saxon court in Dresden, was the leading composer of opera seria, writing in an Italianate style. His wife *Faustina Bordoni* (1700-1781) was one of the century's leading sopranos and sang in most of Hasse's operas. Singers always embellished the written line, especially at the reprise.   **Music: NAWM 88**

IV. Opera Reform (CHWM 302–5, NAWM 91)

Nicolò Jommelli (1714–1774) and *Tommaso Traetta* (1727–1779) sought to make opera more natural and varied, blending French and Italian traits.

1. Gluck

Christoph Willibald Gluck (1714–1787), working with his librettist *Raniero de Calzabigi* (1714–1795), reformed opera by making music once again subservient to the poetry and plot. His *Orfeo ed Euridice* (1762) and *Alceste* (1767) blend Italian, German, and French traits; emphasize the chorus, dance, and orchestra and link them to the dramatic action; restrict the vocal display of singers; lessen the gulf between aria and recitative; and unify a variety of elements in extended scenes. Gluck brought his new style to Paris with *Iphigénie en Aulide* in 1774 and scored a great triumph, beginning a new tradition of serious opera in French.   **Music: NAWM 91**

Etude: The *Querelle des bouffons*

Serious French opera had been in decline since the *Querelle des bouffons* (quarrel of the comic actors), a debate in 1752 about the relative merits of traditional French opera and the new comic Italian opera. Gluck appealed to the public by showing that good opera could be written in French.

V. Instrumental Music: Sonata, Symphony, and Concerto (CHWM 305–13, NAWM 92–96)

A. *Sonata*

1. Domenico Scarlatti

Domenico Scarlatti (1685–1757), son of Alessandro Scarlatti, worked in Portugal and Spain. His 555 harpsichord *sonatas* are typically in one movement (or two paired movements) in binary form: two sections, both repeated, the first moving from tonic to dominant or relative major, the second modulating back to the tonic and ending with a tonic-key restatement of the material that closed the first section. Rather than themes, Scarlatti presents a series of ideas that plainly project the key through pedal points, arpeggiation, and other figuration.   **Music: NAWM 92**

2. Early symphonies
The Italian opera overture or *sinfonia* of the early eighteenth century had three movements in the order fast-slow-fast, ending with a dance. These were also performed independently, and composers such as *Giovanni Battista Sammartini* (1701–1775) began to write *symphonies* for concert performance.   **Music: NAWM 93**

3. Sonata form
Sonatas, symphonies, and chamber works typically have three or four movements in contrasting moods and tempos. The first movement is usually in *sonata form*, which comprises (1) an *exposition* with a first theme in the tonic, a modulatory transition, and second and closing themes in the dominant or relative major; (2) a *development* section which modulates to new keys and may fragment and vary the themes; and (3) a *recapitulation*, restating all three themes in the tonic, sometimes followed by a *coda*. The exposition was usually repeated and the development and recapitulation normally repeated as a unit, showing the derivation of this form from rounded binary form as used by Scarlatti and Sammartini.

B. *The* Empfindsam *Style*

The *empfindsam* style is closely identified with *Carl Philipp Emanuel Bach* (1714–1788), the most famous of Johann Sebastian Bach's sons and an influential composer in his own right. He is best known for his keyboard music, especially several sets of sonatas marked by constantly changing rhythms, sudden surprising changes of harmony, texture, or dynamic level, and instrumental evocations of recitative and aria.   **Music: NAWM 94**

C. *German Symphonic Composers*

Composers at *Mannheim*, Vienna, and Berlin were the leading German symphonists at mid-century. The Mannheim orchestra, led by *Johann Stamitz* (1717–1757), was renowned for its virtuosity, dynamic range, and controlled crescendo.   **Music: NAWM 95**

Etude: The Eighteenth-Century Orchestra
The Classic-era orchestra had about twenty to thirty-five players, including strings, winds in pairs, horns, and harpsichord. The practice of basso continuo was gradually abandoned, and conducting duties passed to the leader of the violins. The winds, often used to double the strings and fill in harmonies, gained more independent roles late in the century.

D. *J. C. Bach's Concertos*

Johann Christian Bach (1735–1782), J. S. Bach's youngest son, studied and worked in Italy before going to London. There he had a successful career and met the young Mozart, on whom he had a profound influence.

His *concertos* for piano or harpsichord and orchestra follow in their first movements a form that alternates orchestral ritornellos with solo episodes, as in the Baroque concerto, but also features the key structure and contrasting themes of sonata form.   **Music: NAWM 96**

STUDY QUESTIONS

Prelude (CHWM 287–91)

1. What was the Enlightenment? How did the wider cultural climate of the eighteenth century affect music? How did musical life change in response to a growing public interested in music?

2. According to Johann Joachim Quantz (quoted in CHWM, p. 290) and others in the late eighteenth century, what were the characteristics of the best music?

General Characteristics of the New Style (CHWM 291–94)

3. What general characteristics distinguish music of the later eighteenth century from music of the Baroque period?

Opera Buffa (CHWM 294–98, NAWM 87 and 89–90)

4. What are the characteristics of an *opera buffa*? How does an *intermezzo* differ, and how are the two genres similar?

Music to Study

NAWM 87: Giovanni Battista Pergolesi, *La serva padrona* (The Maid as Mistress), intermezzo, excerpt: Recitativo and Recitativo obbligato, *Ah quanto mi sta male,* and Aria, *Son imbrogliato io* (1733)
CD 7.1–6 (Concise 3.1–6)   Cassette 7.A (Concise 3.A)

5. What is funny in Uberto's recitative soliloquy in this scene from Pergolesi's *La serva padrona* (NAWM 87)? How do his vocal line, the changes of harmony, and the interjections of the string orchestra convey yet parody his emotions?

6. How are repeated notes and phrases and sudden changes of texture and mood used in Uberto's aria *Son imbrogliato io* to create a comic flavor? What other humorous touches do you notice?

---

7. What are the distinctive features of comic opera in France, England, and Germany in the eighteenth century?

Music to Study
>   **NAWM 89:** Jean-Jacques Rousseau, *Le Devin du village* (The Village Sooth-
>   sayer), opéra comique, excerpt: Scene 1, Air, *J'ai perdu tout mon
>   bonheur* (1752)
>   CD 7.12–15   Cassette 7.A
>   **NAWM 90:** John Gay (librettist and arranger), *The Beggar's Opera*, ballad
>   opera, excerpt: Scenes 11–13 (1728)
>   CD 7.16–20   Cassette 7.A

8. How does the scene from Rousseau's *Le Devin du village* (NAWM 89) compare to Pergolesi's *La serva padrona* (NAWM 87)? What musical characteristics do the two works share, and how do they differ? What elements in the
music mark the Rousseau as distinctively French?

9. In what ways does the Rousseau reflect the new musical tastes of the middle
to late eighteenth century (as described earlier in this chapter)?

10. In what ways does *The Beggar's Opera* differ from Italian opera and French comic opera? What is this type of musical theater called? What did John Gay do to "compose" this work?

Opera Seria (CHWM 298–302, NAWM 88)

11. What are the characteristics of the *opera seria* libretto as established by Pietro Metastasio? What moral lessons did his operas aim to teach?

12. What does "da capo" mean, and what does it ask the performer to do?

    What does "dal segno" mean, and what does it signify?

Music to Study
   NAWM 88: Johann Adolph Hasse, *Cleofide,* opera seria, excerpt: Act II, Scene 9, *Digli ch'io son fedele* (1731)
      CD 7.7–11   Cassette 7.A

13. Compare Cleofide's aria *Digli ch'io son fedele* (NAWM 88) to the standard da capo form in CHWM, p. 299. Where does each section begin and end? In what respects does it follow this form? Where does it deviate?

14. Where does material from the opening ritornello (mm. 1-10) return later in the aria, either in the vocal statements or in later ritornellos, and how is it changed?

15. In what ways does the B section contrast with the A section?

16. What characteristics of the new Classic-era styles (as described in the first section of this chapter) are apparent in the music of both sections of this aria?

17. How does the embellished melody in the upper staff of Example 13.3 in CHWM (p. 301) relate to the written melody in the staff below? It was transcribed (by King Frederick the Great of Prussia, no less) from a live performance. What can you deduce from this example about how singers embellished arias in opera seria? (You may also consider the embellishments added by Emma Kirkby in the performance that accompanies NAWM.)

Opera Reform (CHWM 302–5, NAWM 91)

18. How did Jommelli and Traetta seek to reform Italian opera in the 1750s?

Music to Study
> **NAWM 91:** Christoph Willibald Gluck, *Orfeo ed Euridice*, opera, excerpt
> from Act II, scene 1 (1762)
> CD 7.21–25   Cassette 7.A

19. What operatic reforms did Gluck introduce in *Orfeo ed Euridice* and *Alceste*? How are those reforms apparent in the scene from *Orfeo ed Euridice* in NAWM 91? How does this differ from the other operas we have seen so far in this chapter, and particularly from Hasse's *Cleofide* as composed and performed?

20. What dramatic musical devices does Gluck use to set the scene and portray the characters (the Furies in the underworld, and Orfeo, who has come down to bring back his beloved Euridice)?

Instrumental Music: Sonata, Symphony, and Concerto (CHWM 305–13, NAWM 92–96)

Music to Study
    NAWM 92: Domenico Scarlatti, Sonata in D Major, K. 119 (ca. 1749)
        CD 7.26–27 (Concise 3.7–8)   Cassette 7.A (Concise 3.A)

21. In the first half of his Sonata in D Major, K. 119 (NAWM 92), Scarlatti introduces a string of ideas with contrasting figuration and function. For each of the following passages (indicated by measure numbers), indicate the implied key when it is tonally stable or "mod." if it changes key, and briefly describe the figuration (e.g., arpeggios, scales, octaves, repeated notes or chords, trills, stepwise melody, or a combination of these).

    Of these ideas, some return in the second half, and some do not. For those that do, indicate where in the second half they begin and in what key they are presented.

	Mm.	Implied key	Figuration	Where in 2nd half?
a.	1–5	_____	_____	_____
b.	6–13	_____	_____	_____
c.	14–17	_____	_____	_____
d.	18–35	_____	_____	_____
e.	36–55	_____	_____	_____
f.	56–64	_____	_____	_____
g.	65–72	_____	_____	_____
d'.	73–95	_____	_____	_____

22. Based on your answers above, write a brief description of the form and the kinds of figuration Scarlatti uses in his sonata.

23. In this sonata, how does Scarlatti imitate the sound or style of Spanish guitar music?

24. What role did opera play in the birth of the independent symphony?

Music to Study
   NAWM 93: Giovanni Battista Sammartini, Symphony No. 32 in F Major, first movement (ca. 1744)
      CD 7.28–30   Cassette 7.A
   NAWM 94: Carl Philipp Emanuel Bach, Sonata in A Major, H. 186, Wq. 55/4, second movement (1765)
      CD 7.31–32 (Concise 3.9–10)   Cassette 7.B (Concise 3.A)
   NAWM 95: Johann Stamitz, Sinfonia a 8 in E-flat Major, first movement (published 1758)
      CD 7.33–37   Cassette 7.B

25. How does the first movement of Sammartini's Symphony No. 32 in F Major (NAWM 93) compare in style to the aria from Pergolesi's *La serva padrona* in NAWM 87 or the Scarlatti sonata in NAWM 92? What elements does it have in common with each?

26. In the second movement of C. P. E. Bach's Sonata in A Major (NAWM 94), where does the opening material repeat, and in what key? What else is repeated, and in what key does it appear each time? Diagram the form of the piece. How does it relate to sonata form, and how is it different?

27. What elements of this movement are typical of Bach's expressive style?

28. Compare the melodic writing in this sonata movement to the vocal embellishments added to Hasse's aria from *Cleofide* (NAWM 88), as shown in the upper staff of Example 13.3 in CHWM (p. 301; see also question 17, above). Although the melodic range is too wide for a singer, how does Bach create the sense in this instrumental work of a vocal melody, like a slow aria?

29. Compare the Stamitz symphony movement in NAWM 95 to the Sammartini symphony movement in NAWM 93. How are they similar, and how are they different, in instrumentation, style, and form?

32. How large was the orchestra in the Classic period? In addition to the strings, what other instruments were members, about how many of each were there, and what was their function?

     Who conducted? _____

Music to Study
    NAWM 96: Johann Christian Bach, Concerto for Harpsichord or Piano and
          Strings in E-flat Major, Op. 7, No. 5, first movement (ca. 1770)
    CD 7.38–50   Cassette 7.B

30. What traits mark Johann Christian Bach's keyboard concerto movement (NAWM 96) as *galant* in style? How does it differ from the *Empfindsamkeit* of C. P. E. Bach's sonata movement (NAWM 94)?

31. How does the form of this first movement resemble a Baroque concerto movement in ritornello form (in which the orchestra interjects transposed and often abbreviated statements of the ritornello between solo episodes), and how does it differ? How does it resemble a Classic-era movement in sonata form, and how does it differ?

TERMS TO KNOW

Terms Reviewed from Earlier Chapters

recitative
aria

Singspiel
da capo aria

Terms Related to the Classic Style

Classic style
galant style
Empfindsamkeit (empfindsam
    style)

the Enlightenment
periodicity
Alberti bass

Terms Related to Opera and Vocal Music

opera buffa
intermezzo
opéra comique
vaudeville

ariette
ballad opera
opera seria
querelle des bouffons

Terms Related to Instrumental Music

keyboard sonata
sinfonia (eighteenth-century)
symphony
sonata form

exposition, development, recapitulation,
    coda
concerto (late-eighteenth-century)

NAMES TO KNOW

Names Related to the Classic Style and to Opera

Joseph Joachim Quantz
La serva padrona
Giovanni Battista Pergolesi
Le Devin du village
Jean-Jacques Rousseau
John Gay
The Beggar's Opera
Pietro Metastasio
Johann Adolph Hasse

Faustina Bordoni
Nicolò Jommelli
Tommaso Traetta
Christoph Willibald Gluck
Raniero de Calzabigi
Orfeo ed Euridice
Alceste
Iphigénie en Aulide

Names Related to Instrumental Music

Domenico Scarlatti
Giovanni Battista Sammartini
Carl Philipp Emanuel Bach

Mannheim
Johann Stamitz
Johann Christian Bach

REVIEW QUESTIONS

1. Make a time-line for the pieces, composers, librettists, and theorists discussed in this chapter.

2. How did the Enlightenment ideals of reason and naturalness help to create a climate in which the older Baroque styles were replaced by simpler, immediately pleasing styles with wide appeal?

3. Describe the varieties of comic opera in the eighteenth century in Italy, France, England, and Germany.

4. Describe opera seria of the 1730s to 1750s. How is the reform opera of Gluck and Calzabigi different?

5. What elements of form do all or most of the instrumental works in NAWM 92–96 have in common? (For instance, do they all have similar harmonic plans? Do they repeat musical material in similar ways? What elements does each share with the standard model of sonata form?) Can you distill from these five movements a short list of formal strategies that are shared by all or most of these pieces?

THE LATE EIGHTEENTH CENTURY: HAYDN AND MOZART

14

CHAPTER OBJECTIVES

After you complete the reading, study of the music, and study questions for this chapter, you should be able to:

1. trace the careers of Haydn and Mozart and the development of their musical idioms;
2. describe the principal genres and forms practiced by Haydn, Mozart, and their contemporaries; and
3. name several important works by each of these composers and describe some works by each in their mature styles.

CHAPTER OUTLINE

Prelude (CHWM 315–16)

The greatest composers of the Classic era were *Franz Joseph Haydn* (1732–1809) and *Wolfgang Amadeus Mozart* (1756–1791). They were friends and influenced each other, yet their careers were strikingly different.

I. Franz Joseph Haydn (1732–1809) (CHWM 316 and 318–19)

Haydn learned music through lessons, as a choirboy, and by studying counterpoint. He served the Esterházy family for most of his career.

Etude: Music at Eszterháza and Haydn's Career
Haydn's patron from 1762 to 1790 was *Prince Nicholas Esterházy*, who lived most of the year at his country estate, *Eszterháza*. Haydn's duties were to compose music as requested, conduct frequent performances, train and supervise the musicians, and maintain the instruments. Writing so much music for immediate performance allowed Haydn to experiment and develop a fresh, effective style that made him the most popular composer in Europe. He also wrote music for publication and on commission. When

Prince Nicholas died in 1790, his son Anton disbanded the orchestra and gave Haydn a pension. In 1791–92 and 1794–95 Haydn went to London, where he gave concerts for the impresario *Johann Peter Salomon* and wrote symphonies Nos. 93–104 (the *London* Symphonies). He returned to Vienna as music director for Anton's son Prince Nicholas II with much lighter duties. His major late works are Masses and two oratorios, *The Creation* (1798) and *The Seasons* (1801).

II. Haydn's Instrumental Music (CHWM 316–31, NAWM 97–101)

A. *Symphonic form*

Many early Haydn symphonies use the three-movement plan of the opera sinfonia or four movements in the order Andante, Allegro, Minuet, Presto. Soon he adopted a standard pattern of four movements: Allegro, Andante, *Minuet-and-Trio,* and Allegro or Presto. The first movement is in sonata form, alternating harmonically stable and symmetrically phrased themes with unstable transitions and developments. There may be a slow introduction, and in the later symphonies the second thematic section may rework the first theme. The development varies and recombines elements from the exposition, often with sudden digressions or silences, and the recapitulation recalls the themes in the tonic. The slow movement offers a lyrical respite after the strong contrasts of the first. The Minuet-and-Trio pairs two minuets, the second of which (the Trio) is more lightly scored and is followed by a return of the first. The fourth movement is faster and shorter than the first and is usually full of high spirits and surprises.

B. *The Symphonies of 1768–74*

The symphonies of 1768–74 are longer and more serious than earlier and require the listener's full attention. They feature startling dynamic contrasts, rich harmonies, distant modulations, and more counterpoint. The agitated emotions of some in minor keys has been linked to the slightly later literary movement *Sturm und Drang* (storm and stress).

C. *The Symphonies of 1774–88*

The symphonies after 1774 are cheerful and infused with the appealing style of comic opera. The six Paris symphonies (Nos. 82–87) were commissioned for a concert series in Paris. In Nos. 88–92, Haydn often begins with a slow introduction; uses contrasting second themes less often; features the winds; and infuses the finale with counterpoint, increasing its weight without sacrificing popular appeal. **Music: NAWM 97–98**

D. London *Symphonies*

Haydn wrote music to suit particular occasions, performers, and halls and to please both the expert and the untutored music lover. His *London* Symphonies were aimed at the public, with greater tunefulness (including Slovenian and Croatian peasant tunes), more varied orchestration, and striking changes of key. First movements tend to focus on the first theme rather than introducing a contrasting second theme; the slow movements use theme and variation or a variant of sonata form; and the Minuet-and-Trio movements are fast and often humorous. The finales use sonata form, *rondo form*, or a blend of the two.   **Music: NAWM 99**

E. *The String Quartets*

Haydn's Opp. 17 (1771) and 20 (1772) collections established him as the first great master of the *string quartet*. The same movement types are used as in the symphony, although the minuet may precede the slow movement. Three finales in Op. 20 are fugal. The Op. 33 quartets (1781) are lighter, with the minuet transformed into a *scherzo* (joke) through fast tempos and unusual rhythms. Quartets were intended primarily for amateurs to play for their own pleasure, and Haydn's playfulness adds to the fun. The quartets of 1785–90 tend toward monothematic first movements. His late quartets, written 1793–1803, are marked by widely ranging harmonies and stark juxtapositions of contrasting styles.   **Music: NAWM 100–101**

F. *Keyboard Sonatas*

Haydn's early keyboard sonatas are suitable for harpsichord, clavichord, or piano, but his later ones are intended for the piano. His sonatas generally develop in parallel with his symphonies and quartets.

III. Haydn's Vocal Works (CHWM 331–34)

1. Operas

Haydn wrote many operas, most of them Italian comic operas. They met with success but soon passed from the repertory and are now rarely heard.

2. Church music

Haydn's most important works for church were six festive Masses he wrote between 1796 and 1802 for Prince Esterházy. These were in symphonic style, with full orchestra, soloists, and chorus.

3. Oratorios

While in England, Haydn heard some of Handel's oratorios, and his own late oratorios *Die Schöpfung* (The Creation, 1798) and *Die Jahreszeiten* (The Seasons, 1801), both on librettos by *Baron Gottfried van Swieten*, show Handel's influence.

IV. Wolfgang Amadeus Mozart (1756–1791) (CHWM 334–35)

Mozart was born in Salzburg, where his father *Leopold Mozart* served the archbishop. Wolfgang and his sister Marianne ("Nannerl") were child prodigies, and their father took them on tour around Europe. Mozart began composing at age five. His more than 600 works are identified by their number in the catalogue of his works by Ludwig von Köchel.

Etude: Mozart's Teachers

Mozart's first teacher was his father Leopold. Through touring, Mozart learned every style of music then current in western Europe and imitated each one in his own compositions. His mature works synthesize these various styles and types in music of unprecedented variety.

V. Mozart's Years in Salzburg (CHWM 335–38)

Mozart was in Salzburg for most of 1774–81 but actively sought a position elsewhere. He was commissioned to write an opera seria, *Idomeneo*, for Munich. He wrote piano variations for his pupils and piano sonatas for his own concert performances. The sonatas are varied in form, style, and content. Mozart's themes are often graceful, singing melodies that grow without apparent effort from the initial ideas. He also wrote sonatas for violin and piano, *serenades* and *divertimentos*, and violin concertos.

VI. Mozart's Vienna Years (CHWM 338–49, NAWM 102–3)

Mozart moved to Vienna in 1781, hoping to earn a living as a freelance performer and composer. He met with great initial success, but he failed to find a permanent position and his popularity and earnings later declined. His music struck a perfect balance between immediate universal appeal and the depth of feeling and technique that earned the respect of the learned. He was strongly influenced by Haydn and by Johann Sebastian Bach, whose music he discovered through Baron Gottfried van Swieten. Among Mozart's important works from this time are the piano Fantasia and Sonata in C Minor, K. 475 and 457, and six quartets dedicated to Haydn.

A. *Symphonies*

Mozart wrote only six symphonies after 1781, but they were longer and more substantial than their predecessors, with more difficult wind parts, more harmonic and contrapuntal complexity, and weightier finales. The last two characteristics are exemplified in the finale of Symphony No. 41 in C Major (*Jupiter*), which combines its fugal first theme in counterpoint with five other motives.

B. *Piano Concertos*

Mozart wrote 17 piano concertos in Vienna for his own performances as a soloist, primarily during his first five years there. In them, as in all his music, he sought to please both the connoisseur and the less learned listener, although they challenge the best players. The first movements are like those of Johann Christian Bach's concertos in blending ritornello and sonata–form procedures. Before the final tutti, the orchestra pauses on a tonic six-four chord and the soloist plays a *cadenza*. Mozart's second movements are like slow arias, and the finales are rondos or sonata-rondos. **Music: NAWM 102**

C. *Operas*

In Vienna, Mozart composed a Singspiel, *Die Entführung aus dem Serail* (The Abduction from the Harem, 1786); three Italian comic operas on librettos by *Lorenzo da Ponte* (1749–1838), *Le nozze di Figaro* (The Marriage of Figaro, 1786), *Don Giovanni* (premiered at Prague in 1787), and *Così fan tutte* (Thus Do They All, 1790); an opera seria, *La clemenza di Tito* (The Mercy of Titus, 1791); and a German opera, *Die Zauberflöte* (The Magic Flute, 1791). Mozart's music captured each character, and the ensembles showed them interacting in dramatic ways. *Don Giovanni* was the first opera on the Don Juan theme to take the character seriously, resulting in characters and a drama of unprecedented depth. *Die Zauberflöte* mixes comedy with the humanistic imagery and symbolism of the Freemasons, and Mozart's music blends elements of opera seria, Singspiel, opera buffa, accompanied recitative, sacred choral style, and Baroque counterpoint.   **Music: NAWM 103**

D. *Church Music*

Mozart's Masses are written in symphonic-operatic style, alternating chorus and soloists. His Requiem was left unfinished at his death and completed by Mozart's student and collaborator Franz Xaver Süssmayr.

Window: Mozart and His Father (CHWM 346–47)

Mozart had a complex relationship with his father Leopold, who was an unselfish mentor when Mozart was young but turned unforgiving when Mozart moved to Vienna and married against Leopold's wishes.

STUDY QUESTIONS

Prelude (CHWM 315–16)

1. What are some significant differences between the careers of Haydn and Mozart? (See also the accounts of their careers throughout the chapter.)

Franz Joseph Haydn (1732–1809) (CHWM 316 and 318–19)

2. Who was Haydn's main patron? What was Haydn required to do as part of his employment?

3. Trace Haydn's career after 1790, including his sources of income and his major compositions.

Haydn's Instrumental Music (CHWM 316–31, NAWM 97–101)

4. What are the standard four movements of a Haydn symphony, and what are the main characteristics of each?

Music to Study
   NAWM 97: Franz Joseph Haydn, Symphony No. 56 in C Major, first movement (1774)
      CD 7.51–57 (Concise 3.11–17)   Cassette 7.B (Concise 3.A)
   NAWM 98: Franz Joseph Haydn, Symphony No. 92 in G Major (*Oxford*), second movement (1789)
      CD 7.58–61   Cassette 7.B
   NAWM 99: Franz Joseph Haydn, Symphony No. 104 in D Major (*London*), finale (1795)
      CD 7.62–72   Cassette 7.B

(Note on reading scores: Instruments like the horn and clarinet are written as they are fingered to allow players to move easily between different members of the same family of instruments. Horns in F and D, for instance, will use the same fingering when they see a C, but the instrument will produce an F and a D respectively. In eighteenth- and nineteenth-century scores, these "transposing instruments" are given in the score as they are notated for the player, which means the conductor or score-reader must transpose in the same way the instrument does to determine the pitch that will sound. In the latter two movements, Haydn uses horns in D, which sound a minor seventh lower than written—D when C is notated; in Symphony No. 104, he also uses trumpets in D, sounding a whole step higher, and clarinets in A, sounding a minor third lower—A when C is notated.)

---

5. In the exposition of Haydn's Symphony No. 56, first movement (NAWM 97), how are the following sections distinguished from each other? Mention these and other features you find significant: harmonic stability or instability; key (when stable); use of chromaticism; phrasing (clearly articulated or continuous and overlapping); dynamics; orchestration; and melodic content.

first theme area (mm. 1–28)

transition (mm. 29–52)

second theme area (mm. 53–67, with a contrasting extension in mm. 68–78)

closing group (mm. 79–99)

Notice how many different ways there are to follow the form. A listener may attend to any of these distinguishing features and will still be able to follow the course of the music clearly. This is one of the ways in which Classic-era music is notable for its intelligibility to a wide range of listeners.

6. In what measure does the recapitulation begin? _____

The recapitulation repeats material from the exposition, but with some changes. What is different in the recapitulation, in comparison to the exposition?

7. What happens in the development, in terms of harmony and key?

How are orchestration and dynamics used in the development?

What ideas from the exposition are used in the development, where do they appear, and how are they changed from the exposition?

8. Chart the form of the slow movement of Haydn's Symphony No. 92 (NAWM 98), and give the key of each main section.

How do the opening motives of the first two sections relate?

What elements of both sections appear in the coda (mm. 94–111)?

9. Compare the melodic writing in this movement to the vocal embellishments added to Hasse's aria from *Cleofide* (NAWM 88 and Example 13.3 in CHWM, p. 301) and to the melodic style in the slow movement from C. P. E. Bach's piano sonata (NAWM 94; see also chapter 13, questions 17 and 28). How does Haydn embellish his melodies?

10. How are the wind instruments used in this movement? How does this compare to the earlier Haydn symphony movement in NAWM 97?

11. What elements give the finale of Symphony No. 104 (NAWM 99) its popular character?

12. In what ways does the exposition of this sonata-form movement differ in form from the first movement of Haydn's Symphony No. 56 (NAWM 97)? How are these differences typical of Haydn's later symphonies?

13. String quartets were written primarily for amateurs to play for their own enjoyment. What aspects of Haydn's quartets were particularly well suited to give pleasure to the players themselves?

Music to Study
   NAWM 100: Franz Joseph Haydn, String Quartet in D Major, Op. 64, No. 5,
       finale (1790)
       CD 8.1–8 (Concise 3.18–25)   Cassette 8.A (Concise 3.A)
   NAWM 101: Franz Joseph Haydn, String Quartet in C Major, Op. 76, No. 3,
       second movement (1797)
       CD 8.9–13   Cassette 8.A

14. The theme of a Haydn rondo is normally a little binary form with two
    repeated sections, often a rounded binary form (in which both halves end
    with the same music) in the pattern ‖: a :‖: b a :‖. This is true of the finale
    of Haydn's String Quartet in D Major, Op. 64, No. 5, where the theme
    appears in mm. 1–28. In what measures does this theme reappear in its
    entirety (without the repeat signs)? What is changed on its reappearance?

15. The chart and discussion in NAWM, p. 155, compare this rondo theme to a
    sonata exposition. But mm. 1–28 could not possibly be a sonata exposition.
    Why not? How is this segment of music *unlike* a sonata exposition, as exem-
    plified by mm. 1–99 of Haydn's Symphony No. 56, first movement (NAWM
    97)? (Hint: One way to answer is to list things that happen in this passage that
    do not happen in a sonata exposition, and vice versa.)

16. On the other hand, the episode that begins at m. 29 sounds and behaves more
    like a sonata-form development section than it does like an episode in a
    rondo. What makes this section like a development?

    So this finale blends features of rondo and sonata form, without fulfilling our
    expectations for either. We may conclude from this example that the
    "forms" of the Classic era are best thought of as procedures to be used—
    and, in this and many other cases, mixed with each other—rather than molds
    to be filled. The flexibility with which Haydn and other composers applied
    these procedures is amazing.

17. In the second movement of his String Quartet in C Major, Op. 76, No. 3 (NAWM 101), Haydn presents a series of variations on a tune that later became the Austrian and German national anthems. In each variation, how is the tune varied? How is the accompaniment changed?

variation I:

variation II:

variation III:

variation IV:

Haydn's Vocal Works (CHWM 331–34)

18. Whose music was a major influence on Haydn's late Masses and oratorios?

_____

Wolfgang Amadeus Mozart and Mozart's Years in Salzburg (CHWM 334–38)

19. Describe Mozart's career and the influences on his music to 1781.

Mozart's Vienna Years (CHWM 338–49, NAWM 102–3)

20. How did Mozart become acquainted with the music of Johann Sebastian Bach? How was he influenced by Bach's music?

Music to Study
    NAWM 102: Wolfgang Amadeus Mozart, Piano Concerto in A Major, K. 488, first movement (1786)
        CD 8.14–29   Cassette 8.A

21. In this Mozart concerto movement, what segments of the opening orchestral ritornello return later in the work, and where does each return? How is it varied on its return?

22. How does the form of this first movement resemble a Baroque concerto movement in ritornello form, how does it resemble a sonata-form first movement, and how does it differ from each? How does it compare with the first movement of J. C. Bach's concerto in NAWM 96 (see chapter 13, question 31)?

---

23. In Mozart's view, what was the proper relationship between the words and the music in opera?

Music to Study

NAWM 103: Wolfgang Amadeus Mozart, *Don Giovanni*, K. 527, opera, Act I, Scene 5 (1787)

103a: No. 3, Aria: *Ah chi mi dice mai*
CD 8.30–31 (Concise 3.26–27)   Cassette 8.A (Concise 3.A)
Recitative: *Chi è là?*
CD 8.32 (Concise 3.28)   Cassette 8.A (Concise 3.A)
103b: No. 4, Aria: *Madamina! Il catalogo è questo*
CD 8.33–34 (Concise 3.29–30)   Cassette 8.A (Concise 3.A)

---

24. How does Mozart's music help to delineate the three characters and portray their feelings in *Ah chi mi dice mai* from *Don Giovanni* (NAWM 103a)?

25. In what ways does the form of this aria resemble sonata form? What element of sonata form does it omit?

26. In Leporello's "catalogue" aria (103b), how are the different characteristics of Don Giovanni's victims depicted in the music? That is, what musical means does Mozart use to depict the images in the text?

TERMS TO KNOW

Minuet-and-Trio
Sturm und Drang
rondo form
string quartet

scherzo
serenade
divertimento
cadenza

NAMES TO KNOW

Franz Joseph Haydn
Wolfgang Amadeus Mozart
Prince Nicholas Esterházy
Eszterháza
Johann Peter Salomon
the *London* Symphonies
Die Schöpfung (The Creation)
Die Jahreszeiten (The Seasons)
Baron Gottfried van Swieten
Leopold Mozart

Idomeneo
Mozart's *Haydn* quartets
Die Entführung aus dem Serail (The
    Abduction from the Harem)
Lorenzo da Ponte
Le nozze di Figaro (The Marriage of
    Figaro)
Don Giovanni
Così fan tutte (Thus Do They All)
Die Zauberflöte (The Magic Flute)

REVIEW QUESTIONS

1. Add Haydn, Mozart, and the major events and works discussed in this chapter to the time-line you made for chapter 13.

2. Compare the careers of Haydn and Mozart, including the circumstances of their lives and the genres and styles they cultivated. What are the main similarities between their careers, and what are the major differences?

3. Briefly describe each of the following genres as practiced by Mozart and Haydn in terms of form, style, content, and social function: symphony, string quartet, piano sonata, concerto, and comic opera.

4. Describe the principal characteristics of Haydn's mature style in his instrumental works. Use NAWM 97–101 as examples for your discussion, referring to and describing passages as appropriate.

5. Building on the previous question, what aspects of Haydn's style did Mozart absorb into his own? And in what ways does Mozart's mature music differ from that of Haydn? Use NAWM 102–3 and other works described in HWM as examples for your discussion, referring to and describing passages as appropriate.

LUDWIG VAN BEETHOVEN

15

CHAPTER OBJECTIVES

After you complete the reading, study of the music, and study questions for this chapter, you should be able to:

1. briefly recount Beethoven's career and the circumstances of his life;
2. list the main characteristics of the music of each of his three periods; and
3. name several important works and describe at least one complete movement for each period.

CHAPTER OUTLINE

Prelude (CHWM 350–52)

> *Ludwig van Beethoven* (1770–1827) was born in Bonn in northwest Germany and was taught music by his father and a local organist. In 1792, he went to Vienna and studied with Haydn and other composers. He was neither as prolific nor as speedy a composer as Haydn or Mozart, but took each piece through many drafts and revisions, as we can see in his surviving *sketchbooks*. His career is divided into three periods. In the first, to about 1802, he assimilated the musical language, genres, and styles of his time. In the second, ca. 1803–16, his works were more individual, longer, and grander than before. In the third period, his music became more introspective (and often more difficult to play and understand).

I. First Period (CHWM 352–55, NAWM 104–5)

1. Patrons

Beethoven was supported by aristocratic patrons, three of whom gave him an annuity to keep him in Vienna. He also sold his works to publishers, performed as a pianist, and taught piano. Thus he was able to make a living without being employed by a single patron, as Haydn had been.

190

2. Piano Sonatas

Beethoven's piano sonatas follow Haydn's example but include individual features. Several traits of his piano style may be indebted to the sonatas of *Muzio Clementi* (1752–1832). **Music: NAWM 104–5**

3. Chamber music

Beethoven's first six string quartets, Op. 18 (1798–1800), follow Haydn in motivic development and use of counterpoint but show Beethoven's individuality in their themes, surprising modulations and turns of phrase, and formal structure. Other chamber works of the first period include piano trios, violin sonatas, cello sonatas, and a septet for strings and winds.

4. First and Second Symphonies

Beethoven's Symphony No. 1 in C Major (1800) has a scherzo as the third movement and features long codas in the other movements. His Second Symphony in D Major (1802) is longer than previous symphonies, with more thematic material and long codas that develop the main ideas.

II. Second Period (CHWM 356–65, NAWM 106)

By his early thirties, Beethoven was renowned as a pianist and composer, had many aristocratic patrons, and was sought after by publishers.

1. The *Eroica* Symphony

The *Third Symphony* (*Eroica*, 1803), was unprecedented in length and complexity, with many unusual features. The opening theme is treated as a person in a drama, struggling and finally triumphing. Beethoven first titled the work *Bonaparte*, after Napoleon, but changed the title to *Sinfonia Eroica* (Heroic Symphony). The second movement is a funeral march that evokes the style of French Revolutionary marches. **Music: NAWM 106**

2. *Fidelio*

In Beethoven's one opera, *Fidelio* (1804-5, rev. 1806 and 1814), Leonore assumes the disguise of a man in order to free her husband from wrongful imprisonment. Beethoven revised the work repeatedly before it was a success.

3. The *Rasumovsky* Quartets

Beethoven's second set of string quartets was Op. 59 (1806), dedicated to Count Rasumovsky, Russian ambassador to Vienna. These three quartets are novel in style, and two movements include Russian themes.

Etude: Beethoven's Deafness

Starting in his twenties, Beethoven gradually went deaf, writing movingly of his suffering in an 1802 letter called the *Heiligenstadt Testament*. His deafness tended to isolate him from society.

4. Symphonies

Beethoven's Fourth and Fifth Symphonies project opposite moods; the Fourth (1806–7) is jovial, while the Fifth in C Minor (1807–8) portrays struggle and final triumph. The Sixth (*Pastoral*) Symphony in F Major (1808) evokes country scenes. The Seventh Symphony in A Major (1811-12) is expansive, while the Eighth in F Major (1812) is quite condensed.

Beethoven also wrote several overtures, which resemble in form the first movement of a symphony (without the reprise of the exposition).

5. Piano sonatas

Many of Beethoven's sonatas show individual features. For example, the *Moonlight* Sonata, Op. 27, No. 2 (1801), begins with a fantasia movement; the Sonata in D Minor, Op. 31, No. 2 (1802), uses a melody that resembles a recitative; and the *Waldstein* Sonata in C Major, Op. 53 (1803-4), uses traditional forms with intense themes and strongly contrasting textures.

6. Piano concertos

Beethoven's first three piano concertos belong to his first period, and the Fourth in G Major (1805-6) and Fifth (*Emperor*) in E-flat Major (1809) to his middle period, along with his one Violin Concerto (1806).

III. Third Period (CHWM 365–71, NAWM 107)

Although Beethoven was famous across Europe and well supported by patrons and publishers, his deafness led to greater social isolation. His music became more abstract and introspective, with extremes from the meditative to the grotesque conjoined in works that referred to classical conventions without being constrained by them.

1. Characteristics of Beethoven's late style

Beethoven's late compositions work out the full potential of themes and motives. The *Diabelli Variations* (1819-23) do not simply embellish the theme as do earlier variation sets but rework material from it to create a new design, mood, and character in each variation. Beethoven's late style is also marked by changes in other aspects:

1. He creates a new sense of continuity by blurring phrase and section divisions and deemphasizing cadences.
2. He includes passages that have an improvisatory character or use *instrumental recitative*.
3. He often uses fugal textures in developments, and several movements or large sections are fugues.
4. He uses new sonorities, including wide spacings and unusually dense textures.
5. He often uses an unusual number of movements and unusual kinds of movements.

The *String Quartet in C-sharp Minor*, Op. 131 (1826), exemplifies all of these characteristics.   **Music: NAWM 107**

2. *Missa solemnis*

The *Missa solemnis* (1819–23), or Mass in D, is a grandiose work that recalls the choral style of Handel while resembling the symphonic conception and mix of chorus and soloists typical of Haydn's late Masses.

3. The Ninth Symphony

Beethoven's Ninth Symphony is longer than his others. Its finale is novel in recalling themes from the earlier movements and introducing soloists and chorus to sing stanzas from Friedrich von Schiller's *Ode to Joy*.

Window: Beethoven's Immortal Beloved (CHWM 366–67)

Beethoven never married, but an impassioned love letter found in his effects after his death has left the mystery of the identity of the woman he called his "Immortal Beloved." The most likely candidate is Antonie Brentano, a Viennese woman married to a businessman in Frankfurt.

Postlude: Beethoven and the Romantics (CHWM 372)

Building on the genres, styles, and procedures of the Classic era, Beethoven created highly individual works that brought him unprecedented success and became models for later composers. His middle-period works were the most influential, particularly for the concept of music as a vehicle to express the composer's own feelings and experiences. (This was the most novel aspect of Beethoven's music; this idea became so influential that modern listeners often assume that this is what all composers have had in mind, when earlier composers sought only to convey the feelings in a text or represent the generalized affections.) Through this and his innovations in form and procedure, he became a revolutionary force in music history.

STUDY QUESTIONS

Prelude (CHWM 350–52)

1. What are two reasons that Beethoven wrote fewer symphonies than Haydn or Mozart? (For a reason that he could afford to do so, see question 3 below.)

2. Beethoven's career is often divided into three periods. Provide the dates for each period and a brief characterization of each.

   First period:

   Second period:

   Third period:

First Period (CHWM 352–55, NAWM 104–5)

3. How did Beethoven make a living in Vienna? How was his situation different from that of Haydn?

Music to Study
NAWM 104: Ludwig van Beethoven, *Sonate pathétique* for piano, Op. 13, finale (1797–98)
CD 8.35–44 (Concise 3.31–40)   Cassette 8.A (Concise 3.A)
NAWM 105: Muzio Clementi, Sonata in G Minor, Op. 34, No. 1, first movement (1795)
CD 8.45–53   Cassette 8.B

4. What are some of the effects Beethoven uses to make the rondo finale of his *Pathétique* Sonata (NAWM 104) dramatic?

5. Compare the later repetitions of the rondo refrain to its initial presentation. What changes are made, if any? How do these changes contribute to the dramatic quality of the music?

6. Compare the rondo's first episode (mm. 25-61) to the reprise of this episode near the movement's end (mm. 134-69). In the reprise, how is it changed from its initial presentation? How does this reflect the influence of sonata form?

7. Both the first movement of Clementi's Sonata in G Minor, Op. 34, No. 1 (NAWM 105), and the finale of Beethoven's *Pathétique* Sonata use sudden changes in harmony, texture, or dynamic level for dramatic effect or to demarcate the form. Find and describe two such moments of sudden change in each movement.

8. Name the string quartets and symphonies Beethoven wrote during his first period, and give a date and a brief description for each.

Second Period (CHWM 356–65, NAWM 106)

Music to Study
>   **NAWM 106:** Ludwig van Beethoven, Symphony No. 3 in E-flat Major
>   (*Eroica*), first movement (1803)
>   CD 8.54–68   Cassette 8.B

9. According to CHWM and NAWM, the principal theme of the first movement
   of Beethoven's *Eroica* Symphony (NAWM 106) is treated as a person in a
   drama, struggling against other players and triumphing in the end. How does
   Beethoven use changes in the principal motive (mm. 3-8) to convey struggle
   and triumph? (Hint: Look at the versions of this idea in the development, at
   mm. 408 and 424 in the recapitulation, and at mm. 639ff. in the coda.)

10. What other devices does Beethoven use in this movement to suggest a heroic
    struggle ending in triumph? How do the very long development and coda
    contribute to this effect?

11. What unusual features of this movement can be explained or understood
    better through an examination of the sketches (as shown in NAWM, pp. 277–
    284)?

12. What do Beethoven's *Eroica* Symphony and his opera *Fidelio* owe to the arts and politics of France in the Revolutionary period?

13. Name the string quartets and symphonies Beethoven wrote during his second period, and give a date and a brief description for each.

14. How does the *Pastoral* Symphony suggest scenes from life in the country?

15. What is the *Heiligenstadt Testament*? What does it discuss, and what attitudes does Beethoven express? What does Beethoven say in it about his relations with other people and about the role of his art in his life?

198 15 LUDWIG VAN BEETHOVEN

Third Period (CHWM 365–71, NAWM 107)

16. For each of the following aspects of music, how does Beethoven's late style differ from Haydn, Mozart, and his own earlier style?

   a. juxtaposition of disparate elements

   b. variation technique

   c. delineation of phrases and sections

   d. evocation of improvisation and recitative

   e. use of fugue

   f. sonority

   g. number of movements

Music to Study
 NAWM 107: Ludwig van Beethoven, String Quartet in C-sharp Minor, Op.
  131 (1826), excerpts
  107a. First movement: Adagio ma non troppo e molto espressivo
   CD 8.69–71 (Concise 3.41–43)   Cassette 8.B (Concise 3.A)
  107b. Second movement: Allegro molto vivace
   CD 8.72   Cassette 8.B

17. Beethoven's String Quartet in C-sharp Minor, Op. 131, is in seven movements. Give the tempo marking, meter, key, and form for each movement.

	Tempo	Meter	Key	Form
1.				
2.				
3.				
4.				
5.				
6.				
7.				

  How can this sequence of movements be reconciled with the traditional four-
  movement plan of a string quartet?

18. The key scheme of the quartet is unusual, and there is a correspondence
  between the keys used for each movement and the important pitches of the
  opening fugue subject. Write out the following notes for the fugue subject in
  violin I (mm. 1–4) and the answer in violin II (mm. 4–8):

                    subject in violin I   answer in violin II

  first note (same as last note): _____   _____

  highest note: _____   _____

  lowest note: _____   _____

  longest, loudest note: _____   _____

  Of these notes, circle the ones that are used as the key of one of the movements in the quartet, as you listed them in question 17.

19. What aspects of the music give the second movement its particularly light and folklike character?

20. Where in the second movement is there a recollection of the key of the first movement, to match the hint in the first movement of the key of the second?

21. In what ways does this quartet exemplify the characteristics of Beethoven's late style as you described them in question 16 above? (Hint: Answers for part d. of question 16 will be found in CHWM and for parts e. and g. in the questions above. For parts a., b., c., and f., look both in CHWM and at the two movements in NAWM.)

a. juxtaposition of disparate elements

b. variation technique

c. delineation of phrases and sections

d. evocation of improvisation and recitative

e. use of fugue

f. sonority

g. number of movements

22. What does Beethoven's *Missa solemnis* owe to Handel, and what does it owe to Haydn?

23. What is unusual about Beethoven's Ninth Symphony? Describe the sequence of events in the finale.

Postlude: Beethoven and the Romantics (CHWM 372)

24. In what ways was Beethoven "one of the great disruptive forces in the history of music"?

TERMS TO KNOW

Beethoven's sketchbooks   instrumental recitative
Beethoven's three periods

NAMES TO KNOW

Ludwig van Beethoven   *Diabelli* Variations, Op. 120
Muzio Clementi   String Quartet in C-sharp Minor, Op. 131
Eroica Symphony   *Missa solemnis*
Fidelio   Beethoven's Ninth Symphony
Heiligenstadt Testament   *Ode to Joy*

REVIEW QUESTIONS

1. Write an essay in which you recount Beethoven's career, including the changing circumstances of his life, his three major style periods, and major compositions of each period.

2. What other composers particularly influenced Beethoven's music, and what did he absorb from each?

3. You have examples in NAWM 104, 106, and 107 of movements from each of Beethoven's three periods. For each of these works, describe the form and other significant features of the movements in NAWM and explain what makes this work characteristic of its period.

ROMANTICISM AND NINETEENTH-CENTURY ORCHESTRAL MUSIC

16

CHAPTER OBJECTIVES

After you complete the reading, study of the music, and study questions for this chapter, you should be able to:

1. describe some of the differences between music of the Classic and Romantic periods, particularly in their aesthetic orientation;
2. explain how nineteenth-century symphonic composers responded to the example and influence of Beethoven;
3. identify some of the most important symphonic composers in the nineteenth century and suggest what makes each composer individual; and
4. briefly describe one or more characteristic works for each one.

CHAPTER OUTLINE

Prelude (CHWM 373–74)

There is more historical continuity than contrast between the Classic and Romantic periods. Romanticism held that instrumental music could convey emotion without words, and orchestral music was a central focus.

I. Romanticism (CHWM 374–75)

Most music between 1770 and 1900 uses a common set of conventions. The main differences from Classic music are of degree: Romantic music is more individual in expressing feelings and transcending conventions. Music was seen as the most Romantic art. But music was also closely identified with literature, particularly in the *art song* and in *program music*.

II. Orchestral Music (CHWM 375–88, NAWM 108–9)

A. *Schubert (1797–1828)*

Franz Schubert composed almost 1000 works in his short life, including more than 600 lieder. His *Unfinished Symphony* has been called the first

Romantic symphony for its lyrical themes and striking orchestration, traits also true of his *"Great" C-major Symphony.*

B. *Berlioz (1803–1869)*

The *Symphonie fantastique* (1830) by *Hector Berlioz* is a musical drama whose words are not spoken or sung but are written in a program handed out to the audience. The central theme, or *idée fixe* (fixed idea or fixation), stands for the artist's beloved and appears in every movement, sometimes transformed; this procedure helped to initiate the cyclic symphony. *Harold en Italie* (Harold in Italy, 1834) is also a program symphony, with a solo violist playing the protagonist, and *Roméo et Juliette* (1839) is a "dramatic symphony" for orchestra, soloists, and chorus. These innovative works influenced all later program music and began a new era of colorful orchestration.   **Music: NAWM 108**

C. *Mendelssohn (1809–1847)*

Felix Mendelssohn combined Classical forms with themes reminiscent of foreign lands in his Symphonies Nos. 4 (*Italian,* 1833) and 3 (*Scottish,* 1842). Among his other important orchestral works are his *concert overtures* (independent one-movement works) and his incidental music for Shakespeare's *A Midsummer Night's Dream.*   **Music: NAWM 109**

D. *Liszt (1811–1886)*

Franz Liszt wrote twelve *symphonic poems* between 1848 and 1858 and another in 1881–82. He was the first to use the term, which designates a programmatic work in one movement that evokes ideas and feelings associated with its subject. His symphonies are also programmatic. Liszt used *thematic transformation,* transforming a theme or motive into new themes and thus providing both motivic unity and variety of mood, as in the symphonic poem *Les Préludes.* Many later composers wrote symphonic poems, and Liszt's harmonies influenced Wagner and others.

E. *Brahms (1833–1897)*

Johannes Brahms composed four symphonies, two overtures, and four concertos. He combined Classic structure with Romantic melodic gesture and intensity. Middle movements are often in keys a third away from the main key of the symphony, instead of in the dominant or subdominant. Brahms often superimposes duple and triple divisions of the beat.

F. *Dvořák (1841–1904)*

Antonín Dvořák is best known for his Symphony No. 9 (*From the New World,* 1893), written during his sojourn in the United States.

Window: The Symphony Orchestra (CHWM 380–81)

The Romantic orchestra was more than twice the size of that of Haydn and Mozart, with many more strings and a greater number and variety of winds, brass, and percussion. Individual instruments were also more powerful. The orchestra now required a permanent conductor rather than being directed from the harpsichord or by the leader of the violins.

Postlude: The Beethoven Legacy (CHWM 388–90)

Beethoven cast a long shadow. Later composers sought to differentiate their music from his, typically by extending some elements of his music while rejecting others. Schubert introduced song-like themes into the symphony; Berlioz found precedents in Beethoven's symphonies for the programmaticism and thematic drama of his *Symphonie fantastique*; Mendelssohn and Brahms continued the symphony in individual ways; and Wagner saw the choral finale of Beethoven's Ninth Symphony as pointing to the union of music with words and drama.

STUDY QUESTIONS

Romanticism (CHWM 374–75)

1. According to Liszt and Schopenhauer, what is special about music as an art?

2. What are some of the links between music and literature in the nineteenth century?

Orchestral Music (CHWM 375–88, NAWM 108–9)

3. What does Schumann praise in Schubert's "Great" Symphony in C Major (see the passage in CHWM, p. 377)?

Music to Study
> **NAWM 108:** Hector Berlioz, *Symphonie fantastique* (1830), excerpts
>> III. *Scène aux champs* (Scene in the Country)
>> not on recordings
>> IV. *Marche au supplice* (March to the Scaffold)
>>> CD 9.1–6 (Concise 3.44–49)   Cassette 9.A (Concise 3.B)

4. What devices of orchestration, melody, and rhythm does Berlioz use to suggest that the third movement of his *Symphonie fantastique* (NAWM 108) is set in the country? (One device not mentioned in the commentary is the dotted siciliano rhythm, long associated with pastoral settings, first introduced in mm. 28–30.)

5. Where does the *idée fixe* (printed in NAWM p. 336 and CHWM p. 379) appear in this movement? How is it transformed, and how is it introduced and developed, to suit the program (given in NAWM, pp. 336–37)?

6. Where does the *idée fixe* appear in the fourth movement, *Marche au supplice*? How is it treated, and how do its treatment and the surrounding music fit the program of the movement?

7. What special instrumental effects does Berlioz use in this movement, and how do they suit the program? What other aspects of the music help to support the program?

8. What was Berlioz's significance for later generations?

9. What is "Italian" in Mendelssohn's *Italian* Symphony (No. 4)? What is "Scottish" in his *Scottish* Symphony (No. 3)?

Music to Study
> **NAWM 109:** Felix Mendelssohn, Incidental Music to *A Midsummer Night's Dream*, Op. 61 (1843), excerpt: Scherzo
> CD 9.7–9   Cassette 9.A

10. What musical techniques does Mendelssohn use in the scherzo from the incidental music to *A Midsummer Night's Dream* (NAWM 109) to suggest the fairies in flight? How does he suggest the braying of Bottom, a character whose head has been changed by a spell into the head of a jackass?

11. How does the form of this scherzo differ from the traditional form of a scherzo? How does it resemble a sonata form without the repetition of the exposition?

12. What is a *symphonic poem*? Who invented it, and when?

13. How did Liszt use thematic transformation in his *Les Préludes*? What did this procedure allow him to accomplish?

14. In what ways do the Brahms symphonies continue the Classic tradition, and in what ways are they Romantic?

Window: The Symphony Orchestra (CHWM 380–81)

15. How did the nineteenth-century orchestra differ from that of Haydn's time, in size, composition, sound, and method of direction? How is this reflected in the differences between Romantic orchestral works such as the *Symphonie fantastique* (NAWM 108) and a symphony of Haydn (NAWM 97–99)?

Postlude: The Beethoven Legacy (CHWM 388–90)

16. According to CHWM, how did each of the following composers confront the influence of Beethoven's symphonies and find an individual path?

Schubert

Berlioz

Brahms

Wagner

TERMS TO KNOW

art song
program music
idée fixe

concert overture (nineteenth-century)
symphonic poem
thematic transformation

NAMES TO KNOW

Franz Schubert
Unfinished Symphony
"Great" C-major Symphony
Hector Berlioz
Symphonie fantastique
Harold en Italie

Roméo et Juliette
Felix Mendelssohn
Franz Liszt
Les Préludes
Johannes Brahms
Antonin Dvořák

REVIEW QUESTIONS

1. Make a time-line for the nineteenth century, and place on it the composers and most significant pieces discussed in this chapter. Add to it the three periods of Beethoven's career and his most important works, as discussed in chapter 15. Make your time-line large enough to allow further additions, as you will be adding to it in chapters 17–19.

2. How are Classic and Romantic music similar, and how are they different? Use examples from the orchestral works you know in NAWM 97–99, 102, and 108–9 to illustrate these similarities and differences.

3. Describe the symphonic works of Schubert, Berlioz, Mendelssohn, Liszt, and Brahms. What traits distinguish each composer's works from those of Beethoven, and from the other composers discussed here?

SOLO, CHAMBER, AND VOCAL MUSIC IN THE NINETEENTH CENTURY

17

CHAPTER OBJECTIVES

After you complete the reading, study of the music, and study questions for this chapter, you should be able to:

1. name some of the principal nineteenth-century composers of piano music and chamber music, characterize their styles, trace influences upon them, and describe representative works by Schumann, Chopin, and Brahms; and
2. describe the nineteenth-century German lied as practiced by Schubert, Robert Schumann, and Clara Schumann.

CHAPTER OUTLINE

Prelude (CHWM 391–92)

While orchestras were expanding and orchestral music becoming more monumental, composers also cultivated more intimate genres for solo piano, voice and piano, and chamber ensembles. The nineteenth-century piano had a larger range, more varied dynamics, and faster response than the eighteenth-century piano, allowing greater expressivity and virtuosity and making it an attractive medium. (It was also now mass-produced and thus widely available and affordable, so that it became the most common household instrument.) The best chamber music of the period came from composers who felt closest to the Classic tradition. The *lied* or German art song, combining literary and lyrical tendencies, reached its peak in this era.

I. Solo Music for Piano (CHWM 392–401, NAWM 110–13)

The most frequent forms of Romantic piano music were short dances and lyrical pieces. Longer works included sonatas, variations, and fantasias.

A. *Schubert*

Schubert wrote marches, dances, and lyrical works that create a distinctive mood. His longer works include eleven sonatas and the *Wanderer Fantasy*

(1822), which uses a theme from his song *The Wanderer*. His sonatas often present three keys in the exposition, rather than two, and while following Classic form use lyrical themes that resist development.

B. *Mendelssohn*

Mendelssohn wrote a variety of piano works, including preludes and fugues that show his interest in Bach. Most popular are his *Lieder ohne Worte* (Songs without Words), which are like songs for piano alone.

C. *Robert Schumann (1810–1856)*

Robert Schumann aimed to be a concert pianist, but after injuring his right hand he turned to composition and to writing about music in the journal he founded, the *Neue Zeitschrift für Musik*. All his published music before 1840 was for piano. He specialized in short character pieces grouped into collections, such as *Phantasiestücke* (Fantasy Pieces, 1837). His pieces carry titles that suggest extramusical associations. In his criticism and his music, he used the imaginary characters Florestan, Eusebius, and Raro to reflect different sides of his own character.   **Music: NAWM 110**

D. *Chopin (1810–1849)*

Fryderyk Chopin wrote almost exclusively for piano. He was born in Poland and lived in Paris from 1831. His *mazurkas* and *polonaises* are stylized Polish dances and are among the first nationalist works of the nineteenth century. His playing style was more personal than theatrical, and his music is accordingly introspective. He used *tempo rubato,* in which the right hand pushes forward or holds back the tempo while the left hand accompanies in strict time. He followed *John Field* (1782–1837) in composing *nocturnes*. Chopin also wrote preludes, *ballades* (a term he apparently coined), scherzos, fantasias, and sonatas. His *études* are studies in piano technique, but are unusual for études in that they are also for concert performance.   **Music: NAWM 111–12**

E. *Liszt*

Born in Hungary and trained in Vienna, Liszt was a touring virtuoso from a young age. He sought to match on the piano the dazzling virtuosity of the violinist *Nicolò Paganini* (1782–1840). Liszt ceased touring in 1848 and became court music director at Weimar, later moving to Rome. He made many transcriptions for piano of other music. His original compositions for piano include Hungarian rhapsodies, two concertos, and a one-movement Sonata in B Minor that uses thematic transformation, as in his symphonic poems. Liszt experimented with chromatic harmony, especially in his late works.   **Music: NAWM 113**

Window: A Ballad of Love (CHWM 398–399)

George Sand (1804–1876) left her husband, adopted a male name and men's clothing, and wrote more than 80 novels. Her romantic relationship with Chopin coincided with his most productive years.

II. Chamber Music (CHWM 401–6, NAWM 114)

A. *Schubert*

Schubert wrote several significant chamber works, notably the *Trout* Quintet, three late string quartets, and the String Quintet in C Major, widely regarded as his best chamber work.

B. *Brahms*

Brahms is Beethoven's true successor in the realm of chamber music, with a large body of works of high quality. Like most of Brahms's music, the Piano Quintet in F Minor, Op. 34 (1864), uses *developing variation,* in which a musical idea is varied to create a string of interrelated but different ideas, producing both unity and variety. His chamber works with clarinet are peaks of the clarinet literature.   **Music: NAWM 114**

III. Vocal Music: The Lied (CHWM 406–10, NAWM 115–18)

Ballads were long narrative poems that required more variety and drama in the music than did a lyrical strophic poem. The piano became equal with the voice in conveying the meaning of the poetry.

A. *Schubert*

Schubert's song melodies are both lovely in themselves and perfectly suited to the text. He often used chromaticism and harmonic contrast to create drama or highlight the meaning of the words. Many songs are strophic; those that are through-composed are based on recurring themes and a clear tonal structure. The accompaniments often include figures that convey an image or feeling in the text. He set dozens of poems by Goethe and composed two *song cycles* (groups of songs intended to be performed in sequence and often implying a story) to poems by Wilhelm Müller, *Die schöne Müllerin* (The Beautiful Miller, 1823) and *Winterreise* (Winter's Journey, 1827).   **Music: NAWM 115–16**

B. *Robert Schumann*

In Schumann's lieder, the piano is equal to the voice in interest and expressivity. He wrote more than 100 songs in 1840, the year of his marriage, including the song cycle *Dichterliebe* (A Poet's Love) on poems by Heinrich Heine.   **Music: NAWM 117**

C. *Clara Schumann (1819–1896)*

Clara Wieck Schumann was a child prodigy on the piano and became an important soloist and composer. Her marriage to Robert Schumann and raising a family limited her touring, but she continued to perform, compose, and teach. Her works include a piano concerto, a piano trio, pieces for piano solo, and lieder.   **Music: NAWM 118**

STUDY QUESTIONS

Solo Music for Piano (CHWM 392–401, NAWM 110–13)

1. How do Schubert's sonatas differ from Beethoven's?

2. What were Mendelssohn's most popular piano pieces, and what are they like?

Music to Study

NAWM 110: Robert Schumann, *Phantasiestücke*, Op. 12 (1837), excerpts
    4: *Grillen* (Whims)
        CD 9.10–12 (Concise 3.50–52)   Cassette 9.A (Concise 3.B)
    5: *In der Nacht* (In the Night)
        CD 9.13–15   Cassette 9.A

3. What is the form of Schumann's *Grillen* (NAWM 110)?

   How does it compare to a traditional ABA form?

   How does this piece, titled "Whims," convey a sense of whims or whimsy?

4. What is the form of Schumann's *In der Nacht*?

   How does this piece convey passionate emotions? How does its form resemble a narrative—that is, how does it suggest that it is relating a story?

---

5. What textures does Schumann use in these piano pieces that are different from textures used by Classic-era composers such as C. P. E. Bach (NAWM 94), Mozart (NAWM 102), or Beethoven (NAWM 104)?

6. What was Chopin's national heritage, and how is this reflected in his music?

Music to Study
   NAWM 111: John Field, Nocturne in A Major, No. 8 (1815)
      CD 9.16   Cassette 9.A
   NAWM 112: Fryderyk Chopin, Nocturne in E-flat Major, Op. 9, No. 2
      (1830–31)
      CD 9.17 (Concise 3.53)   Cassette 9.A (Concise 3.B)

7. In what ways does Field embellish the melodic line in his Nocturne in A Major (NAWM 111)? How do his melodies resemble the style of opera?

8. How does Chopin embellish the melodic line of his Nocturne in E-flat Major (NAWM 112)? How is it like operatic singing? How is it like Field's nocturne?

9. What elements of style, sound, and texture distinguish Chopin's Nocturne from Schumann's *Phantasiestücke* (NAWM 110) and from earlier keyboard styles? Describe Chopin's style, based on this example.

10. Who was Nicolò Paganini? What was his significance for Liszt's career?

Music to Study
> **NAWM 113:** Franz Liszt, *Nuages gris* (Grey Clouds), for piano (1881)
> CD 9.18 (Concise 3.54)   Cassette 9.A (Concise 3.B)

11. What is unusual about the harmony of *Nuages gris* (NAWM 113)?

Chamber Music (CHWM 401–6, NAWM 114)

12. Which Schubert chamber works borrow material from his songs, and how is that material used?

13. What is *developing variation*? How does Brahms use it in the first movement of his Piano Quintet in F Minor, Op. 34 (excerpted in CHWM, p. 405). How does it compare to Liszt's thematic transformation? (For Liszt, see chapter 16, question 13.)

Music to Study
   NAWM 114: Johannes Brahms, Piano Quintet in F Minor, Op. 34 (1864), excerpt: Scherzo
   CD 9.19–25 (Concise 3.55–61)   Cassette 9.B (Concise 3.B)

14. How does the scherzo movement of Brahms's Piano Quintet in F Minor (NAWM 114) recall the style of Beethoven?

15. Chart the form of the scherzo, indicating changes of meter, thematic ideas, and keys.

16. How do the piano and strings interact with each other in this movement?

17. What elements of this movement strike you as typical of Romantic music?

Vocal Music: The Lied (CHWM 406–10, NAWM 115–18)

18. What is a *ballad*? Why did ballads call for greater variety and expressivity from composers? What effect did this have on the piano accompaniments to art songs?

Music to Study

NAWM 115: Franz Schubert, *Gretchen am Spinnrade* (Gretchen at the Spinning Wheel), Lied (1814)
CD 9.26–30 (Concise 3.62–66)   Cassette 9.B (Concise 3.B)

NAWM 116: Franz Schubert, *Der Lindenbaum* (The Linden Tree), lied, from the song cycle *Winterreise* (1827)
CD 9.31–34   Cassette 9.B

NAWM 117: Robert Schumann, two lieder from *Dichterliebe* (A Poet's Love), song cycle (1840)

117a: *Im wunderschönen Monat Mai* (In the marvelous month of May)
CD 9.35   Cassette 9.B

117b: *Ich grolle nicht* (I bear no grudge)
CD 9.36   Cassette 9.B

---

19. Schubert's *Gretchen am Spinnrade* (NAWM 115) sets a scene from Goethe's *Faust* in which Gretchen sits spinning thread while thinking of Faust. How is the spinning wheel depicted in this song? Why is this an effective device for depicting the spinning wheel?

How does this device also capture Gretchen's mood?

Where does the wheel suddenly stop, and then gradually start again? What does this suggest about Gretchen's feelings at this point?

20. Diagram the form of this song. How does Schubert use changes in melody, harmony, and key to portray Gretchen's changing emotions?

21. In *Der Lindenbaum,* how does Schubert use figuration in the piano and contrasts between major and minor to suggest the images and meaning of the poem?

22. The text of *Im wunderschönen Monat Mai* (NAWM 117a) speaks of new love. How does Schumann's music imply, through melody and harmony, that this love is unrequited—as yet all "longing and desire" and no fulfillment? How are the opening piano prelude and closing postlude crucial in conveying this meaning?

23. What is the key of this song? Where does the tonic chord appear? What is unusual about the beginning and ending harmonies?

24. How does Schumann alter the poetry in his setting of *Ich grolle nicht* (NAWM 117b)?

25. In what way is the setting ironic, with the emotional tone of the music contradicting what the words claim?

26. Briefly trace the career of Clara Wieck Schumann.

Music to Study
   NAWM 118: Clara Wieck Schumann, *Geheimes Flüstern hier und dort* (Secret whispers here and there), lied (1853)
      CD 9.37   Cassette 9.B

27. In Clara Schumann's song *Geheimes Flüstern hier und dort* (NAWM 118), how does the figuration in the piano capture the imagery in the poem? In what other ways does the music suit the poetry?

TERMS TO KNOW

lied (nineteenth-century)	ballade (for piano)
mazurka	étude
polonaise	developing variation
tempo rubato	ballad
nocturne	song cycle

NAMES TO KNOW

Wanderer Fantasy	John Field
Lieder ohne Worte (Songs without Words)	George Sand
	Nicolò Paganini
Robert Schumann	*Die schöne Müllerin*
Neue Zeitschrift für Musik	*Winterreise*
Phantasiestücke	*Dichterliebe*
Fryderyk Chopin	Clara Wieck Schumann

REVIEW QUESTIONS

1. Add the composers and major works discussed in this chapter to the time-line you made for chapter 16.

2. Trace the history of piano music in the nineteenth century. Include in your discussion the changed character of the piano and the genres composers used, as well as describing the styles and works of the most prominent composers for the instrument.

3. What are the distinctive features of chamber music in the nineteenth century?

4. Describe the German lied as composed by Schubert and the Schumanns.

OPERA, MUSIC DRAMA, AND CHURCH MUSIC IN THE NINETEENTH CENTURY

18

CHAPTER OBJECTIVES

After you complete the reading, study of the music, and study questions for this chapter, you should be able to:

1. trace the history of opera in France, Italy, and Germany in the nineteenth century and distinguish among the characteristics of each national tradition;
2. define and use terminology associated with nineteenth-century opera;
3. name the most significant composers in each nation and describe the style and approach of each of them;
4. describe characteristic excerpts from operas by Rossini, Bellini, Verdi, Weber, and Wagner; and
5. describe some of the varieties of choral music in the nineteenth century and name some important composers of choral music.

CHAPTER OUTLINE

Prelude (CHWM 412–13)

Nineteenth-century Paris was a center for opera. *Grand opera* combined spectacle and Romantic elements and appealed to a wide audience. Opera was the leading genre in Italy. German Romantic opera joined traits of the Singspiel and grand opera with Romantic literature, and Richard Wagner devised the new form he called *music drama*. Religious choral music varied from revivals of older styles to monumental works intended only for concert performance.

I. French Grand (and Not-So-Grand) Opera (CHWM 413–16)

Grand opera was established by the librettist *Eugène Scribe* (1791–1861) and the composer *Giacomo Meyerbeer* (1791–1864) with *Robert le diable* (Robert the Devil, 1831) and *Les Huguenots* (1836). In these historical dramas, structure and style convey grandeur as well as the plot.

Etude: *Les Huguenots,* Closing Scenes of Act II
Les Huguenots dramatizes the sixteenth-century religious wars in France. Typical of grand opera are massed choruses, soaring melodies, and strong contrasts of mood and sonority.

1. Opéra comique
   Opéra comique used spoken dialogue rather than recitative and featured a smaller cast and simpler music than grand opera. Its plots were comic or romantic rather than historical.

2. Opéra bouffe
   After the 1851 declaration of the Second Empire under Napoleon III, the satiric genre of *opéra bouffe* emerged with *Jacques Offenbach* (1819–1880). His comic style influenced the later operettas of Gilbert and Sullivan in England and of Johann Strauss and others in Vienna.

3. Lyric opera
   Lyric opera lies between comic and grand opera in scale, with romantic plots and a focus on melody. A famous example is *Faust* (1859) by *Charles Gounod* (1818–1893). *Carmen* (1875) by *Georges Bizet* (1838–1875) reflects *exoticism* and a taste for realism.

4. Berlioz
   Berlioz's *La Damnation de Faust* (1846) is a series of scenes for concert rather than stage performance. *Les Troyens* (1856–58) is a Romantic contribution to the operatic tradition of Lully, Rameau, and Gluck.

II. Italian Opera (CHWM 416–18, NAWM 120–21)

1. Rossini
   Gioachino Rossini (1792–1868) was the most successful Italian opera composer of the early nineteenth century. His thirty-two operas include both serious and comic works, all with a strong emphasis on shapely, ornamented melody. Best known today are his comic operas, such as *Il barbiere di Siviglia* (The Barber of Seville, 1816). Many arias move from a slow, highly embellished *cavatina* to a faster, brilliant *cabaletta*. Rossini often combined repetition of an idea with a crescendo to build excitement. He moved to Paris in 1824, wrote some operas in French, and then wrote smaller vocal and piano works.   **Music: NAWM 120**

2. Donizetti
   Gaetano Donizetti (1797–1848) composed about seventy operas, both serious and comic, in a style attuned to the public taste.

3. Bellini
   Vincenzo Bellini (1801–1835) wrote ten serious operas in a refined style. His melodic style influenced Chopin's nocturnes.   **Music: NAWM 121**

III. Giuseppe Verdi (1813–1901) (CHWM 418–22, NAWM 122)

Giuseppe Verdi (1813–1901) was the major figure in Italian opera after Donizetti. He continued the Italian operatic tradition and was a strong nationalist. His operas focus on human drama conveyed through song. His career divides into three periods: to 1853 (the year of *Il trovatore* and *La traviata*), to 1871 (the year of *Aida*), and his last two operas.

1. Early operas
Most of his operas are in four main segments, with ensemble finales in the middle two, a big duet in the third, and a prayer or meditation for the heroine to begin the fourth. His early operas are notable for their choruses. He often mixed a variety of musical forces in a single scene to create a more compelling drama. **Music: NAWM 122**

2. Second-period operas
After 1853 Verdi wrote fewer operas, as he experimented with Parisian grand opera (*Les Vêpres siciliennes,* 1855, and *Don Carlos,* 1867), daring harmonies, comic roles, and *reminiscence motives.*

3. Late operas
After a hiatus, Verdi returned to opera with *Otello* (1887), responding to intervening developments in German and French opera by making the music more continuous and by using several unifying motives. *Falstaff* (1893) takes comic opera to a new level, particularly the ensemble.

Etude: *Otello,* Act IV
In Verdi's *Otello,* the conclusion of the drama unfolds without pause, contrasting lyrical aria with dialogue and interludes to carry the action.

IV. German Romantic Opera (CHWM 422–23, NAWM 123)

Carl Maria von Weber (1786–1826) established the tradition of German Romantic opera with *Der Freischütz* (1821), whose humble characters, supernatural events, wilderness setting, and use of folklike style are typical. The famous Wolf's Glen scene uses *melodrama* (spoken dialogue over music), startling chromatic harmony, and unusual orchestral effects to create an eerie scene. **Music: NAWM 123**

V. Richard Wagner (1813–1883) and the Music Drama (CHWM 423–29, NAWM 124)

Richard Wagner was the most important German opera composer and has been a pivotal figure for music since the middle of the nineteenth century.

1. Early operas
Wagner's *Der fliegende Holländer* (The Flying Dutchman, 1843) set the pattern for his operas with a libretto by the composer himself, a plot based on legend, the use of recurring themes, and the hero's redemption through the loving sacrifice of the heroine. *Lohengrin* (1850) is more continuous, with less division into numbers, more use of recurring themes, and the association of keys with characters.

2. Music dramas
The 1848 Revolution forced Wagner into exile in Switzerland, where he wrote essays on his musical theories and the librettos to his cycle of four music dramas, *Der Ring des Nibelungen* (The Ring of the Nibelungs), whose music he completed over two decades (1853–74). His other music

dramas include *Tristan und Isolde* (1857–59), *Die Meistersinger* (1862–67), and *Parsifal* (1882).

Etude: The Ring of the Nibelungs: A Brief Overview
The four music dramas of *The Ring of the Nibelungs* are linked by a continuous story, common characters, and shared motives.

3. *Gesamtkunstwerk*
Wagner's notion of music drama links drama and music in the service of a single dramatic idea. Together with scenery, staging, and action, they comprise a *Gesamtkunstwerk* (total artwork). Vocal lines are only part of a complete texture in which the orchestra plays a leading role, and music is continuous throughout an act rather than being broken into separate numbers, despite echoes of earlier types such as recitative, aria, and scene.

4. The Leitmotif
In Wagner's music dramas, a person, thing, or idea may be associated with a motive called a *Leitmotif*. By recalling and developing these motives, Wagner creates unity and and makes the music itself the locus of dramatic action.   **Music: NAWM 124**

5. Endless melody
Wagner sought to create an endless melody, a "musical prose" in place of the "poetic" four-square phrases of other composers.

6. Wagner's influence
The complex chromatic chords, constant modulation, and evasion of resolutions that characterize Wagner's harmony in *Tristan und Isolde* created ambiguities that depart from common-practice tonality and led in the music of later composers to new systems of harmony. His concept of opera as a combination of many arts and his notion of continuous music ("endless melody") strongly influenced later composers.

VI. Church Music (CHWM 429–31, NAWM 119)

Some Romantic composers wrote large works on liturgical texts, intended for special occasions or performance in concert rather than in church. Berlioz's *Requiem* (1837) and *Te Deum* (1855) are dramatic symphonies with voices, scored for large orchestras with interesting instrumental effects. Several of Liszt's works are on a similarly large scale. Rossini's *Stabat Mater* (1832, rev. 1841) and Verdi's *Requiem* (1874) are in operatic style, dramatizing their subjects. Brahms's *Ein deutsches Requiem* (A German Requiem, 1868) is a masterpiece of choral writing. Music meant for church services was more modest. *The Cecilian movement,* named after St. Cecilia, the patron saint of music, worked within the Catholic church to revive the style of Palestrina and restore Gregorian chant to purer form. *Anton Bruckner* (1824–1896) was a church organist; his Masses share qualities and some themes with his symphonies, and his motets show the influence of the Cecilian movement.   **Music: NAWM 119**

STUDY QUESTIONS

French Grand (and Not-So-Grand) Opera (CHWM 413–16)

1. What is *grand opera*? In what ways does *Les Huguenots* exemplify the style?

   Who were the librettist and composer for *Les Huguenots*?

   librettist: _____   composer: _____

2. What is *opéra bouffe*, and when and why did it come into existence?

   Who was a major composer of *opéras bouffes*? _____

   Who were major composers of comic opera or operetta in England and Vienna?

   England: _____   Vienna: _____

3. What is *lyric opera*? How does it differ from grand opera and opéra bouffe?

Italian Opera (CHWM 416–18, NAWM 120–21)

4. Briefly trace Rossini's career.

Music to Study
   NAWM 120: Gioachino Rossini, *Il barbiere di Siviglia* (The Barber of
         Seville), opera (1816), Act II, Scene 5: Cavatina, *Una voce poco fa*
      CD 9.39–42   Cassette 9.B
   NAWM 121: Vincenzo Bellini, *Norma,* opera (1831), Act I, Scene 4: Scena e
         Cavatina, *Casta diva*
      CD 10.1–5   Cassette 10.A

5. What is a *cavatina*? What is a *cabaletta*? Where are these types represented in
   Rosina's aria *Una voce poco fa* from Rossini's *Il barbiere di Siviglia*
   (NAWM 120)? How do they correspond to and help to convey what Rosina is
   saying and feeling?

6. How does Rossini's style compare to the operatic styles of Pergolesi (NAWM
   87), Hasse (NAWM 88), Gluck (NAWM 91), and Mozart (NAWM 103)?

7. In the scene from *Norma* (NAWM 121), how does Bellini use the contrast of
   cavatina and cabaletta to convey Norma's inner conflict?

8. What does Bellini add to the scene, beyond the cavatina and cabaletta sections of an aria? How do these added elements heighten the conflict? (If it is useful, chart out the scene, noting changes of tempo and performing forces.)

9. Compare the melodic writing of Bellini's Andante section to that in the Andante section of Rossini's *Una voce poco fa* (NAWM 120). What differences and similarities do you see? What characteristics mark the styles of Rossini and Bellini in their slow arias?

10. Now compare both to the melodic writing in Chopin's Nocturne in E-flat Major (NAWM 112). What does Chopin's melodic style have in common with Rossini's? With Bellini's?

Giuseppe Verdi (1813–1901) (CHWM 418–22, NAWM 122)

11. In what ways was Verdi a nationalist composer? How was his name used as a nationalist emblem?

12. Describe the three periods of Verdi's career and the main features of each.

Music to Study

> **NAWM 122:** Giuseppe Verdi, *Il trovatore* (The Troubadour), opera (1853),
> Part 4, Scene 1, No. 12: Scene, Aria, and *Miserere*
> CD 10.6–9 (Concise 3.67–68)   Cassette 10.A (Concise 3.B)

13. How does Verdi use various musical forces, textures, and types to further the drama in this scene from *Il trovatore* (NAWM 122)? How does this compare with the textures and types used in the excerpts from Rossini's *Il barbiere di Siviglia* (NAWM 120) and Bellini's *Norma* (NAWM 121)?

14. In the slow aria section of the scene, *D'amor sull'ali rosee*, how does Verdi's melodic style compare to that of the slow arias in the excerpts from Rossini and Bellini (NAWM 120–21, and see question 9 above)?

German Romantic Opera (CHWM 422–23, NAWM 123)

Music to Study
   NAWM 123: Carl Maria von Weber, *Der Freischütz* (The Free Shot), opera
      (1821), Act II, Finale (Wolf's Glen Scene)
   CD 10.10–20   Cassette 10.A

15. What is *melodrama*? How is it used in the Wolf's Glen scene from Weber's
   Der Freischütz (NAWM 123)? Why do you think it might be more effective
   here than recitative?

16. What supernatural events happen in the Wolf's Glen scene? For each one,
   how does Weber depict it in the music? How does he use tritones, diminished
   or augmented harmonies, orchestration, sudden dynamic change, or other
   effects to create a feeling of the supernatural or spooky? (Note: In examining
   the harmony, remember that the clarinets in A sound a minor third lower
   than written; the horns in D a minor seventh lower than written; and the
   trumpets in D a whole step higher than written.)

Richard Wagner and the Music Drama (CHWM 423–29, NAWM 124)

17. Who wrote the librettos for Wagner's operas and music dramas? _____

18. What does *Gesamtkunstwerk* mean? What is its importance for Wagner?

Music to Study
   NAWM 124: Richard Wagner, *Tristan und Isolde* (1857–59), excerpt from
         Act I, Scene 5
   CD 10.21–29 (Concise 4.1–9)   Cassette 10.B (Concise 4.A)

19. How do text, action, scenery, and music reinforce each other in this scene
    from *Tristan und Isolde* (NAWM 124)? How is this like, and how is it differ-
    ent from, the scene from Verdi's *Il trovatore* in NAWM 122?

20. In the section from m. 132 to 188, how do the singers' melodies relate to the
    melodies in the orchestra? Where does the musical continuity lie, with the
    singers or with the orchestra? How does this compare to the excerpts from
    operas by Rossini, Bellini, and Verdi in NAWM 120–22?

21. How do Wagner's vocal melodies here and throughout the scene compare to
    those of Rossini, Bellini, and Verdi in NAWM 120–22? Include observations
    on phrasing and overall shape as well as on vocal embellishment. What are
    the main characteristics of Wagner's vocal style?

22. What is a *Leitmotif*? Where do leitmotifs appear in this scene from *Tristan und Isolde*, and how are they used? (Note: Several appeared earlier, in the overture, and will recur in Acts II and III.)

23. How does the harmonic language used for the sailors (e.g., at mm. 196–203, "Hail! King Mark, hail!") differ from that used for Tristan and Isolde after they have drunk the love potion? Why is this contrast appropriate, and how does it heighten the drama?

24. What aspects of Wagner's music were especially influential on later composers?

Church Music (CHWM 429–31, NAWM 119)

25. How do Berlioz's *Requiem* and *Te Deum* differ from traditional church music of the previous hundred years?

26. What was the *Cecilian movement*, and what were its goals?

Music to Study
   NAWM 119: Anton Bruckner, *Virga Jesse,* motet (1885)
      CD 9.38   Cassette 9.B

27. How does Bruckner evoke or suggest sixteenth-century polyphony in his
    motet *Virga Jesse* (NAWM 119)?

28. What elements in the music make clear that this could not have been written
    earlier than the nineteenth century?

TERMS TO KNOW

grand opera
music drama
opéra comique
opéra bouffe
lyric opera
exoticism
cavatina

cabaletta
reminiscence motive
melodrama
Gesamtkunstwerk
Leitmotif
the Cecilian movement

NAMES TO KNOW

Names Related to French Opera

Eugène Scribe
Giacomo Meyerbeer
Robert le diable
Les Huguenots
Jacques Offenbach
Faust

Charles Gounod
Carmen
Georges Bizet
La Damnation de Faust
Les Troyens

Names Related to Italian Opera

Gioachino Rossini
The Barber of Seville
Gaetano Donizetti
Vincenzo Bellini
Giuseppe Verdi
Il trovatore

La traviata
Aida
Les Vêpres siciliennes
Don Carlos
Otello
Falstaff

Names Related to German Opera and Music Drama

Carl Maria von Weber
Der Freischütz
Richard Wagner
Der fliegende Holländer (The Flying Dutchman)

Lohengrin
Der Ring des Nibelungen
Tristan und Isolde
Die Meistersinger
Parsifal

Names Related to Church Music

Berlioz: Requiem, Te Deum
Rossini: Stabat Mater
Verdi: Requiem

Ein deutsches Requiem (A German Requiem)
Anton Bruckner

REVIEW QUESTIONS

1. Add the composers and major works discussed in this chapter to the time-line you made for chapter 16.

2. What types of opera were written for production in Paris in the nineteenth century? Trace the emergence of the new types of opera, name a significant composer and opera for each type, and briefly describe what makes each type distinctive.

3. Describe the operas and operatic styles of Rossini, Bellini, and Verdi, noting the similarities and differences among them. Use examples from NAWM 120–22 to illustrate your points.

4. Trace the development of Verdi's operas through his three periods. What changed, and what remained constant?

5. How does the German Romantic opera of Weber and early Wagner differ from Italian and French opera in the first half of the nineteenth century? Use examples from the works excerpted in NAWM or described in CHWM to support your answer.

6. Describe the mature style of Wagner in his music dramas, using the scene from *Tristan und Isolde* in NAWM 124 as an example. At the end of your essay, explain the elements of this style that were particularly influential on later composers.

7. Choose two composers of choral music in the nineteenth century (such as Berlioz and Bruckner) and contrast their approaches. As part of your answer, describe at least one work by each composer.

EUROPEAN MUSIC FROM THE 1870s TO WORLD WAR I

19

CHAPTER OBJECTIVES

After you complete the reading, study of the music, and study questions for this chapter, you should be able to:

1. name some of the most prominent European composers active in the late nineteenth and early twentieth centuries, characterize their styles, and describe some of their music;
2. describe the varieties of musical nationalism that were prominent at this time;
3. define and describe impressionism and related trends in music of this period.

CHAPTER OUTLINE

Prelude (CHWM 433)

After Wagner, the search for an individual voice led composers in many different directions, undermining the shared conventions of the Classic and Romantic eras, including tonality. Nationalism prompted composers in Russia and eastern Europe to forge independent idioms, and new currents developed in France and Italy.

I. The German Tradition (CHWM 434–44, NAWM 125–27)

A. *Hugo Wolf*

Hugo Wolf (1860–1903) brought to his 250 lieder Wagner's harmony and ideal of fusing voice and instrument. Wolf chose excellent poets and sought equality between words and music. The musical continuity is often in the piano, while the voice has a speechlike arioso.   **Music: NAWM 125**

B. *Gustav Mahler*

Gustav Mahler (1860–1911) made a career as a conductor, directing the Vienna Opera (1897–1907) and the New York Philharmonic (1909–11). He completed nine symphonies and five song cycles with orchestra.

1. Symphonies

   Mahler's symphonies are long and often programmatic. He used a large orchestra but frequently created delicate effects with unusual instruments and combinations. Several symphonies are based in part on his songs, and four include voices. Four symphonies begin and end in different keys.

Etude: Mahler's Fourth Symphony

   Mahler included a greater diversity of elements and styles than did earlier symphonists, seeking to "construct a world" in all its variety, as in the Fourth Symphony. His music often suggests irony or parody.

2. Songs with orchestral accompaniment

   The orchestral song cycle *Kindertotenlieder* (Songs of Dead Children, 1901–4) uses the large orchestra and chromatic harmony of Wagner in a spare, haunting style. *Das Lied von der Erde* (The Song of the Earth, 1908), on poems translated from Chinese, alternates between ecstasy and resignation. **Music: NAWM 126**

C. *Strauss*

   Richard Strauss (1864–1949) is renowned for his symphonic poems, most of them written before 1900, and operas, most of them from after 1900. Like Mahler, he was also well known as a conductor.

1. Symphonic poems

   Symphonic poems may have a philosophical program, like Strauss's *Also sprach Zarathustra* (So Spoke Zoroaster, 1896, after a poem by Nietzsche), or a descriptive tale, like his *Till Eulenspiegels lustige Streiche* (Till Eulenspiegel's Merry Pranks, 1895) and *Don Quixote* (1897). In each, the transformation of motives with extramusical connections helps to convey the plot, as in Wagner's music dramas. **Music: NAWM 127**

2. Operas

   Strauss achieved new fame as an opera composer with *Salome* (1903–5), whose decadent subject he captured with heightened dissonance that soon influenced the growth of musical expressionism and the dissolution of tonality. *Der Rosenkavalier* (The Rose-Bearing Cavalier, 1910) has a lighter setting and plot and is thus less dissonant and more melodious.

Etude: Strauss's *Elektra*

   Elektra (1908) uses sharp, apparently unresolved dissonance contrasted with diatonic passages to tell the tragic story, along with leitmotifs and the association of certain keys with characters.

II. Nationalism (CHWM 444–51, NAWM 128–29)

   Nationalism in the nineteenth and early twentieth centuries was an attempt to capture in music the character of one's own people, through the choice of patriotic subjects or topics drawn from national literature and the use of national, folk, or folklike melodies or rhythms. Composers in Russia, eastern Europe, England, France, and the United States especially sought a national style.

A. *Russia*

1. Glinka
Mikhail Glinka (1804–1857) was the first Russian composer to be recognized for a distinctively Russian style, notably in his operas.

2. Tchaikovsky
Piotr Il'yich Tchaikovsky (1840–1893) was more a cosmopolitan than a nationalist, but chose Russian subjects for his operas.

3. The Mighty Handful
The Mighty Handful (or Mighty Five) was a group of five composers who sought a fresh Russian style founded on folk music and exoticism. The group included Alexander Borodin, César Cui, Mily Balakirev, *Modest Musorgsky* (1839–1881), and *Nikolay Rimsky-Korsakov* (1844–1908.)

4. Musorgsky
Musorgsky was the most original of the Five. In his opera *Boris Godunov* (premiered 1874) and his songs, his vocal melodies follow Russian speech accents closely and imitate Russian folksong, his harmony is innovative, and his music depicts physical gestures realistically.   **Music: NAWM 128**

5. Rimsky-Korsakov
Rimsky-Korsakov was one of the Five but later developed a broader, still nationalist idiom. He taught at the St. Petersburg Conservatory and was a master of orchestration. His principal works are symphonic poems and operas, which often render human characters in a diatonic, modal style and supernatural characters and events in a chromatic, fanciful style marked by *whole-tone* and *octatonic scales* (respectively, scales made up of all whole tones or whole and half steps in strict alternation).

6. Rakhmaninov
Sergei Rakhmaninov (1873–1943), a virtuoso pianist, wrote passionate, melodious piano concertos and symphonic works in a style that was Romantic and sometimes Russian but not deliberately nationalist.

7. Skryabin
Alexander Skryabin (1872–1915) wrote mostly for the piano, beginning in a style derived from Chopin and evolving to an individual style that was no longer tonal but used a complex chord or collection of notes as a reference point akin to a tonic chord. He sought a synthesis of the arts and intended his orchestral work *Prometheus* (1910) to be performed with changing colored lights.   **Music: NAWM 129**

B. *Nationalism in Other Countries*

1. Bohemia
Bedřich Smetana (1824–1884) and Antonin Dvořák, the principal Czech composers of the nineteenth century, chose national subjects for program music and operas. *Leoš Janáček* (1854–1928) collected folk music and based his style on Moravian speech and song.

2. Norway

   Edvard Grieg (1843–1907) was a nationalist who incorporated Norwegian national traits particularly in his short piano pieces and vocal works.

3. Finland

   Finnish composer *Jean Sibelius* (1865–1957) drew programs and song texts from the literature of Finland. He does not use or imitate folksongs. He is known for symphonies, symphonic poems, and the Violin Concerto.

4. England

   Edward Elgar (1857–1934) wrote in a style derived from Brahms and Wagner rather than from English folksong.

5. Spain

   Spanish nationalism was sparked by the operas of *Felipe Pedrell* (1841–1922) and piano music of *Isaac Albeniz* (1860–1909). The major Spanish composer of the early twentieth century was *Manuel de Falla* (1876–1946), who used rhythms and melodic turns from Spanish popular music.

III. New Currents in France (CHWM 451–59, NAWM 130–32)

The *National Society for French Music* (founded 1871) performed music of living French composers and revived French music of the sixteenth through eighteenth centuries, helping to strengthen an independent French musical tradition. Three traditions coexisted in French music after 1871: a cosmopolitan tradition around Franck, a French tradition around Camille Saint-Saëns and Fauré, and a new style developed by Debussy.

1. Cosmopolitan tradition

   César Franck (1822–1890) worked in instrumental genres and oratorio, enriching a restrained, traditional idiom with counterpoint and cyclic form.

2. French tradition

   French music from Couperin to Gounod is typified by emotional reserve, lyricism, economy, refinement, and interest in well-ordered form rather than self-expression.

3. Fauré

   Gabriel Fauré (1845–1924) worked as an organist, taught composition at the Paris Conservatoire, and became its director. His refined songs, piano pieces, and chamber works are marked by lyrical melodies, lack of virtuosic display, and harmony that does not drive toward a resolution, but instead suggests repose. His students include Ravel and *Nadia Boulanger* (1887–1979), who taught many later composers.   **Music: NAWM 130**

4. Debussy

   Claude Debussy (1862–1918) had a major influence on twentieth-century music. He blended traits of French music, Wagner, and Musorgsky. Although his music usually has a tonal center, the harmony is often coloristic and the strong pull to resolution is missing, creating a sense of movement without direction and of pleasure without urgency. His orchestration features a great variety of sounds and colors. His most important music includes orchestral pieces, piano works, and the opera *Pelléas et Mélisande* (1902).   **Music: NAWM 131**

5. Satie

Erik Satie (1865–1925) consistently opposed sentimentality, from his early deliberately simple works to his later piano pieces marked by parody, wit, surreal titles, and satirical commentary printed in the score.

6. Ravel

Maurice Ravel (1875–1937) looked back to the eighteenth-century French tradition in *Le Tombeau de Couperin* (for piano 1917, orchestrated 1919) and other works. His music features clear forms, functional harmonies, and colorful orchestration.   **Music: NAWM 132**

Window: Impressionism (CHWM 456–57)

Debussy's style, called *impressionism* by analogy with the impressionist painters, suggests a mood or atmosphere rather than expressing the deep emotions of Romanticism.

IV. Italian Opera (CHWM 459–60)

One trend in Italian opera in the late nineteenth century is *verismo* (realism or naturalism), which sought a realistic depiction of everyday people in extreme dramatic situations. *Giacomo Puccini* (1858–1924) was an eclectic composer who combined realism and exoticism with intense emotion through a style focused on melody over spare accompaniment.

STUDY QUESTIONS

The German Tradition (CHWM 434–44, NAWM 125–27)

1. What texts did Wolf choose for his songs, and what was his approach to the relationship of music and poetry?

Music to Study
   NAWM 125: Hugo Wolf, *Kennst du das Land,* Lied (1888)
      CD 10.30–37   Cassette 10.B

2. Compare Wolf's vocal style in *Kennst du das Land* (NAWM 125) to that of Schubert's lieder (NAWM 115–16) and to that of Wagner's *Tristan und Isolde* (NAWM 124). What are the similarities and differences in each comparison? Which earlier composer does Wolf's style resemble most?

3. How does the piano part in Wolf's song compare to the piano parts in Schubert's lieder? What aspects of Wagner's operatic style does it incorporate?

4. Describe the characteristics of Mahler's symphonies that distinguish them from other nineteenth-century symphonies. How are these characteristics exemplified in the Fourth Symphony, as excerpted and discussed in CHWM, pp. 437–39? How does Mahler suggest a varied world in this work?

Music to Study
> **NAWM 126:** Gustav Mahler, *Kindertotenlieder*, song cycle with orchestra
> (1901–4), No. 1: *Nun will die Sonn' so hell aufgeh'n* (Now the sun
> will rise again)
> CD 10.38–39 (Concise 4.10–11)   Cassette 10.B (Concise 4.A)

5. Mahler's setting of *Nun will die Sonn' so hell aufgeh'n* (NAWM 126) high-
lights the irony in the poem. In the poem, the tragedy that has befallen the
speaker—the death of his child during the night—is ignored by the sun,
which rises as if nothing bad has happened. Mahler heightens the irony by
mismatching sad, lonely music to the bright, warm images in the first line of
the poem, and bright, warm music to the sadness of the second line. Later
repetition or reworking of these contrasting musical ideas is also ironic.

a. How is the effect of sadness and loneliness achieved in the music for the
first line? How does the contour of the vocal line negate the poetic image of a
rising sun?

b. How does the music of the second line suggest the rising sun and the
warming earth?

c. How does the varied repetition of this opening section in mm. 22–40 continue or expand upon the ironic setting of the first two lines of the poem?

d. How does the music in mm. 40–63 work against the apparently comfort-
ing message of the text?

e. What indication is there in the music at the end of the song that the protagonist utters the final line, "Blessed be the joyous light of the world," with
irony rather than with sincerity?

6. How does Mahler use the orchestra in this song? How is it different from Wagner's use of the orchestra in the excerpt from *Tristan und Isolde* (NAWM 124)?

7. What two kinds of program did Richard Strauss use in his symphonic poems? Which does he use in *Don Quixote* (NAWM 127)?

Music to Study
    NAWM 127: Richard Strauss, *Don Quixote*, symphonic poem (1897), excerpts: Themes and Variations 1 and 2
    CD 10.40–45 (Concise 4.12–17)   Cassette 10.B (Concise 4.A)

8. How does Strauss depict Don Quixote? How does he depict Sancho Panza?

How are these themes treated and varied in the first two variations, given in NAWM 127?

---

9. Based on the descriptions of *Salome, Elektra,* and *Der Rosenkavalier* in CHWM, pp. 442–44, what is distinctive about each of these operas?

Nationalism (CHWM 444–51, NAWM 128–29)

10. What was the role of Glinka in the creation of a Russian national music?

Music to Study
   NAWM 128: Modest Musorgsky, *Bez solntsa* (Sunless), song cycle (1874),
      No. 3, *O konchen praedny* (The idle, noisy day is over)
      CD 11.1–2 (Concise 4.18–19)   Cassette 11.A (Concise 4.A)

11. What is unusual about the harmony in Musorgsky's *O konchen praedny*
    (NAWM 128)? Describe some unusual progressions.

12. How does the vocal line in Musorgsky's song compare to that of the other
    nineteenth-century songs you have studied, by Schubert, Robert Schumann,
    Clara Schumann, and Hugo Wolf (NAWM 115–18 and 125)?

---

13. Briefly describe the styles and contributions of Rimsky-Korsakov and
    Rakhmaninov.

Music to Study
> **NAWM 129:** Alexander Skryabin, *Vers la flamme* (Toward the flame), poem
> for piano, Op. 72 (1914)
> CD 11.3–5   Cassette 11.A

14. *Vers la flamme* (NAWM 129) is not tonal in a traditional sense. What kinds of
    chords does Skryabin use? How does he create a sense of tonal motion? What
    chord progressions (or root progressions) does he use most frequently?

15. What is the relationship between the opening passage of the piece and the
    closing passage (mm. 107–37) in terms of theme, rhythm, and harmony?
    How is a sense achieved of ending on a kind of tonic chord?

16. Describe the rhythm of this piece. Does it suggest a strong forward motion,
    or a static hovering? How is the effect achieved?

17. Name nationalist composers active in Czech regions, Norway, Finland, and
    Spain in the late nineteenth and early twentieth centuries and briefly describe
    what made their music nationalist.

New Currents in France (CHWM 451–59, NAWM 130–32)

18. What was the National Society for French Music? When was it founded, what did it do, and what was its importance?

Music to Study
    NAWM 130: Gabriel Fauré, *La bonne chanson* (The Good Song), Op. 61, song cycle (1891), No. 6, *Avant que tu ne t'en ailles* (Before you depart)
        CD 11.6–10   Cassette 11.A
    NAWM 131: Claude Debussy, *Nocturnes*, tone poem suite (1899), No. 1: *Nuages* (Clouds)
        CD 11.11–16 (Concise 4.20–25)   Cassette 11.A (Concise 4.A)

19. What are the characteristics of Fauré's melodic and harmonic style, and how are they exemplified in *Avant que tu ne t'en ailles* (NAWM 130)?

20. How does Debussy use harmony in *Nuages* (NAWM 131) to create a sense of movement without direction, like clouds?

21. The motive in the English horn (here notated C–B–A–G#–F# and sounding a fifth lower) is never played by another instrument (while the English horn never plays anything else), it is never transposed, and it is changed only by omitting notes until all that remains is B–A–F# (as notated). How does this treatment of a motive differ from motivic development as practiced in the nineteenth century? If motivic development suggests a drama or story, with the motives as characters, in what ways does Debussy's approach suggest a visual impression, rather than a plot?

22. How does the section at mm. 64–79 imitate a Javanese gamelan?

23. How does Debussy use the orchestra? How does this reinforce the sense of a visual impression moving without direction, rather than a drama with conflict and resolution?

24. Briefly describe Satie's musical aesthetic and style.

Music to Study

    NAWM 132: Maurice Ravel, *Le Tombeau de Couperin,* suite (1917, orchestrated 1919), excerpt: Menuet

        CD 11.17–22   Cassette 11.A

25. What does Ravel's minuet have in common with eighteenth-century music?

26. Compare Ravel's minuet to Debussy's *Nuages* (NAWM 131). How are they similar? What is most different?

Italian Opera (CHWM 459–60)

27. What is *verismo*? What are some notable examples of it?

TERMS TO KNOW

nationalism   impressionism
whole-tone scale   verismo
octatonic scale

NAMES TO KNOW

Names Related to the German Tradition

Hugo Wolf   *Also sprach Zarathustra*
Gustav Mahler   *Till Eulenspiegels lustige Streiche*
Mahler's Fourth Symphony   *Don Quixote*
Kindertotenlieder   *Salome*
Das Lied von der Erde   *Elektra*
Richard Strauss   *Der Rosenkavalier*

Names Related to Nationalism in Eastern and Northern Europe and Spain

Mikhail Glinka	Bedřich Smetana
Piotr Il'yich Tchaikovsky	Leoš Janáček
The Mighty Handful	Edvard Grieg
Modest Musorgsky	Jean Sibelius
Boris Godunov	Edward Elgar
Nikolay Rimsky–Korsakov	Felipe Pedrell
Sergei Rakhmaninov	Isaac Albeniz
Alexander Skryabin	Manuel de Falla

Names Related to French and Italian Music

National Society for French Music	*Pelléas et Mélisande*
César Franck	Erik Satie
Gabriel Fauré	Maurice Ravel
Nadia Boulanger	*Le Tombeau de Couperin*
Claude Debussy	Giacomo Puccini

REVIEW QUESTIONS

1. Add the composers and major works from the nineteenth century discussed in this chapter to the time-line you made for chapter 16. Make a new time-line for the entire twentieth century, and place on it the twentieth-century composers and major works discussed here. Leave plenty of space, as you will be adding to it in chapters 20–22.

2. How did Wolf, Mahler, and Strauss respond to the German Romantic tradition from Beethoven through Wagner? What elements did they continue in their music, what aspects did they further intensify or develop, and what did they introduce that was new and individual?

3. What is nationalism, and how is it manifest in music of the nineteenth and early twentieth centuries?

4. Beethoven's music conveys a sense of drama and forward motion toward a goal, as in the first movement of his *Eroica* Symphony (NAWM 106). Some of the music studied in this chapter conveys a different sense, of harmonic and rhythmic stasis, or of movement that is not directed toward a goal. Compare the works you have studied by Musorgsky, Skryabin, Fauré, and Debussy (NAWM 128–31) with Beethoven and with each other, seeking to show what musical techniques these later composers use to avoid tension, negate forward momentum, and create a musical experience of being present in the moment, rather than striving toward a goal.

5. For any of the following pairs of composers, compare and contrast their musical styles and aesthetics, showing what they have in common as composers from the same nation and what is individual about each: Mahler and Strauss; Musorgsky and Skryabin; Debussy and Ravel.

THE EUROPEAN
MAINSTREAM IN THE
TWENTIETH CENTURY

20

CHAPTER OBJECTIVES

After you complete the reading, study of the music, and study questions for this chapter, you should be able to:

1. identify some of the factors that have led to a diversity of style and technique in the twentieth century that is greater than in any previous era;
2. name some of the most significant composers active after World War I in Hungary, Russia, England, Germany, and France and describe what makes their music individual;
3. describe the synthesis of folk and classical elements in the music of Bartók;
4. describe the music of Shostakovich and his circumstances under the Soviet regime;
5. summarize the careers and describe the musical styles of Hindemith and Stravinsky.

CHAPTER OUTLINE

Prelude (CHWM 462–64)

After World War I, the division of the former Austro-Hungarian Empire and the rise of totalitarian regimes in Russia, Italy, Spain, and Germany reduced cultural interaction between nations and led to a growing diversity in musical trends. Some composers abandoned common-practice tonality and thematic development. Folk and traditional music from Eastern Europe and Asia suggested new possibilities in rhythm and pitch organization. Recordings, radio, and television broadened the audiences for both popular and art music around the world. Composers of film music and of *Gebrauchsmusik* (music for use) for schools and amateurs sought more accessible idioms. *Neo-Classic music* evoked forms and styles of the eighteenth century. In some times and places, government control limited what composers could do; elsewhere, composers went beyond what audiences would accept. The diversity of music in the twentieth century is unprecedented, as composers have sought individual paths even within wider trends.

I. Ethnic Contexts (CHWM 464–69, NAWM 133)

New recording technologies aided the collection and study of the music of traditional peoples. Rather than changing this music to fit art music, as had been done in the previous century, composers used it to create new styles.

1. Bartók

Béla Bartók (1881–1945) collected and published folk tunes from his native Hungary, Romania, and elsewhere. Besides arranging or borrowing folk tunes in his music, he synthesized a personal style that united folk and art music. He was also a pianist and a piano teacher, and his *Mikrokosmos* (1926–37) is a series of graded piano pieces that encapsulates his style. He worked in traditional forms, with a distinguished series of string quartets, sonatas, and concertos. From the Western tradition he took imitative and fugal techniques, sonata and other forms, and thematic development; from eastern Europe, modal and other scales, irregular meters, harmonic seconds and fourths, and certain types of melody. Most of his music has a tonal center, but this is established in novel ways. **Music: NAWM 133**

Etude: Bartók's *Music for Strings, Percussion, and Celesta*
Music for Strings, Percussion, and Celesta (1936) has a tonal center on A, with a secondary center a tritone away. The middle movements also feature a tritone relationship, between C and F-sharp. The piece shows Bartók's fondness for symmetry and his incorporation of elements of folk style.

2. Kodály

Zoltán Kodály (1882–1967) collected Hungarian folk tunes and developed a strongly nationalist style. He was well known as a music educator.

II. The Soviet Orbit (CHWM 469–73, NAWM 134–35)

1. Prokofiev

Sergey Prokofiev (1891–1953) left Russia after the 1917 Revolution, toured as a pianist, and composed on commission. He returned to the Soviet Union in 1934 and wrote some of his most popular music there. Soviet authorities demanded that composers adhere to the concept of *socialist realism* and attacked Prokofiev for *formalism*.

2. Shostakovich

Dmitri Shostakovich (1906–1985) was the most prominent composer to spend his entire career under the Soviet state, which supported him yet sought to control him. His opera *Lady Macbeth of Mtsensk* (1932) was a success until it was condemned by the official newspaper *Pravda* in 1936. **Music: NAWM 135**

Etude: Shostakovich's Fifth Symphony
The Fifth Symphony shows Shostakovich's blending of Russian influences with international ones, especially Mahler.

3. Post-Soviet music
The relaxation of state control in the 1970s allowed younger composers to learn more about music in the West, and exchanges have intensified since the 1991 dissolution of the Soviet Union. *Alfred Schnittke* (b. 1934) often incorporates existing music or refers to Baroque and popular styles to produce music that is *polystylistic. Sofia Gubaidulina* (b. 1931) writes music with a spiritual dimension, often inspired by Christian themes.   **Music: NAWM 134**

III. England (CHWM 473–75)

1. Vaughan Williams
Ralph Vaughan Williams (1872–1958) drew on English folksong, hymnody, and earlier English composers and wrote in a mixed tonal and modal style. (His first name is pronounced "Rafe," and his last name is "Vaughan Williams," not "Williams.")

2. Britten
Benjamin Britten (1913–1976) is known for his choral works, especially the *War Requiem* (1962), and his operas. Mixing diatonic tonality with modal and chromatic effects, his music uses simple means to convey deep human emotions.

IV. Germany (CHWM 475–78, NAWM 136)

Nazi policies in the 1930s hindered modern music in Germany and led many musicians to leave.

1. Hindemith
Paul Hindemith (1895–1963) was important as a composer and teacher. Concerned about the growing gulf between composers and the public, in the late 1920s he began to compose *Gebrauchsmusik* in an accessible style. His opera *Mathis der Maler* (Matthias the Painter, 1934-35) examines the role of the artist in a time of political turmoil.   **Music: NAWM 136**

2. Weill
Kurt Weill (1900–1950) composed operas on librettos by Bertolt Brecht, notably *Die Dreigroschenoper* (The Threepenny Opera, 1928). After the Nazis rose to power in 1933, Weill emigrated to the United States and had a second career writing Broadway musicals.

Etude: Weill's *Mahagonny*
In *The Rise and Fall of the City of Mahagonny* (1927–31), Brecht and Weill sought to promote a social ideology. Weill used an easily understood musical language that parodied American popular music.

V. Neo-Classicism in France (CHWM 479–81)

Composers in the first half of the twentieth century often imitated styles and genres from earlier periods. Music that referred to eighteenth-century models was frequently called *neo-Classic*. When the reference is to the early eighteenth century, some writers now prefer the term neo-Baroque.

1. Honegger
Arthur Honegger (1892–1955) is best known for his opera-oratorio *King David* (1921).

2. Milhaud
Prolific in almost every genre, *Darius Milhaud* (1892–1974) absorbed a variety of influences, from earlier French composers to Brazilian music, ragtime, and blues. He frequently used *polytonality,* in which two or more streams of music, each implying a different key, are superimposed.

3. Poulenc
Francis Poulenc (1899–1963) wrote in an engaging style influenced by French popular song and eighteenth-century French composers.

VI. Stravinsky (CHWM 481–91, NAWM 137)

Igor Stravinsky (1882–1971) took part in most major compositional trends during his lifetime. He made his reputation with three early ballets commissioned by Sergei Diaghilev for the Russian Ballet in Paris. All use Russian folk melodies and plots from Russian culture.

1. *The Fire Bird*
The Fire Bird (1910) continues the exoticism and colorful orchestration of Rimsky-Korsakov, Stravinsky's teacher.

Etude: Stravinsky's *Petrushka*
Some of Stravinsky's distinctive stylistic traits emerge in the second ballet, *Petrushka* (1911), including independent superimposed layers of sound, blocks of sound that alternate without transitions, repetitive melodies and rhythms over static harmony; and octatonic and polytonal sonorities.

2. *Le Sacre du printemps*
Le Sacre du printemps (The Rite of Spring, 1913) adds to those elements new orchestral effects, heightened dissonance, and rhythm whose changing meters and unexpected accents negate regular meter and emphasize instead the basic pulse, suggesting a musical *primitivism. Le Sacre* precipitated a riot at its premiere, but all three ballets have since become Stravinsky's most popular works. **Music: NAWM 137**

3. 1913–1923
Partly due to economic necessity, Stravinsky's works during and just after World War I are for smaller ensembles.

4. Stravinsky's neo-Classicism
From the 1920s to 1951, Stravinsky adopted a neo-Classic approach that abandoned the Russian tunes and extramusical concerns of his earlier works and sought to create abstract, objective music based on historical models. This was inaugurated by his reworkings of eighteenth-century music in the ballet *Pulcinella* (1919) and continued in a series of works that evoked earlier styles, particularly the Classic era, yet continued to show the personal characteristics exemplified in *Le Sacre du printemps*. In works of the 1950s and 1960s, Stravinsky adapted the serial techniques of Schoenberg and Webern.

Etude: *The Rake's Progress*

Stravinsky's opera *The Rake's Progress* (1951) is based on engravings by William Hogarth and modeled after eighteenth-century opera.

Window: Nijinsky's Lost Ballet (CHWM 486–87)

Vaslav Nijinsky (1888–1950) was the Russian dancer and choreographer who created the dance for Stravinsky's *Le Sacre du printemps*. The dance was not filmed, but a reconstruction was made in the 1980s by choreographer Robert Joffrey and danced by his company, the Joffrey Ballet.

STUDY QUESTIONS

Prelude (CHWM 462–64)

1. What were some of the factors that led to the diversity of musical aesthetics, styles, and procedures in the twentieth century?

Ethnic Contexts (CHWM 464–69, NAWM 133)

2. What were Bartók's activities in music, in addition to composing?

Music to Study

    NAWM 133: Béla Bartók, *Music for Strings, Percussion, and Celesta,* suite (1936), third movement: Adagio
        CD 11.23–28 (Concise 4.26–31)   Cassette 11.A (Concise 4.A)

3. In the slow movement of *Music for Strings, Percussion, and Celesta* (NAWM 133), how does Bartók use mirrors, retrogrades, and palindromes? (A palindrome is its own retrograde, as in the palindrome about Napoleon, "Able was I ere I saw Elba.")

---

4. What elements of East European folk music are used in this movement?

5. This movement also uses techniques derived from Western art music, in addition to the use of traditional orchestral instruments and a complex arch form. Find instances of the following:

   imitation and canon _____

   ostinato _____

   inversion of melodic material _____

   rhythmic diminution of material _____

6. Bartók's synthesis of the folk and art music traditions creates something new within the realm of the orchestral repertory. List the ways in which this movement offers new sounds and ideas, in comparison with twentieth-century symphonic music. (You may use NAWM 106, 108, 109, and 127 as points of comparison.)

The Soviet Orbit (CHWM 469–73, NAWM 134–35)

7. As used by Soviet authorities, what is *socialist realism*? What is *formalism*? How did Prokofiev and Shostakovich attempt to conform to the demand for socialist realism?

Music to Study

>   **NAWM 135:** Dmitri Shostakovich, *Lady Macbeth of Mtsensk,* opera (1932), Act IV, Scene 9, excerpt
>   CD 11.33–37   Cassette 11.B
>   **NAWM 134:** Sofia Gubaidulina, *Rejoice!* Sonata for violin and violoncello (1981), fifth movement, "Listen to the still small voice within"
>   CD 11.29–32 (Concise 4.32–35)   Cassette 11.A (Concise 4.B)

8. What characteristics of Shostakovich's *Lady Macbeth of Mtsensk* displeased the Soviet authorities? Once you translate the negative words of the *Pravda* article into neutral or positive ones, which of these traits, if any, appear in the excerpt in NAWM 135?

9. Describe the main elements of Shostakovich's style in this excerpt. How does it compare to the operatic style of Wagner (see NAWM 124) and Verdi (see NAWM 122)? How does it differ from Bartók's style in *Music for Strings, Percussion, and Celesta* (NAWM 133), written around the same time?

10. What spiritual lesson does Sofia Gubaidulina seek to convey in the movement from *Rejoice!* (NAWM 134)? How is it conveyed in the music?

11. How does Gubaidulina use repetition, variation, and contrast in this movement? How is this like traditional eighteenth- and nineteenh-century procedures, and how is it different?

England (CHWM 473–75)

12. Briefly describe the music of Vaughan Williams and Britten. If their work is representative, how does English music contrast with that of Bartók (NAWM 133) in its relation to tonality and diatonicism?

Germany (CHWM 475–78, NAWM 136)

13. Briefly summarize Hindemith's career.

Music to Study
    NAWM 136: Paul Hindemith, *Mathis der Maler* (Matthias the Painter), opera
       (1934–35), Sixth Scene, excerpt
    CD 11.38–42   Cassette 11.B

14. In the theme presented in mm. 198–213, how does Hindemith use consonant and dissonant chords to delineate the phrases?

15. Where else in the excerpt in NAWM does this theme appear?

16. In mm. 320–29, Regina sings a chorale, "Es sungen drei Engel" (Three angels sang). How does the quotation of this chorale fit the dramatic moment, after Mathis has described a vision that he will paint as one panel of the Isenheim altarpiece?

    Where else in the excerpt in NAWM does this tune appear, in voices or instruments?

17. What were Kurt Weill's "two careers"? What were his musical aims? Describe his musical style, and explain how it suited his aims and the types of music he composed.

Neo-Classicism in France (CHWM 479–81)

18. If a work is *neo-Classic*, what are some characteristics one might expect to find in it?

19. Describe the music and musical style of Milhaud.

Stravinsky (CHWM 481–91, NAWM 137)

Music to Study
> **NAWM 137:** Igor Stravinsky, *Le Sacre du printemps* (The Rite of Spring), ballet (1913), excerpt from Part I: *Danse des adolescentes* (Dance of the Adolescent Girls)
> CD 11.43–46 (Concise 4.36–39)   Cassette 11.B (Concise 4.B)

20. Find and describe two passages in *Danse des adolescentes* from *Le Sacre du printemps* (NAWM 137) that exemplify each of the following characteristics of Stravinsky's style.

ostinatos

repetitive melodies over static harmony

blocks of sound that succeed each other without transitions

independent layers of sound that are superimposed on one another

unexpected accents that negate regular meter and emphasize pulsation

novel orchestral effects

Note: Here is a guide to some of Stravinsky's orchestral markings:
- In m. 1 he asks the strings to play each beat with a down-bow instead of bowing up and down; this will create a forceful, detached effect.
- "Con sord." in m. 18 means "with mute," which on the trumpet yields a thin, metallic sound.
- "Flttzg." on the chromatic scales in the winds in mm. 27–31 means fluttertonguing, which creates a sort of buzzy effect.
- The cellos in mm. 78–81 have a harmonic glissando, an effect Stravinsky invented; bowing the C string while moving the finger rapidly along it without touching the string to the fingerboard creates this effect by allowing only certain overtones to sound.
- "Col legno" (m. 82) means to hit the string with the stick of the bow.

21. Summarize Stravinsky's career, including where he lived, his major compositions, and the main elements of his style in each period.

22. In what ways is *Symphony of Psalms* neo-Classic and/or neo-Baroque?

    Which of the characteristics of Stravinsky's style listed above in question 20 are also true of the excerpt from *Symphony of Psalms* in Example 20.13 in CHWM, p. 490?

TERMS TO KNOW

Gebrauchsmusik
neo-Classic music
socialist realism
formalism

polystylistic music
polytonality
primitivism

NAMES TO KNOW

Béla Bartók
Mikrokosmos
Music for Strings, Percussion, and Celesta
Zoltán Kodály
Sergey Prokofiev
Dmitri Shostakovich
Lady Macbeth of Mtsensk
Alfred Schnittke
Sofia Gubaidulina
Ralph Vaughan Williams
Benjamin Britten
War Requiem
Kurt Weill
The Rise and Fall of the City of Mahagonny

Die Dreigroschenoper (The Threepenny Opera)
Paul Hindemith
Mathis der Maler
Arthur Honegger
Darius Milhaud
Francis Poulenc
Igor Stravinsky
The Fire Bird
Petrushka
Le Sacre du printemps (The Rite of Spring)
Pulcinella
The Rake's Progress

REVIEW QUESTIONS

1. Add the composers and major works discussed in this chapter to the twentieth-century time-line you made for chapter 19.

2. Write an essay in which you summarize the major trends in European music between about 1915 and 1950 (excepting the atonal and twelve-tone music of Schoenberg and his associates, treated in chapter 21).

3. How does Bartók achieve an individual style within the Western art music tradition by integrating traditional procedures with elements abstracted from East European folk music? Describe how this synthesis works in *Music for Strings, Percussion, and Celesta.*

4. Compare the music of Shostakovich and Gubaidulina, using the excerpts in NAWM 134–35 as examples. What was each trying to achieve in these works, and what musical procedures or traditions did each find useful in achieving these aims? What did Soviet authorities ask of composers in the Soviet Union, and how did Shostakovich and Gubaidulina relate to the Soviet state?

5. Describe the musical style of Hindemith, using *Mathis der Maler* (NAWM 136) as an example. How does it compare to the styles of Beethoven, Brahms, Wagner, and Bartók (NAWM 106–7, 114, 124, and 133)?

6. Trace the career of Igor Stravinsky, naming major pieces and describing the changes in his style. What distinctive characteristics of his music, established in *Petrushka* and *Le Sacre du printemps*, continued throughout his career, and how are these traits embodied in his neo-Classical music?

Atonality, Serialism, and Recent Developments in Twentieth-Century Europe

21

Chapter Objectives

After you complete the reading, study of the music, and study questions for this chapter, you should be able to:

1. describe the music and innovations of Schoenberg, Berg, and Webern;
2. describe in simple terms how twelve-tone music works and analyze a brief passage;
3. describe the style of Messiaen and some of his characteristic devices; and
4. define expressionism, total serialism, electronic music, musique concrète, and indeterminacy and name and describe at least one work representing each trend.

Chapter Outline

Prelude (CHWM 462–64)

The twentieth century has seen a continuing pursuit of new resources, among them atonality, serialism, electronic technology, and indeterminacy.

Chapter Outline

I. Schoenberg and His Followers (CHWM 493–503, NAWM 138–41)

Arnold Schoenberg (1874–1951) was born in Vienna and first composed in a Romantic style derived from Wagner, Mahler, and Strauss.

1. Second period: Atonality
   About 1905, Schoenberg turned to smaller forms and a more concentrated language with complex rhythms and counterpoint. He began around 1908 to write music that was *atonal*, meaning that it avoided any sense of a tonal center (whether through traditional tonal harmony or any new way of establishing a central pitch). Instead of treating each pitch and chord in terms of its function within a key and requiring dissonant notes and chords

to resolve, all notes were equal and all sonorities possible; Schoenberg called this *"the emancipation of the dissonance"* (since dissonance was freed of its need to resolve to consonance). *Pierrot lunaire* (Moonstruck Pierrot, 1912) for female voice and chamber ensemble is his best-known atonal piece. The voice uses *Sprechstimme* (speech-voice or speech-song).

Etude: *Pierrot Lunaire*
Without tonality, Schoenberg creates unity in *Pierrot lunaire* through canons, motives, and reliance on the text.   **Music: NAWM 138**

2. Third period: Twelve-tone method
Seeking a way to compose unified longer works without a tonal center and without depending on a text, Schoenberg by 1923 devised the *twelve-tone method*. The twelve chromatic notes are ordered in a *row* or *series*. Tones from the series (or from a contiguous segment of the series, such as the first three or four notes) may be sounded in succession as a melody or simultaneously as a chord, in any octave and rhythm. (The order of notes in the row is not arbitrary, but is based on the melodic motives and chords the composer plans to use in the piece, which are embedded in the row.) The series may be used in its original (*prime*) form, in *inversion* (upside down), in *retrograde* (backward), in *retrograde inversion* (upside down and backward), and in any transposition of these four forms. Each statement of a row includes all twelve notes (but different statements can appear simultaneously). Schoenberg wrote many twelve-tone works, most of them in standard forms.

Etude: Schoenberg's *Variations for Orchestra*
The *Variations for Orchestra* (1927–28) show Schoenberg's blending of traditional and twelve-tone methods.   **Music: NAWM 139**

3. Fourth period
Schoenberg fled Nazi Germany in 1933 and settled in the United States. Most of his late music is twelve-tone, but some works are tonal or blend aspects of tonal and atonal or twelve-tone music.

4. *Moses und Aron*
In Schoenberg's unfinished twelve-tone opera *Moses und Aron* (1930–32), Moses speaks in Sprechstimme, symbolizing his inability to convey his vision of God.

5. Alban Berg
Alban Berg (1885–1935) was Schoenberg's student and adopted many of his techniques, but infused his music with warmth of feeling and with sounds borrowed from tonal music. Berg's expressionist opera *Wozzeck* (1917–21) is atonal (*not* twelve-tone). It uses leitmotifs and continuous music (as did Wagner) and casts each scene as a traditional form, such as suite or passacaglia.   **Music: NAWM 140**

Etude: *Wozzeck,* Act III, Scene 3
This scene is an invention on a rhythm. Announced at the outset in the piano, it pervades the entire texture and symbolizes Wozzeck's obsession.

6. Anton Webern
Anton Webern (1883–1945) also studied with Schoenberg and adopted his atonal and twelve-tone methods. But Webern's works are usually brief, spare, often canonic, and without tonal references. His melodies may change timbre as well as pitch, as a single line passes from one instrument to others in turn.   **Music: NAWM 141**

Window: Expressionism (CHWM 502–3)

Expressionism in art and music portrayed extreme inner feelings such as anxiety, fear, and despair through extreme means. In music, this included dissonance, angular melodies, and distortion of past styles and conventions.

II. After Webern (CHWM 504–6, NAWM 141)

After World War II, several younger composers (as well as Stravinsky) took up the twelve-tone system, usually looking to Webern as a model.

1. Total serialism
By 1950, composers began to apply the serial procedures of twelve-tone music to aspects other than pitch, such as duration and dynamics, resulting in *total serialism. Pierre Boulez* (b. 1925) practiced total serialism, then moved beyond it to a more flexible language in works such as *Le Marteau sans maître* (The Hammer without a Master, 1954).

2. Messiaen
Olivier Messiaen (1908–1992) was an organist, composer, and teacher. His music often has religious subjects, as in the *Quatuor pour la fin du temps* (Quartet for the End of Time, 1940–41), on the Apocalypse. He devised his own musical system, incorporating transcribed birdsongs, modal and octatonic scales, repeated rhythmic series (related to medieval isorhythm and the music theory of India), durational patterns that are the same forward and backward, and other devices.   **Music: NAWM 142**

III. Recent Developments (CHWM 506–14)

Throughout the century, composers introduced new sounds into music.

1. *Musique concrète* and electronic resources
Musique concrète used recorded sounds that were manipulated through tape and electronic procedures. *Electronic music* used electronically generated sound. Unlike music for live performers, music on tape allowed composers total control and an unlimited range of sounds.

2. New technology
Technology developed quickly, from oscillators, to *synthesizers,* to computers and digital encoding of music. Since the invention of portable synthesizers, and especially since the rise of portable computers and the MIDI interface, it has become possible to create electronic music in real time, rather than solely on tape.

3. Influence of electronic music

Electronic music in turn suggested new sounds for traditional instruments and voices and brought a renewed interest in the spatial effects of locating performers in different places around a performing space. Edgard Varèse's *Poème électronique* was a tape piece played at the 1958 World's Fair through 425 loudspeakers while colored lights and slides were projected on the walls, giving a sense of sounds moving through space.

4. The pitch continuum

Partly influenced by electronic music, composers increasingly used the entire continuum of pitch, not only the discrete pitches of the chromatic scale. *Threnody for the Victims of Hiroshima* for string orchestra (1960) by *Krzysztof Penderecki* (b. 1933) uses traditional instruments to play glissandos, extremely high notes, and bands of pitch within which every quartertone is played simultaneously. *György Ligeti* (b. 1923) also used traditional instruments to achieve quasi-electronic effects in *Atmosphères* for orchestra (1961).

5. Indeterminacy

Throughout the history of notated music, performers have made choices or filled in what is not specified in the notation. In the twentieth century, some composers tried to exercise greater control through very specific indications in the score. Others have explored *indeterminacy,* in which certain aspects of the music, such as the order of events, are not determined by the composer.

6. Stockhausen

Karlheinz Stockhausen (b. 1928) used indeterminacy in several pieces. Some works use fragments of existing music.

7. Lutosławski

Witold Lutosławski (1913–1994) used indeterminacy to allow individual players to play at varying speeds or create a cadenza-like elaboration on a figure within controlled boundaries.

8. New notations and new concepts of composition

Indeterminacy has brought new systems of notation and a new concept of a piece as the sum of its possible performances.

STUDY QUESTIONS

Schoenberg and His Followers (CHWM 493–503, NAWM 138–41)

1. What is *atonal* music? What did Schoenberg mean by *"the emancipation of the dissonance"*?

Music to Study
> **NAWM 138:** Arnold Schoenberg, *Pierrot lunaire,* song cycle for female speech-song voice and chamber ensemble (1912), excerpts
> 138a: No. 8, *Nacht* (Night)
> 　CD 11.47–48　　　　　　　　　Cassette 11.B
> 138b: No. 13, *Enthauptung* (Decapitation)
> 　CD 11.49–52　　　　　　　　　Cassette 11.B
> **NAWM 139:** Arnold Schoenberg, *Variations for Orchestra,* Op. 31 (1926–28), excerpts
> 139a: Theme
> 　CD 11.53 (Concise 4.40)　　　　Cassette 11.B (Concise 4.B)
> 139b: Variation VI
> 　CD 11.54 (Concise 4.41)　　　　Cassette 11.B (Concise 4.B)

(Note: The score for *Variations for Orchestra* is at sounding pitch. This means that transposing instruments like clarinet and horn are written as they *sound,* and not according to the once standard practice of writing them in the score as they are notated for the player. Notice also that in the first excerpt the cello is in tenor clef, in which the second line from the top is middle C.)

2. What is *Sprechstimme*? How is it notated, and how is it performed?

How is Sprechstimme used in the two numbers from *Pierrot lunaire* in NAWM 138? Where is it *not* used by the voice?

3. What musical gestures does Schoenberg use to express or illustrate the text in these two songs?

4. What is *expressionism*? What characteristics of these two songs mark them as expressionist works?

5. In the theme of Schoenberg's *Variations for Orchestra* (NAWM 139a), the main melodic line is in the cello, later joined by violin I (marked "I. Gg"—for Geige—in the score). Just considering these melodies, what rhythmic and melodic motives does he introduce, and how are these motives varied as the melodies unfold?

6. In what sense is Variation VI (NAWM 139b) a variation of the theme? What stays the same, and what is changed?

7. As shown in Example 21.1 in CHWM, p. 497 (also in NAWM, p. 746), the first half of the theme (NAWM 139a, mm. 34–45) presents the row in the cello, in two forms: the untransposed prime form (P-0, meaning prime transposed up zero semitones), and the retrograde inversion transposed up nine semitones (RI-9). These are accompanied by chords drawn from I-9 (the inversion transposed up nine semitones) and R-0 (the untransposed retrograde) respectively. With the first half of the theme as an example, the following questions will help you figure out what happens in the second half of the theme (mm. 46–57).

a. What form of the row appears in the cello in mm. 46–50? _____
(Hint: See the diagram of row forms in Example 21.1.)

b. What form of the row is used for the accompanying chords? _____
(Hint: Look at the three-note chord in m. 46. Which form of the row as shown in Example 21.1 begins with those three notes, in some order?)

c. Measures 46–47 include all twelve tones of the chromatic scale, six in the melody, and the other six in the accompaniment. What is the relationship between these two forms of the row that makes this possible? (Hint: Look at the row chart in Example 21.1, and compare the first six notes and last six notes in each row to the same groupings in the other row.)

d. What form of the row appears in Violin I (I. Gg) in mm. 51–57? What row form appears in the accompanying chords in the winds and horn?

    in Violin I   _____   in winds and horn   _____

What is the relationship between these two rows? (Hint: See section c. above.)

e. A new transposition of the prime form of the row appears in the cello in mm. 52–57. By how many semitones up is it transposed, in comparison to P–0? If P–0 is the prime form transposed up zero semitones, what would you call this form of the row?

    number of semitones by which it is transposed up: _____   name: _____

The point of Schoenberg's twelve-tone music is neither to be the musical equivalent of crossword puzzles nor to create completely arbitrary music, but to create logical, unified music based on motives that are developed and accompanied by harmonies derived from them. In that respect, twelve-tone pieces continue the nineteenth-century tradition of thematic development.

Music to Study
>   **NAWM 140:** Alban Berg, *Wozzeck,* opera (1917–21), Act III, Scene 3
>   CD 11.55–57 (Concise 4.42–44)   Cassette 11.B (Concise 4.B)
>   **NAWM 141:** Anton Webern, Symphony, Op. 21, for nine solo instruments
>   (1928), first movement
>   CD 12.1–5   Cassette 12.A

(Note: The Webern Symphony score is written at sounding pitch.)

8. What characteristics of Act III, Scene 3, from Berg's *Wozzeck* (NAWM 140) mark it as an expressionist work?

9. Berg called this scene "Invention on a Rhythm." The rhythmic idea is presented in the right hand of the piano at the beginning of the scene (mm. 122–25) and immediately repeated. Wozzeck then states it in augmentation and with a new melody (mm. 130–36). (Notice that the attacks are in the same rhythm, even though one note is sustained through what was originally a rest.) List below the appearances of this rhythm in mm. 138–54, by the measure in which each statement begins and the instrument(s) or voice that carry it.

Measure	Instrument(s) or Voice	Measure	Instrument(s) or Voice
1. _____	_____	6. _____	_____
2. _____	_____	7. _____	_____
3. _____	_____	8. _____	_____
4. _____	_____	9. _____	_____
5. _____	_____	10. _____	_____

How does the constant reiteration of this rhythm convey the dramatic situation?

10. Where does Berg imitate a polka? A folksong? How does he suggest these types of tonal music, despite using an atonal language?

11. Which characteristics of Webern's style, as described in CHWM, pp. 500–503, are evident in the first movement of his Symphony (NAWM 141)?

12. The opening section of this movement is a double canon. The leading voice of the first canon begins in horn 2, passes to the clarinet, and continues in the cello (see the example in NAWM, p. 773). The canonic answer is in inversion and begins in horn 1. In what instruments does the answer continue?

After Webern (CHWM 504–6, NAWM 141)

13. What is *total serialism*?

Music to Study
> **NAWM 142:** Olivier Messiaen, *Quatuor pour la fin du temps* (Quartet for the
> End of Time) for violin, clarinet, cello, and piano (1940–41), first
> movement: *Liturgie de cristal* (Crystal Liturgy)
> CD 12.6 (Concise 4.45)   Cassette 12.A (Concise 4.B)

14. Messiaen's *Liturgie de cristal* (NAWM 142) has four mutually independent
    layers. The flute and clarinet lines are each based on birdsongs. According to
    NAWM, which bird's song is imitated in each instrument?

    in the clarinet _____   in the flute _____

    How is the opening material in each instrument treated in the rest of the
    movement?

    flute:

    clarinet:

15. The cello has a pitch series, analogous to the *color* of a fourteenth-century
    isorhythmic motet, and a durational series, analogous to the motet's *talea*.
    The entire cello line is in harmonics, which sound two octaves higher than the
    black note. (The notation tells the player to play the black note while touch-
    ing the string at a spot a fourth higher, which creates the harmonic. Once
    again the cello is in tenor clef, as in NAWM 139a.)

    What is the pitch series? _____

    What scale does this set of pitches belong to or suggest? _____

    How many times does the series appear in the movement? _____

    The durational series is given in NAWM, p. 781, in a form that shows it is
    what Messiaen called a "non-retrogradable rhythm." Such rhythms are the
    same forward as backward, which gives them a timeless quality Messiaen
    relished as a symbol of the eternal. In the piece, the last three durations
    always overlap the first three of the next statement of the series.

    How many times does the durational series appear in the movement? _____

    How does the durational series coordinate with the pitch series?

16. The piano also has a durational series and a pitch series, here a series of chords.

   How many chords are in the chord series? _____

   How many times does the chord series appear in the movement? _____

   How many durations are in the durational series? _____

   How many times does it appear in the movement? _____

   How does the durational series coordinate with the pitch series?

17. What is the effect on the listener of this combination of superimposed bird-calls, pitch series, and durational series? Is there a sense of a regular meter? Is there momentum toward a goal?

Recent Developments (CHWM 506–14)

18. What have been some important developments in electronic and tape music since 1945?

19. How did Penderecki and Ligeti use traditional instruments to create novel sounds and textures in *Threnody for the Victims of Hiroshima* and *Atmosphères*?

20. What is *indeterminacy*? How has it been used in composition? Name two European composers who have used it, and describe a piece by each.

TERMS TO KNOW

atonal music, atonality
"the emancipation of the
   dissonance"
Sprechstimme
twelve-tone method
row, series
prime, inversion, retrograde,
   retrograde inversion

expressionism
total serialism
musique concrète
electronic music
synthesizer
indeterminacy

NAMES TO KNOW

Arnold Schoenberg
Pierrot lunaire
Schoenberg: Variations for
  Orchestra
Moses und Aron
Alban Berg
Wozzeck
Anton Webern
Pierre Boulez
Le Marteau sans maître

Olivier Messiaen
Quatuor pour la fin du temps
Poème électronique
Krzysztof Penderecki
*Threnody for the Victims of
  Hiroshima*
György Ligeti
Atmosphères
Karlheinz Stockhausen
Witold Lutosławski

REVIEW QUESTIONS

1. Add the composers and major works discussed in this chapter to the twentieth-century time-line you made for chapter 19.

2. Compare the atonal music of Schoenberg's *Pierrot lunaire* (NAWM 138) to
   the music you know by Wagner, Wolf, Mahler, and Strauss (NAWM 124–27).
   How does Schoenberg continue the late-Romantic German tradition, and
   what does he introduce that is new?

3. How does Schoenberg's twelve-tone music, as exemplified in the *Variations
   for Orchestra* (NAWM 139), continue and extend nineteenth-century procedures?

4. How does Berg's music resemble that of Schoenberg, and how does it differ?
   How does it compare to the music you know by Wagner, Mahler, and
   Strauss?

5. How does Webern's twelve-tone music differ from that of Schoenberg?

6. List the predominant characteristics of Messiaen's style and explain how they
   are exemplified in *Liturgie de cristal* (NAWM 142).

7. What are some of the trends in European art music since 1945? Describe an
   example of each trend.

THE AMERICAN TWENTIETH CENTURY

$\mathcal{22}$

CHAPTER OBJECTIVES

After you complete the reading, study of the music, and study questions for this chapter, you should be able to:

1. summarize the historical background for art music in the United States;
2. outline the history of vernacular music in the United States from ragtime to rock; and
3. name the most significant composers of and trends in art music in the United States during the twentieth century, explain what is individual about each one, and describe pieces by some of the major composers of the century.

CHAPTER OUTLINE

Prelude (CHWM 515–17)

The United States became the center for new music in the classical tradition after World War II. American music grew out of the European tradition, as European composers emigrated to or visited the United States and many Americans studied with Nadia Boulanger in Paris or with other European teachers at summer festivals. But American music also drew from its many ethnic and popular traditions.

I. Traditional Music (CHWM 517–20)

1. Music in the Colonies
   New England colonists sang psalms, and singing schools were established in the eighteenth century to teach singing in parts from notation.

2. William Billings
   William Billings (1746–1800) wrote psalms, hymns, anthems, and canons. Some hymns were *fuging tunes,* which include a middle section in free imitation. Billings did not follow the rules of "correct" counterpoint, but allowed parallel octaves and fifths and often used chords without thirds.

3. Immigration and its influences

Other immigrants brought their musical cultures. The Moravians, German-speaking Protestants from Czech and Slovak regions, encouraged music in church, including arias and motets. German immigrants were prominent as music teachers, and American composers often studied in Germany.

4. Lowell Mason

Lowell Mason (1792–1872), trained by a German immigrant, introduced music into the public school curriculum and sought to replace the music of Billings and others with hymns harmonized in the "correct" European style. Many of his hymns are still in use. The Yankee tunes remained in use in the South. The folk tradition of African-American *spirituals* was popularized after the Civil War by the *Fisk Jubilee Singers.*

5. Brass and wind bands

In the nineteenth century, almost every town and city had an amateur *wind* or *brass band,* and in the twentieth century almost every high school and college has one. The nineteenth-century repertory included marches, dances, song arrangements, and solo display pieces. *John Philip Sousa* (1854–1932) wrote more than 100 marches. Brass bands and dance orchestras played an important role in African-American social life and provided training for black musicians.

II. Vernacular Styles (CHWM 520–26)

1. Ragtime

Ragtime developed from American and African traditions. A typical *rag,* such as *Maple Leaf Rag* (1899) by *Scott Joplin* (1868–1917), uses march form in duple meter and presents a syncopated melody over a steady bass.

2. Blues

Black laments evolved in the early twentieth century into a style called *blues.* Blues have a text in rhymed couplets, the first line repeated, and use *blue notes,* lowering the third, seventh, or fifth degree of the major scale.

Etude: Form of the Blues

The standard blues form has a twelve-bar harmonic framework, often with improvised instrumental "breaks" between lines of the song.

3. Jazz and improvisation

Jazz is a form of group or solo improvisation over a blues or popular tune, developed by black musicians and imitated by white bands by 1915. A leading band was *King Oliver's Creole Jazz Band,* which used the typical instrumentation of cornet, clarinet, trombone, piano, banjo, and drums.

4. Big bands and swing

The popularity of jazz brought larger performing spaces, leading in the 1920s to *big bands,* which had trumpets, trombones, saxophones, and clarinets in sections and a *rhythm section* of string bass, piano, guitar, and drums. Big bands performed from an arrangement or *chart,* which still provided some opportunities for improvised solos. This style is also called *swing,* from the swinging uneven rhythms.

5. Modern jazz and bebop

Bebop (or *bop*) of the 1940s and 1950s used smaller groups, more improvisation, and new techniques, some borrowed from modern classical music, to create a serious art music in the jazz tradition.

6. Country music

Country-and-western or *country music* blended the Anglo-American folk tradition of the hill country with cowboy music and some jazz elements. Singers accompanied themselves on guitar or were backed by a band featuring violins and guitars.

7. Rhythm-and-blues

Rhythm-and-blues was a black urban blues-based style with an unrelenting rhythm emphasizing the offbeats and often using electric guitar and bass.

8. Rock-and-roll

Rock-and-roll or *rock* emerged in the mid-1950s from a blending of white country and black rhythm-and-blues styles. *Elvis Presley* (1935–1977) in the 1950s and *The Beatles* in the 1960s were both enormously popular.

9. Musical comedy

The *Broadway musical* (or *musical comedy*) is the main genre of musical theater in the United States. Many popular songs by Jerome Kern, Irving Berlin, and *George Gershwin* (1898–1937) were written for Broadway shows. Gershwin also wrote works that blend popular with classical traditions, such as his blend of jazz with the Romantic piano concerto in *Rhapsody in Blue* (1924) and his folk opera *Porgy and Bess* (1935).

III. Foundations for an American Art Music (CHWM 526–35, NAWM 143–46)

1. Ives

Charles Ives (1874–1954) blended elements of the American vernacular and European art music traditions in works that evoke nineteenth-century America through modernist techniques, as in his *Second Piano Sonata (Concord, Mass., 1840–60)*. He often used existing music, especially American tunes, as a basis for his own, reworking borrowed material in a variety of ways and with various meanings. His independence of mind, innovations, use of popular materials, and multilayered textures inspired many younger composers. **Music: NAWM 143**

2. Ruggles

Carl Ruggles (1876–1971) wrote atonal, very original works, of which the best known is *Sun-Treader* (1926–31).

3. Cowell

Henry Cowell (1897–1965) explored new effects on the piano, including *tone clusters* in *The Tides of Manaunaun* (1912) and other works and strumming or playing directly on the strings in *The Aeolian Harp* (1923). His later music uses folk and non-Western elements. Cowell was also a promoter and publisher of new music.

4. Crawford Seeger
Ruth Crawford Seeger (1901–1953) composed in a modern atonal style, creating a series of very individual works, before changing her interests to transcribing and arranging American folksongs.   **Music: NAWM 144**

5. Varèse
Edgard Varèse (1883–1965) was born in France and moved to New York in 1915. Rather than using themes, harmony, or conventional rhythm his works use pitch, duration, dynamics, and timbre (including percussion) to create *sound masses* that move and interact in musical space.

Etude: Varèse, *Intégrales*
Intégrales (1925) illustrats Varèse's juxtaposition of elements.

6. Copland
Aaron Copland (1900–1990) studied in France with Nadia Boulanger. His early works use jazz elements and dissonance. In the mid-1930s he turned to a more popular style of simple textures, diatonic writing, and folk tunes, as in *Appalachian Spring* (1944). In the 1950s, his music became more abstract, and he adopted some twelve-tone methods.   **Music: NAWM 145**

7. Harris
Roy Harris (1898–1979) is best known for symphonic music that evokes the American West through modal themes and open textures.

8. Thomson
Critic and composer *Virgil Thomson* (1896–1989) studied with Boulanger but emulated the playful simplicity of Satie. His two operas on texts by Gertrude Stein, *Four Saints in Three Acts* (1928) and *The Mother of Us All* (1947), draws on the styles of American hymns, songs, and dance music.

9. Still and Price
William Grant Still (1895–1978), composer of the *Afro-American Symphony* (1931), and *Florence Price* (1888–1953) are among the best-known African-American composers of art music and incorporated elements from African-American musical styles.   **Music: NAWM 146**

10. National vs. cosmopolitan elements
Many American composers of the first half of the century composed music that was more cosmopolitan than nationalist.

IV. Since 1945 (CHWM 535–51, NAWM 147–52)

A. *Abstract Idioms*

1. Sessions
Roger Sessions (1896–1985) wrote dissonant, complex music in an individual style based on continuous development.

2. Carter
Elliott Carter (b. 1908) often gives each instrument a different rhythmic and melodic character to create a counterpoint of thoroughly independent lines, as in his String Quartet No. 2 (1959).   **Music: NAWM 147**

3. The post-Webern vogue

Webern influenced composers in the universities who sought an objective approach free from Americanism and the influence of popular music.

4. Babbitt

Milton Babbitt (b. 1916) extended twelve-tone music in new directions and was the first to apply serial principles to duration and other parameters.

Etude: The University as Patron

In the United States and Canada, composers of music in the classical tradition have been supported during the twentieth century largely through university teaching positions. This has isolated composers from the public and has sometimes encouraged avant-garde experimentation, but it has also been the major way younger composers have been trained. Important universities for composers have included Yale (where Hindemith taught), UCLA (Schoenberg), and Princeton (Sessions and Babbitt).

B. *New Sounds and Textures*

1. Nancarrow

Conlon Nancarrow (b. 1912) used player-piano rolls to create pieces whose complex and rapid rhythms were beyond human performers.

2. Partch

Harry Partch (1901–1974) rejected equal temperament, formulated a scale of 43 unequal steps using only the pure harmonic ratios of just intonation, and built new instruments that used this scale. His works typically use these instruments to accompany dancing and singing.

3. Johnston

Ben Johnston (b. 1926) applies just intonation to traditional instruments, such as piano or string quartet.

4. Crumb

George Crumb (b. 1929) draws new sounds from traditional instruments to create emotionally powerful music in an eclectic style, as in *Black Angels* (1970) for amplified string quartet.   **Music: NAWM 148**

5. Electronic music

Lacking performers, electronic music is less often played in concert than heard in recording. But several composers have combined live performers with electronic music, as in Babbitt's moving *Philomel* (1964) for soprano and tape.   **Music: NAWM 149**

6. Influence of jazz

Many twentieth-century composers have used jazz elements in classical works. *Gunther Schuller* (b. 1925) merged jazz and classical elements in music he called *third stream*. University-trained jazz pianist *Anthony Davis* (b. 1951) juxtaposed jazz and classical elements in his opera *X: The Life and Times of Malcolm X* (1984).   **Music: NAWM 150**

7. John Cage and Indeterminacy

John Cage (1912-1992) used both *indeterminacy*, in which some aspect of the music is left undetermined by the composer (as in the silent piece

4'33", 1952, where the music is the ambient sounds one hears during the duration of the piece), and *chance,* in which some aspect of the music is determined, not by the composer's will or intentions, but by chance operations (as were the pitches in *Music of Changes,* 1951). (These two are often confused, and must be kept distinct. If something is determined by chance operations, it is not indeterminate.) Cage's aim, inspired by Zen Buddhism, was to allow listeners to hear sounds as sounds in themselves, not as means by which a composer communicates a feeling or idea.

8. Influence of Asia
Asian music exercised a growing influence in American music after 1960.

9. Minimalism
The approach called *minimalism* uses a deliberately restricted set of notes or sounds and a large amount of repetition. *Steve Reich* (b. 1936) has used small repeated units that begin in unison and gradually move out of phase with each other. *Philip Glass* (b. 1937) has written operas and works for his own ensemble using a very repetitive style. *John Adams* (b. 1947) has written operas and orchestral music using repeated ideas that evolve and shift in alignment with each other.   **Music: NAWM 151**

Etude: Reich's *Violin Phase* (1979)
Reich's *Violin Phase* (1967, rev. 1979) involves a short pattern of notes repeated many times and played out of phase with itself.

C. *The Mainstream*
Many American composers continue to write music accessible to a wide public. Three composers are particularly noted for their vocal music: *Ned Rorem* (b. 1923) for his songs, *Gian Carlo Menotti* (b. 1911) for his operas, and *Samuel Barber* (1910–1981) for both. *Joan Tower* (b. 1938) and *Ellen Taaffe Zwilich* (b. 1939) are younger composers who have found a middle road.

1. Post-modern styles
Recent post-modernist architects have incorporated elements of earlier styles into their designs, and so do a number of post-serial composers.

2. Rochberg
George Rochberg (b. 1918) revisits and deconstructs the style of J. S. Bach in *Nach Bach* (After or According to Bach, 1966).

Etude: Rochberg and Bach Compared
Rochberg uses similar gestures to Bach, but a different harmonic language.

3. Del Tredici
David Del Tredici (b. 1937) has written several works based on parts of *Alice's Adventures in Wonderland* and *Through the Looking Glass,* using a style derived from Wagner and Strauss in order to communicate with an audience.   **Music: NAWM 152**

STUDY QUESTIONS

Traditional Music (CHWM 517–20)

1. When did William Billings live? What kinds of music did he write?

2. What is a *fuging tune*? Explain what characteristics make *Washington-Street* (printed in CHWM, p. 518) a fuging tune.

3. What were Lowell Mason's contributions to music in the United States?

4. What was the importance of brass and wind bands in the United States? What was their repertory? What was their significance for African-Americans?

Vernacular Styles (CHWM 520–26)

5. What is *ragtime*? From what traditions did it derive?

6. Describe the style and form of the *blues*.

7. Briefly trace the evolution of *jazz* from early jazz through big bands to modern jazz.

8. Describe the characteristics of *country music*. From what traditions did it derive?

9. Describe the origins and style of *rhythm-and-blues*.

10. Describe the origins and style of *rock-and-roll*.

Foundations for an American Art Music (CHWM 526–35, NAWM 143–46)

11. What are some prominent characteristics of Charles Ives's music? What was his significance for American music?

Music to Study
> **NAWM 143:** Charles Ives, *"They Are There!"*: *A War Song March*, for uni-
> son chorus and orchestra (adapted in 1942 from Ives's 1917 song
> *He Is There!*)
> CD 12.7–9 (Concise 4.46–48)   Cassette 12.A (Concise 4.B)

Most of Ives's works are in European genres and use modernist techniques to
evoke nineteenth-century America. *They Are There!* (NAWM 143) is unusual,
for it uses the verse-chorus format and ragtime-like melodic style of a Tin
Pan Alley tune. But it illustrates several characteristics of Ives's music.

Tin Pan Alley composers often quoted existing tunes. Ives intensifies this
practice, quoting or paraphrasing fragments of the following tunes. Most are
Civil War songs, used here to link what Ives considered the idealism of the
fight to end slavery with the cause of fighting tyranny in World War I and II.

Measures	Parts	Tune
1–2	brass, piano, clarinets	*Country Band March,* by Ives
8–9	voices, trumpets, violin 1 & 2	*Country Band March*
12–14	voices, trumpets, violin 1 & 2	*Marching through Georgia*
18–19	voices, trumpets, violin 1	*Tenting on the Old Camp Ground*
19–21	voices, trumpets, violin 1	*Columbia, the Gem of the Ocean*
20–23	trombones	*The Battle Hymn of the Republic*
21–22	winds	*Dixie*
23	winds	*Marching through Georgia*
23–25	voices, trumpets, trombones, violin 1	*Tramp, Tramp, Tramp*
24	winds	*Yankee Doodle*
25–26	winds	*Marching through Georgia*
27–30	voices, trumpet 1, viola 1	*Columbia, the Gem of the Ocean*
29–30	winds	*Maryland, My Maryland*
31–35	winds	*La Marseillaise*
32–33	voices, brass, viola 1	*Columbia, the Gem of the Ocean*
34–38	voices and brass	*Tenting on the Old Camp Ground*
40–44	voices and brass	*Tenting on the Old Camp Ground*
43–47	winds	*The Battle Cry of Freedom*
44–48	voices, trumpet 1, violin 1	*The Battle Cry of Freedom*
48–50	winds and brass	*The Star-Spangled Banner*
51–53	flutes and trumpets	*Reveille* (bugle call)

12. In the voice part throughout and the upper winds from m. 21 to the end, how
does Ives join these fragments of tunes into a coherent melody?

13. Ives harmonizes his vocal melody with the expected tonal harmonies, in most cases. But he also adds many elements that one would not expect to find in a Tin Pan Alley song, or in a traditional tonal work. What are some of these added elements? How do these added elements affect your experience of the work? In your opinion, how do they affect the work's meaning?

14. Ives often superimposed layers of music, each with its own rhythm, melodic or harmonic character, and instrumental timbre. In mm. 28–29, what rhythmically independent layers are sounding simultaneously? For each layer, name the instruments or voices that are performing it and describe its rhythmic and melodic character.

15. What new musical resources did Henry Cowell introduce in his piano music? For each one, name at least one piece that uses it.

Music to Study
> **NAWM 144:** Ruth Crawford Seeger, Violin Sonata (1926), second move-
> ment
> CD 12.10–12   Cassette 12.A

(Note: In this work, accidentals apply only to the note to which they are
affixed. For example, the fifth note of the piece is A-natural, not A-flat.)

16. The second movement of Ruth Crawford Seeger's Violin Sonata (NAWM
    144) is built on a bass ostinato. How is this figure treated during this move-
    ment? Where is it repeated, where and how is it varied, and where (if ever)
    does it not appear?

17. How is the theme introduced by the violin varied and developed over the
    course of the movement?

18. Describe the music of Edgard Varèse. What resources does he use, and how
    does he deploy them?

19. Outline Aaron Copland's career, indicating distinctive aspects of his style in each period.

Music to Study
> **NAWM 145a:** *'Tis the gift to be simple,* Shaker hymn
> > not on recordings
> **NAWM 145b:** Aaron Copland, *Appalachian Spring,* ballet (1944), excerpt
> > (variations on *'Tis the gift to be simple*)
> > CD 12.13–17 (Concise 4.49–53)   Cassette 12.A (Concise 4.B)

20. How does Copland vary the Shaker tune *'Tis the gift to be simple* in the excerpt from *Appalachian Spring* in NAWM 145b?

21. What kinds of harmonies does Copland use in this excerpt?

---

22. Name two operas by Virgil Thomson on librettos by Gertrude Stein.

_____   _____

What are the characteristics of Thomson's music for these operas? How are they exemplified in the passage in Example 22.4 in CHWM, p. 532?

Music to Study
   NAWM 146: William Grant Still, *Afro-American Symphony* (1931), third
         movement
      CD 12.18–20   Cassette 12.A

23. William Grant Still's *Afro-American Symphony* unites the symphonic and
    African-American traditions. What elements from the symphonic tradition
    does he use in the third movement (NAWM 146)? What elements does it draw
    from African-American traditions (including spirituals, ragtime, blues, and
    jazz)? Refer back to pp. 519–23 in CHWM for a discussion of these types of
    music. (Two elements not mentioned there, both from jazz, are the trumpets
    with Harmon mutes starting at m. 58 and the wire brush used to play the
    drum starting at m. 69.)

Since 1945 (CHWM 535–51, NAWM 147–52)

Music to Study
   NAWM 147: Elliott Carter, String Quartet No. 2 (1959), excerpt:
         Introduction and Allegro fantastico
      CD 12.21–23   Cassette 12.A

24. What are some of the ways in which Elliott Carter gives each of the four
    instruments a distinctive rhythmic and melodic character in his String Quartet
    No. 2 (NAWM 147)?

25. What has been the role of North American colleges and universities in sup-
porting composition of new music? How does this differ from the situation in
Europe?

Music to Study
> **NAWM 148:** George Crumb, *Black Angels: Thirteen Images from the Dark
> Land,* for electric string quartet (1970), excerpts

148a: 4. *Devil-music*	CD 12.24	Cassette 12.A
148b: 5. *Danse macabre*	CD 12.25	Cassette 12.A
148c: 6. *Pavana lachrymae*	CD 12.26	Cassette 12.A
148d: 7. *Threnody*	CD 12.27	Cassette 12.A
148e: 8. *Sarabanda de la muerte oscura*	CD 12.28	Cassette 12.A
148f: 9. *Lost Bells*	CD 12.29	Cassette 12.A

> **NAWM 149:** Milton Babbitt, *Philomel* for soprano and tape (1964), opening
> section
> CD 12.30–34 (Concise 4.54–58)   Cassette 12.B (Concise 4.B)

26. What new playing techniques for string instruments does George Crumb use
in these six movements from *Black Angels* (NAWM 148)? (Hint: Check the
footnotes that explain how to perform certain effects; these footnotes sometimes appear on a different page.) What additional instruments and sounds
does he call for, beyond the four instruments of the string quartet? List all the
new playing techniques, instruments, and other sounds you can find. For
each one, put down one or a few words that describe how the device sounds
and what emotional effect it conveys.

27. Crumb quotes or refers to earlier music several times. *Danse macabre* (NAWM 148b) refers to the piece of the same name by Camille Saint-Saëns and—like Saint-Saëns—quotes the famous chant *Dies irae* from the Gregorian Mass for the Dead. *Pavana lachrymae* (NAWM 148c) is the title of a William Byrd keyboard transcription of a John Dowland song (see NAWM 45 and 47), but Crumb instead quotes Schubert's song *Death and the Maiden*, which Schubert himself had quoted in a string quartet. *Sarabanda de la muerte oscura* (NAWM 148e) presents a sarabande that is apparently not borrowed but written in fifteenth-century style, with double-leading tone cadences, a Landini cadence, and appropriate ornamentation. What is the effect of these references to earlier music within the context of Crumb's music? In your opinion, what might these references mean?

28. How does Milton Babbitt use the singer, taped vocal sounds, and electronic sounds in *Philomel* (NAWM 149)? What is each component like? How do they relate? And how do they work together to suggest the story and the feelings of Philomel?

Music to Study
> **NAWM 150:** Gunther Schuller, *Seven Studies on Themes of Paul Klee* for
>   orchestra (1959), excerpts
> 150a: 3. *Kleiner blauer Teufel* (Little Blue Devil)
>   CD 12.35–36   Cassette 12.B
> 150b: 5. *Arabische Stadt* (Arab Village)
>   CD 12.30–34 (Concise 4.54–58)   Cassette 12.B (Concise 4.B)

29. What is *third stream*? How is it exemplified in *Kleiner blauer Teufel*, the third
    movement of Gunther Schuller's *Seven Studies on Themes of Paul Klee*
    (NAWM 150a)?

30. How does Schuller evoke Arab music in *Arabische Stadt*, the fifth movement
    of his *Seven Studies on Themes of Paul Klee* (NAWM 150b)?

---

31. Why did John Cage use indeterminacy and chance operations in his music?
    How did he use them?

32. What is *minimalism*?

    In what sense is Steve Reich's *Violin Phase* (NAWM 151) minimalist? In what sense is it complex?

33. What is the effect when the parts get out of phase with each other? Can you still hear the original repeated figure? Do other things become more prominent?

34. How can you follow this music? In your opinion, what should you listen for?

35. In *Nach Bach* (NAWM 152), where does Rochberg quote Bach or invoke the Baroque style directly? How do these references to Bach or Baroque style contrast with the other music in the piece? How do the different kinds of music fit together, and what is the overall effect?

36. What is David Del Tredici's attitude toward communication with the audience, as summarized in his statement on p. 550 of CHWM? How does his music reflect his concerns?

TERMS TO KNOW

Terms Related to American Music before 1900 and to Vernacular Music

fuging tunes	rhythm section
spirituals	chart
wind band, brass band	swing
ragtime	bebop (bop)
rag	country music (country-and-western music)
blues	
blue notes	rhythm-and-blues
jazz	rock-and-roll (rock)
big bands	Broadway musical (musical comedy)

Terms Related to 20th-Century American Art Music

tone clusters   indeterminacy
sound masses   chance
third stream   minimalism

NAMES TO KNOW

Names Related to American Music before 1900 and to Vernacular Music

William Billings   King Oliver's Creole Jazz Band
Lowell Mason   Elvis Presley
Fisk Jubilee Singers   The Beatles
John Philip Sousa   George Gershwin
Scott Joplin   *Rhapsody in Blue*
Maple Leaf Rag   *Porgy and Bess*

Names Related to American Art Music Before 1945

Charles Ives   Aaron Copland
Second Piano Sonata (Concord)   *Appalachian Spring*
Carl Ruggles   Roy Harris
Sun-Treader   Virgil Thomson
Henry Cowell   *Four Saints in Three Acts*
The Tides of Manaunaun   *The Mother of Us All*
The Aeolian Harp   William Grant Still
Ruth Crawford Seeger   *Afro-American Symphony*
Edgard Varèse   Florence Price
Intégrales

Names Related to American Art Music Since 1945

Roger Sessions   *4' 33"*
Elliott Carter   *Music of Changes*
Milton Babbitt   Steve Reich
Conlon Nancarrow   *Violin Phase*
Harry Partch   Philip Glass
Ben Johnston   John Adams
George Crumb   Samuel Barber
Black Angels   Ned Rorem
Philomel   Gian Carlo Menotti
Gunther Schuller   Joan Tower
Anthony Davis   Ellen Taaffe Zwilich
X: The Life and Times of   George Rochberg
   Malcolm X   *Nach Bach*
John Cage   David Del Tredici

REVIEW QUESTIONS

1. Add the composers and major works discussed in this chapter to the twentieth-century time-line you made for chapter 19, or to the earlier time-lines you made for chapters 13 and 16, as appropriate.

2. Summarize the eighteenth- and nineteenth-century historical background for music in the United States.

3. What were the major forms of popular music in the United States between the 1890s and the 1960s? Describe each kind, and explain how each relates to the others in historical succession.

4. Trace the course of American art music in the first half of the twentieth century, naming the most important composers and describing their music.

5. What are some of the main trends in American art music since World War II? Define each trend, and describe at least one composer and piece associated with each.

6. Write a brief essay in which you defend or reject the position Milton Babbitt articulates in his statement on p. 539 of CHWM. Whichever position you take, use examples from at least two twentieth-century works in NAWM to support your point of view about the relationship between a composer and his or her listeners.

7. Of the seven pieces in NAWM composed since 1950 (NAWM 134 and 147–52), which one or two do you like the best? Which one or two do you like the least? Write an essay in which you explain what is especially good about the piece(s) you like and what is unappealing about the piece(s) you like less, as if you were writing a review or trying to persuade a friend about which CD to purchase. Explain what it is you find most valuable in music and how your judgments are based on those values.